From Blues to Beyoncé

SUNY series in Feminist Criticism and Theory
———————
Michelle A. Massé, editor

SUNY series in Black Women's Wellness
———————
Stephanie Y. Evans, editor

From Blues to Beyoncé
A Century of Black Women's Generational Sonic Rhetorics

ALEXIS McGEE

Cover image, "Friends at Dawn," used by permission of Cyrena McGee.

Published by the State University of New York Press, Albany

© 2024 State University of New York

All rights reserved

Printed in the United States of America

No part of this book may be used or reproduced in any manner whatsoever without written permission. No part of this book may be stored in a retrieval system or transmitted in any form or by any means including electronic, electrostatic, magnetic tape, mechanical, photocopying, recording, or otherwise without the prior permission in writing of the publisher.

For information, contact State University of New York Press, Albany, NY
www.sunypress.edu

Library of Congress Cataloging-in-Publication Data

Name: McGee, Alexis, 1988– author.
Title: From blues to Beyoncé : a century of black women's generational sonic rhetorics / Alexis McGee.
Description: Albany : State University of New York Press, [2024]. | Series: SUNY series in Feminist Criticism and Theory | Series: SUNY series in Black Women's Wellness | Includes bibliographical references and index.
Identifiers: LCCN 2023022982 | ISBN 9781438496498 (hardcover : alk. paper) | ISBN 9781438496511 (ebook) | ISBN 9781438496504 (pbk. : alk. paper)
Subjects: LCSH: Music and race—United States—History. | Women musicians, Black—United States. | Sound recording industry—United States—History. | Black people—United States—Music—History and criticism. | Music and rhetoric. | Feminism and rhetoric. | Black English—Rhetoric.
Classification: LCC ML82 .M39 2024 | DDC 780.82/0973—dc23/eng/20230922
LC record available at https://lccn.loc.gov/2023022982

10 9 8 7 6 5 4 3 2 1

*For Mildred, Tammy, Cyrena, Lou, Maurice,
and those yet to come*

Contents

Acknowledgments ix

Preface: A Tale of Two Stories: Listening to Liminal Spaces to Listen to Myself xiii

Introduction 1

Chapter 1 Sonic Sharecropping 15

Chapter 2 "Strange Fruit" Sonic Rhetorics 55

Chapter 3 Queer(ing) Sound, Time, and Grammar: Black Women's Methods for Generative Prosodic Rhetoric 97

Chapter 4 Audible Advice, or Mentorship in Sound: A Black (Feminist) Practice of Care through Sonic Rhetorics 139

Chapter 5 Reverb: A Coda for a Quiet, Undisputed Dignity in Sound 179

Notes 185

References 197

Index 209

Acknowledgments

Where do I even begin? I always find the genre of acknowledgments to be daunting and inherently flawed. How can we ever encompass all that goes into making a book? Do we keep a running list to the moments experienced and shared? How do we describe the intangible ways we find help and encouragement from the physical and spiritual planes? How do we record reflections that have not happened yet but know are still very much a part of this making process?

This book was not written by me alone; there are so many people (still with us and not) and things that went into creating this project. I thank God, my ancestors, and the spirits walking with me—guiding me, showing me visions, helping me feel and hear the lower resonating vibrations—who are transforming the spaces and thoughts that fuel my being on a daily basis. Without their guidance, I would not be who I am or where I am today.

The same can be said for my family. Y'all's input, love, and support has helped me grow and come into my own. Thank you mommy and grammy. You both have always supported me and shown me what love and courage look like, how it should feel. You both made sure I knew our stories, remembered them, and encouraged me to embrace all my identities and lean into all my emotions, especially laughter. Mommy, you have been my rock and my everlasting support. Without you I would not have this opportunity, a roof over my head, or food to eat. You cared for me when I could not walk, could not breathe, and could not see. I will never be able to repay you for your love, and I am eternally blessed and thankful to be your daughter. I love you more.

I wish the three of us could sit around the table once more, but I know you and grammy are always with me regardless of my geographical location. I'm also deeply thankful for my big sister, Cyrena, who not only provided the cover art for this work but also always believed in my vision. You've pushed and challenged me since we were little; we might not have always gotten along, but you have always been there to protect me. Because of your strength, I know I will always have someone in my corner who fully understands my/our journey, our tensions, and our suspicions that we constantly grapple with day after day. And while you may not be old enough to comprehend this book, Anthony Zion, this is for you: so you know the true beauty of our family and our roots. Aunty loves you! Even though we all share blood, Louis Maraj shares my heart. I can't even express how much I love, respect, and admire you. You constantly inspire me to do and be better; your patience and kindness are without limits, and have I told you how brilliant you are?! I couldn't dream of a better partner to walk through life with than you. I am beyond blessed to have found you in this world, and to be able to raise our child together with so much love makes all the heartache of my past worth it. I'd do it again knowing that you're who is on the other side. Thank you, Lou. "Sweetpea," just because you aren't born yet doesn't mean you aren't very much a part of this work. You have always been the cornerstone of this project, and I hope you can see yourself within these pages with all the beauty and splendor I see in you.

Stephen Dadugblor, Amber Buck, and Cindy Tekobbe, you three have always been so generous with your time and encouragement. You all are inspiring even beyond the page. I am grateful for y'all's thoughtful feedback but even more so for your friendships. I cannot forget my other UA/CRES family and the ever-important Gender and Race writing group. Cassander Smith, Trudier Harris, Yolanda Manora, Lauren Cardon, Jessy Ohl, Utz McKnight, Sara-Maria Sorentino, Megan Gallagher, Erin Stoneking, Garrett Bridger Gilmore, and Alyx Vesey were all instrumental in helping give structure and clarity to this project. That transitional period of my life also blessed me with some amazing graduate students and colleagues: Sara Whitver; James Eubanks, Taylor Waits, and Khadeidra Billingsley gave me so much life. Thank you all for being so generous, thoughtful, and welcoming. I am also thankful for the institutional contributions from the University of Alabama, which supplied me with research funding from National Humanities Research Center & Travel Grant; Williams Fund; College Academy of Research, Scholarship, and Creative Activity Grant; and Office for Research & Economic Development and awarded me with junior research leave to continue writing this book.

Moreover, there are countless scholars whom I look to for inspiration and advice, whom I see as mentors and role models. Carmen Kynard, Tamika Carey, Tonya Perry, and Elaine Richardson have given me advice and opportunity; they helped develop a sense of confidence in myself and my writing just by being open and willing to talk with and listen to me—even when my thoughts were half-formed and scattered. Their genuine support and kindness along the way has made this road easier to navigate.

My gratitude for my academic family, however, extends beyond my first years on the tenure-track. I have the utmost gratitude to my dissertation committee members and lifelong mentors. These individuals inspired my thoughts, encouraged me to keep going, and saved me from unraveling and losing my way. Sonja Lanehart, I am forever thankful for your guidance, compassion, enthusiasm, and encouragement. You always found time to talk to me about my concerns, my well-being, and my progress. You never wavered in your mentorship and persistent uses of calendars and schedules. I would not be so lucky or prepared as I am today if it were not for your constant communication and belief in my abilities. Joycelyn Moody, thank you for the countless reality checks, conversations about productive and effective writing, and the many opportunities to cultivate and share my work and voice. My work would not be as complex and complete without your tremendous knowledge and support. Kinitra Brooks, thank you for always pushing back on my ideas and challenging me to rethink possibilities, meanings, and intentions. Our lively conversations, exercises in listening, and road trips always prompted me to dig deeper, to write more confidently and carefully, and to always think more critically. Your knowledge and presence in my life are incalculable and forever appreciated. Thank you for opening so many doors. Marco Cervantes, I cannot express how thankful I am to have had your keen insight while writing the early version of this project. Adam Banks, your work and mentorship have undoubtedly left their mark on me. Since my first year as a graduate student, you have shown me that it is possible to follow your passion in academia, be successful, and stay true to yourself. Gwendolyn Pough, thank you for taking the time to work with me and introduce me to texts, theories, and current discussions, particularly during the early development of this work. Your mentorship and publications have immensely grounded my ideas and shaped both my writing and outlook on life. You have always inspired me, and I will always be your fangirl.

Even before the dissertation, though, my academic family planted seeds of inspiration, and I'm forever thankful for my time at Texas State

University, where I received some of the most meaningful life lessons and professional development. I cannot express the joy and gratitude I feel for my fellow Bobcats, especially Nancy Wilson, Octavio Pimentel, and Jamie Mejía. I will always hold the MARC program and the Office of Student Diversity and Inclusion close to my heart.

Having written all this, I'm sure I have undoubtedly left someone out or forgotten to name an award or grant I was given to complete this work. Please know I am not trying to do this on purpose. As I asked in the beginning: how can we ever incorporate all the help and support one gets as they journey through life? How can we ever convey just how much people and opportunities mean to us at any given moment—not to mention the fact that we have to fit it all within the first few pages of a book. All I can really say is THANK YOU.

Preface

A Tale of Two Stories:
Listening to Liminal Spaces to Listen to Myself

Growing up in the American South as a product of miscegenation, I was constantly reminded of the social and cultural tensions I embodied. I became acutely aware of how I had to carry myself in spaces; how I had to navigate gazes that rarely acknowledged my intersectionality and my bodies of knowledges; how I had to constantly remake my notions of home because the idea of belonging and identity were luxuries I conjured up as I came of age. Down South, I was often labeled "not Black enough," but up North I was deemed "too Black" to be accepted by society and by some of my own family members. My understanding of self, home, and identity were not fixed, but, like the echoes of a note sung too long, they expanded, moved, transient, and imagined.

I spent some summers and winters at my grandmother's home in central Pennsylvania: sometimes it was a vacation, other times it was a refuge. This small town is rich in American history and is known for being the home of a nationally ranked private liberal arts school. Other than its roots in education, colonial America, and its sometimes-seedy past connected to sports history, this small town remains quiet and sleepy. In all my years growing up there I had not seen or heard of a flourishing nightlife like I did back in San Antonio. There weren't sensationalized crimes being broadcast on a 24-hour loop—just the occasional national headline coming in from larger cities like Harrisburg, Pittsburgh, or Philadelphia. Only a few radio and television stations had strong enough signals to be considered regular programs for the locals, or at least that's what I understood since my grandma didn't have cable or internet.

We usually just sat around the kitchen table, talked, and listened to the radio, the record player, or an old boombox on which we'd play CDs of bluegrass, country, or gospel singers. We visited with my grandma's neighbors to get the daily gossip, and close friends and family dropped in to say "hi," checking on her while they made their way through town on errand runs, spreading the news of which grandkid was getting married, got in trouble, or went off to college, or who was finally coming home. These visitations were the highlight of our days in these small farming and shipping communities.

Her home was different than the home I knew in Texas. As children, my sister and I were always looking for places to go and things to do in this sleepy township. Having spent most of our school year in a large metropolitan city, we continually had to readjust (often without notice) to this slower pace of life, which meant finding ways to occupy our minds and expend our energy. I usually found myself reading or sitting at the table with Grammy and mommy—trying to be grown—when I wasn't arguing with my sister. At different points in the year, I took up running and gardening. After stopping for gas one day, I asked my mom about "that place," as in "hey, what's that place? Can we go in there?" I remember my mother telling me it was not *safe for us* (my sister and myself) to go in there because "Black people were not welcomed." I was taken back by her bluntness, but I was thankful for her protection. How did she know I couldn't go in there? How did she know that kind of attitude existed in such a small town that she'd been away from for so many years?

I asked my mom, "Why? Why was I not allowed to go in there?"

She replied slow and clear: "Lexi, that's a pretty rough bar. At least that's what it was when I went there, and it still looks the same. I used to go there to drink, play pool, listen to music, and meet guys. You wouldn't want to go in even if you went in *with me.*"

It was clear "*with me*" was commenting on more than just my age. I knew my sister and I were looked at differently than my mom; I know some of our family wanted nothing to do with us because my sister and I were not white. Unfortunately, this firsthand knowledge and open communication with my mother couldn't save me from how her answer lingered with me well past our return to San Antonio. It was a heavy observation that weighed my identity as a young, Black[1] (or non-white) woman as "less than" others in that predominately white surrounding. My curiosity about a vaguely marked building and search for social engagement had the power to rescript identities for two generations.

Although my mom talked to me and my sister before this trip and before this conversation about "that place," about being mixed-raced, she made it very clear that in this town, being mixed didn't matter, not in the mid-1990s/early 2000s at least. I knew the city had its fair share of racism and sexism. It is, after all, where my mom grew up, where my mom met my father, and where my mom was disowned by *her* father for loving a Black man. At this point in my life, I had never seen my mother's father; I had only heard stories about how some of her family treated her after their wedding. It wasn't until I was an adult that I met my extended family; not because there weren't any opportunities but because my mother, my sister, and I were taboo subjects for many of them. I could count every one of my family members I knew on both hands: that was the extent of my family tree until I went in search for my roots and forced my own recovery project of myself.

My mother's demonstration of agency through marriage was a deviation from the norm, the expected, the acceptable, and thus something not to be tolerated in the eyes of her father. From her stories, my travels, and my experiences, I began to piece together an understanding of what it meant to be me in particular spaces. I was no longer a child visiting her grandmother during breaks or seeking shelter from the violence that was "home" in the South; I was my mother's daughter who was her mother's daughter; I was embodying and symbolizing the very tensions of a generation before me. I quickly realized that racism was not quarantined to one specific region of the United States; it was ubiquitous, insidious, alive, and well.

Let me be clear: it was not all sunshine and roses growing up in Texas. I am not trying to paint an inverted picture of the North-South binary that many of us know so well. I had a violent, unstable, and often isolating childhood. I found comfort in books and in music. I often played vinyl records and listened to the radio for hours when I was young in the hopes of finding a "safe" place to be myself. As a teenager I was glued to my boombox, still listening to the radio and records, but I was obsessed with making mixtapes and later burning CDs. I was forever dancing to Frankie Smith's "Double Dutch Bus," Janet Jackson's *Rhythm Nation 1814*, Paula Abdul's *Forever Your Girl*, Kurtis Blow's "The Breaks," Michael Jackson's *Thriller*, The Zapp Band's *Zapp* album, Queen's *Greatest Hits* (vol. 1), and Selena's *Dreaming of You* in the 1990s. Music linked time and place to my *conocimiento*, or my "coming to consciousness," as Gloria Anzaldúa discusses in "now let us shift." Music guided my understanding of who I was, how I got there, and who I wanted to be in any given moment. It helped me create safe(r) places, like a home or a classroom could do, to explore my identities. The sounds coming from the speakers gave me a space to tell, to listen, and to witness stories of becoming that I dared to imagined for myself. I used those albums, that background music from my grandma's kitchen, and the concepts from sound to construct my various identities and alter egos: I'd often use music to plan out what would be my floor routines for my pretend debut on the US Women's Olympic gymnastics team like Dominic Dawes. I would practice for hours each day, which meant I would play and dream of a future for myself. I would watch hip-hop videos on tv shows like MTV's *TRL* or BET's *106th and Park* for hours after school on weekdays, and I'd watch *Soul Train* on Saturday mornings to learn new (and old) dance moves and practice how to be "cool" and confident with the world looking at you. My identity was informed and infused by music across generations.

In effect, dancing and music taught me how to heal, how to escape, and how to navigate my identities in public and in private. Hip-hop and soul music, in particular, not only affected why and how I danced, but also influenced how I dressed and how I presented myself as a woman of color in/of the South, negotiating the very tensions I had come to carry with me from my earliest memories: the tensions between white, rural North and Black, urban South. Music has been my way of communicating and understanding how to *be* in the world. Music such as hip-hop has continuously been at the forefront of developing who I am as a person, rhetorician, Black feminist, and scholar but so has the influence of classical, jazz, and even blues music.

After my parents divorced, my sister and I saw very little of our father. What time we did spend with him before he moved back to New Orleans was spent attending jazz festivals and visiting art museums. I rarely listened to what he was actually telling me when we did have to spend time together; much of the time—as I recall it—was spent in fear and anger because I had seen his personality change from charming to volatile as quick as a heartbeat. The home I had with my father was very different than the home I had with my grandmother or the home I had with my mother—before and after the divorce. Sound, however, has always been central to the way I navigate and cultivate space, language, and identity. I always felt at ease with sound reverberating and filling the space around me, with the vibrations of electricity emitting from household appliances, with the rise and fall of the cadence of the cicadas when

I was alone. I could hear the change in frequencies and feel the vibrations more readily than I could join in conversations happening around me.

When my sister and I spent time with my father at his apartment, he would play jazz and classical music all day. He would sit at the dining table, smoke a cigarette, and then lean his head back and listen to the music. Other times, he would be driving in his white, two-door Mazda truck, smoking a cigarette (me sitting in the middle with my sister to my right), listening to classical, jazz, or blues music on the radio. Like I said, my father and I seldom had long conversations, but we always had music—as if the tunes could say it all for my father—an osmotic permeation of language, conveying what William Banfield (2010) describes as "Black music philosophy." Banfield's Black music philosophy and Black cultural codes are the physical manifestations of the aesthetic renderings of one's perceived reality; they are "things" or commodities in which people—for mine and Banfield's purpose, these are people of African descent—impose various types of value. Like Houston Baker's interpretation of the blues as a "text" in *Blues, Ideology, and Afro-American Literature*, Banfield recognizes the Black aesthetic philosophy as evolving into larger signified representations of Black identity, history, and epistemology, which is often translated into or through music. The Black music philosophy allows people to engage in interpretations and understandings (or even productions) of the cultural codes, specifically as consumption of musical discourse even within a larger historical evolution.

The same can be said for language—not just music as a discipline, genre, or profession. Sound simultaneously acts as material and aesthetic; language and entertainment; timely message and historical documentation; call *and* response. Fred Moten surmises that "[w]here shriek turns speech turns song—remote from the impossible comfort of origin—lies the trace of our descent" (22). In *In the Break: The Aesthetics of the Black Radical Tradition*, Moten argues for a repositioning of sound as being on par with other Black modes of communication, even the seemingly inanimate or the unrecognized, to insist on the lived reality and process of knowledge-making for Black folks, which can be found "in the breaks" of Black performance. Moten writes:

> There occurs in such performances a revaluation or reconstruction of value, one disruptive of the oppositions of speech and writing, and spirit and matter. . . . If we return again and again to a certain passion, a passionate response to passionate

> utterance, horn-voice-horn over percussion, a protest, an objection, it is because it is more than another violent scene of subjection too terrible to pass on; it is the ongoing performance, the prefigurative scene of a (re)appropriation—the deconstruction and reconstruction, the improvisational recording and revaluation—of value, of the theory of value, of the theories of value. (14)

I continually went back to those moments with my father and juxtaposed them with moments I had with my mother and grandmother, making and remaking and searching for meaning and identity in the ways we communicated; it took time to find comfort in the ways my understanding of self was forming. Music, sound, and language became intertwined with material and memory in this process.

This is what was happening with my dad: we were consuming our histories and communicating not with our own words, but with his archiving of music. At the time I thought these shared moments with my dad were a cruel type of isolation; however, now I see those moments in a wholly different and significant light. Music was our way of communicating *in* all the silence and trauma. It was his way of giving us part of his identity and of giving us his story, adding another layer of generative tensions I carry with me.

The way I read the world as I came of age is not the way I read the world today. The way I read the world today is, however, informed by how I read the world as I came of age. The stories my mother shared with me about her time in that bar transformed from a rumination to a cautionary tale as it impressed onto my consciousness; the stories I now share with you are both documenting the dynamisms of literacies and rhetorics that can provide counterstories to examine, challenge, and critique the violences of accepted (but false) master narratives—even across disciplines (Journet et al. 2011). Literacies, like representations of the self, are constantly transforming and vacillating between oral and written narratives that guide other—like my own—rhetorics, languages, and epistemologies in practices of intervention.

As Jaqueline Jones Royster points out in *Traces of a Stream: Literacy and Social Change Among African American Women* (2000), "African American women writers across genres . . . are deliberately engaging in the social and political conversations around them. . . . their interests are not just in expressing themselves in writing but in using language in such a way as to affect the reader's heart, mind, and soul. . . . they . . . 'move' the audience, that is, to inspire change—in thinking, feeling, and behavior" (21). Therefore, the boundary between oral and written text is secondary to the meaning behind Black women's rhetorics and literacies. The discursive boundary or privileging of written texts should be scrutinized from a methodological viewpoint in addition to the contemporary works already engaging with decolonial and Black feminist rhetorics questioning discursive practices.

From Blues to Beyoncé continues blurring those disciplinary boundaries by looking at other genres of texts and literacies as having rhetorical purposes and implications. To discuss these figures outside this cultural context (or within a vacuum) would be unethical and would be erasing valuable rhetorical material that has the potential to bridge politics, culture, sound, music, performance, orality, speech, history, gender, sexuality, generations, and much more. It is important to continue searching for those "everyday" rhetorics to not only continue the work Royster and others laid out, but also recover, validate, and amplify the voices, rhetorics, literacies, and identities at the margins. My looking to Black women music artists as rhetors is one contribution to this call.

Introduction

From Blues to Beyoncé, An Introduction

> Black women use the whole of Hip-Hop culture to not only assert agency, claim voice, grapple with and create images, negotiate sexual and body politics, evoke Black feminism, continue lineages, and empower themselves, but also lay claim to the public sphere and subvert stereotypes and domination by bringing wreck.
>
> —Gwendolyn Pough (86)

My husband gave me a vinyl copy of Beyoncé's *Lemonade* for my first birthday we spent together as a couple. Inside the album cover is a large photo book filled with still images from Beyoncé's visual album. The central image in its liner notes is a black-and-white photo of Black women and girls holding hands encircling a large, outdoor picnic table placed under the cover of oak trees draped in Spanish moss. Half of them have their backs turned to the camera; many of them have their heads lowered, but I can see some of their faces. One woman seems contemplative while Beyoncé's smile is captured. All are dressed in various white garments from different centuries adorned with various period-specific accoutrements. This single panoramic image (placed near the end of the booklet) spans two full sheets while most other title images occupy one page. Only two words are embossed on these pages, centered and at the bottom: "Hope" and "Freedom." Sure, one of these words represents a song title from the album, but "Hope," written in a slanted, almost cursive font, isn't listed on the discography. These two words symbolize much more. They represent two of the most urgent and long-standing goals we aim toward.

Sometimes we name it (i.e., "freedom") and other times we don't; we feel it instead (i.e., hope). Either way, both words work in tandem and move us both individually and collectively across time and space. This opening image, along with the quote from Gwendolyn Pough, sets the tone for this work, for my work, and for the work that so many of us Black feminists, Black women, and Black girls do daily.

The Black women (and girls) gathered here represent the diversity and richness of Blackness; they represent the ongoing attempts at survival, liberation, and health. The image and the words resonate with and in the foregrounded sound, movement, emotion, reflection, intellect, creativity, and action produced by Black women music artists/writers/actors/activists/mentors/collaborators/daughters/aunts/mothers/friends/neighbors. The fact that we come from all walks of life doesn't dampen our ability to connect with each other. Blackness is not monolithic. Because our histories are so robust, so old, so ingenious, and so varied, we are bound to have created a plethora of strategies to help us navigate and interrupt so many ongoing antiBlack acts. As such, there is no one "right" way to challenge oppression; we, in fact, have many tactics for circumventing systemic inequities as well as individual microaggressions stemming from centuries of hatred, bigotry, and ignorance—not to mention certain kinds of world-building. Resistance from Black women (music artists), such as Ruth Brown's testimony to Congress, Ida B. Wells' anti-lynching campaign, and Cardi B's attempted trademark, documents our ongoing efforts to disrupt insidious, oppressive attempts that try to "freeze" Blackness in and out of place. Their contributions, along with others named in this book, provide instructive blueprints for understanding how to use our everyday realities to survive and give insight into how to interpret the practical applications employed by Black women and girls across time and space.

By pointing to these Black women's (music artists') interferences, *From Blues to Beyoncé: A Century of Black Women's Generational Sonic Rhetoric* ties together "Rhetoric and Composition, Literacy Studies, African American Studies, and other spaces beyond studies of Black women's expressive and rhetorical lives," as one reviewer mentioned, and demonstrates how deep and wide these antiBlack roots are. *From Blues to Beyoncé* prioritizes the responses that challenge the very logic and purpose of these problematic acts. Recognizing these varied counterattacks, which is still necessary in 2023, begins closing the gap between the "exceptional moments" and lifting the veil on disciplinary containment of injustices.

After all, antiBlackness is not just a problem that surfaced in writing studies, or sound studies more specifically, in the last five years; it has been here for eons and precedes disciplinary silos. Thus, this work embraces Black women's sonic rhetorical connections and tries to learn from our similarities and differences even though these exchanges form in some of the most intangible, mysterious, yet wholly present and perfectly concrete ways. I hope we can learn with each other even though (as others have said before) we are "shape-shifters" and "time-benders" (Adam Banks 2011), and even as we crisscross through various cultural moments and engage with generations of information.

Each generation puts pressure on the last to fix what they broke or (at the very least) acknowledge its culpability in creating the world we have today. Tenuous relationships between race, class, gender, sexuality, and many other factors influencing and reflecting identity are constantly put to the test when the old guard ushers in the new. However, we can learn from these momentary ideological clashes or exchanges when we are motivated to reflect on how we can move forward and how our actions are/have been altered by our interpretations of reality: what we believe in, what we are told, or what is heard in passing. Each generation can learn from the previous one; each generation can leave its mark on the world. *From Blues to Beyoncé* examines these exchanges when Black women and girls hold hands around the table, making connections within and between each other across time and space. I see Black women's use of music, sound, imagery, and voice as part of those generational rhetorical methodologies and generational conversations, facilitating pathways for intersecting, blurring, and cross-pollinating pedagogies as well as activism in, across, and between generations.

Generations of Black women and girls, like those identified by the image and within the quote, have cultivated identities, rhetorics, languages, and literacies to navigate similar acts of oppression with and without music. Generation, as defined by Cathy Sandeen's reading of Strauss and Howe, is "a cohort of people born within a particular period of time" who encompass a "generational interval" of "approximately 20 years in length. Twenty years represents the average length of time between birth and childbearing—or the beginning of the next generation" (12). This quantification may also align with one's productive years within a profession or discipline. This span of twenty years is flexible (give or take five years in either direction), and it is generally accepted as an elastic classificatory system for grouping individuals who share similar personality characteristics and experiences; it is often grounded by traditional, Western notions of the human life span. While I accept Sandeen's bound period of twenty years as a kind of temporal marker, I do also want to nuance it by emphasizing the affiliation and shared experiences of cohorts across time by exposing the kinds of conversations Black women engage with across "generations" to unsettle such a neatly packaged unit. The cases used in the following chapters do not strictly adhere to or exemplify changes happening in Black communities every twenty to twenty-five years; rather, the examples used here reinforce the overlap, doubling back, and jumping ahead that happens when Black folks envision a more just future by holding the past accountable.

This work explores conversations from the 1850s through the 2020s, providing a through line of how sound can connect over a century of Black women's rhetorics and how sound can connect multiple generations. As new types of media surface and document society's "evolution," more and more possible venues open our analysis to assess the kinds of dialogues Black women have to pressure for change and progress as well as reflect on the communities that made change possible—much of which is symbolized in the chapter's opening image and quote. Black women are proficient at reading and interpreting culturally relevant timelines because we are often signified as the litmus test for change. Thus, our rhetorical methodologies do, indeed, hold the world accountable and try to fix what's been broken, not solely by blaming someone else but by healing, surviving, building together and acknowledging each other's agency. These strategies don't just happen overnight, and they don't always happen within the span of twenty to twenty-five years. Black women have been successful in thwarting continued moves of devaluation, in large part because we operate with the understandings of Sankofa and collectivity.

Black women's generational sonic rhetorics demonstrate the messy interconnectivity of rhetoric, identity, literacy, and context. Black women's rhetoric can limit the power of white supremacy; we can challenge the systematic erasure of Black bodies when we voice the existence of ourselves and our multiple (collective) identities namely by proclaiming and negotiating the spaces we inhabit. Black women's generational rhetorics are inherently radical because citizenship (in an American context, at least) has historically been limited, denied, or intended to erase the agency of Black folk altogether (Ore 2019; Sharpe 2016; Browne 2015; McKittrick 2006; Hartman 1997; Mills 1997). The traditional systems that cultivate a normative citizenship often (re)enforce oppressive policies hindering the agency of people of color in systemic fashions. The use of these insidious, intersecting, oppressive systems like standard education, or a mythologized "standard English," can have lasting psychological effects that damage perceptions of the self (DeGruy 2005) and propagate harmful stereotypes (Harris-Perry 2011). So the fact that we can recognize ourselves across generations is a testament to how long we've been here fighting for each other, asserting our rhetorical agency, and blurring generational boundaries.

This generational shift in scholarship, specifically Black women's intentional intervention in these conversations, signals a pivotal turn in sound studies where Black women are changing the game—in usual fashion. Recent works from Daphne A. Brooks (2021), Emily Lordi (2020), and Regina Bradley (2017; 2021) draw attention to the dynamic and ongoing legacy of Black women's sonic traditions, which have been often overlooked because their critiques don't fit neatly into a box—or, to be honest, the old boys' club did everything they could to keep us out. To say that I wrote this work to see myself within ongoing scholarly conversations would be cliché, but it would also be true. I began my initiation into sound studies/sonic rhetorics as I was trying to finish my dissertation (which was the original blueprint for this work). I was researching the blues and trying to connect language with music—not a particularly "new" endeavor in the academy—but that was when I was confronted with a group of sound studies scholars and hit in the face with the stark Whiteness of it all. Many conversations within these traditional acoustic dialogues stripped the music of the persons embedded within its texts or glossed over the importance of identity as an influential feature of sound, including the social, cultural, political, and historical baggage we all carry with us. When race and gender were engaged, Sun Ra and Miles Davis were the exemplary models to examine. Not to take away from these two essential figures, but what about the work Black women continue doing in these spaces and histories of sound? While I don't dismiss the importance of Sun Ra (or more broadly iconic Black male musicians) within the subfield of sonic rhetoric, and not that I'm suggesting that these conversations weren't helpful or necessary, I do think sound studies/sonic rhetorics still have a lot to grapple with, explore, and learn from Black women (broadly defined). So, yes, I did write this book to see myself in the conversation. I wrote myself into the larger sonic narratives, as Toni Morrison has suggested and as Pough, Brooks, Lordi, and Bradley have done before me. Like them, I write from a space as both a Black woman scholar and fan girl of Black music. Vantage points like these offer the field (and subfield) something more accessible, more relatable, and just plain fun if you ask me—and that's what may be missing from these static critiques of sound. Rather than a myopic view of composing, *From Blues to Beyoncé* offers an intimate, intersectional, and global perspective on the history of sound as applied through the lives of Black women. But even this work has its limitations.

For the purposes of this work, generational sonic rhetorics are mechanized concepts (i.e., "the sonic") of *being* transmitted in and across sound (e.g., laughs, shrieks, or crescendos); they have an intentional and often long-lasting impact on one person or many people that energizes the translation of being across time, space, and media. Said another way, generational sonic rhetorics are the collective moments of sound that act as methods for communicating knowledge that can be used to persuade or inform (younger) generations about topics like survival, liberation, and care, for instance. Generational sonic rhetorics are the vernacular ways one learns about the stories that are passed on (to teach children life lessons); they are shared lessons and epistemologies about how to enact agency. These rhetorical practices are passed on by ancestors, picked up by individuals interacting with communities, or rediscovered in the future and reinvented with the advent of new technologies for storytelling and counternarratives. Embedded within Black women's generational sonic rhetorics is the often-employed shifting—or the conscious change in positionality dependent on situation, place, and audience—as a way of survival or resistance.

Sound, in this project, refers to more discrete examples of communication, including nonverbal gestures—like moans, grunts, hums, rhythmic beat-making with various parts of the body—the speed, tempo, pitch, duration, and instrumentation accompanying voice (to name a few), all of which are audible to other people/listeners. In *Just Vibrations: The Purpose of Sounding Good*, William Cheng defines sounds as "things we say, music we make, noises we hear, pressures we feel" and suggests that sounds "are too often and too facilely conceived as just (*mere*) vibrations" (15). Moreover, sound, as it is discussed here, varies in tempo, pitch, vibration, frequency, and volume. It is constructed within dynamic ecologies and can be used as a rhetorical practice, making it a sonic kind of rhetoric. Sound, music, and voice are parts of a sonic rhetoric that serves as a foundational point of reference to better recognize when to listen for the rhetorical practices of race, gender, class, sexuality, ethnicity, and other intersections of fluid identities for Black women that are engaged with day-to-day meaning-making. In other words, sound is to characteristics as sonic is to praxis.

As oral and written histories matter to rhetoric, so, too, do the sonic histories. They expand our understanding of communication and audience, challenge our awareness of distribution as a rhetorical function, and nuance our repertoire of literacies. I stretch these dialogues into a sonic third space by engaging with rhetoric that bridges the intersections of sound and performance, race and time, location and class with collaborative Black feminist praxes. I argue that the very use of sound, music, and voice as texts by Black women holds significance as a dynamic, rhetorical function operating within and outside Western notions of self, time, and linearity.

The interdisciplinarity and quotidian engagement with sound and the sonic, time and time again, lead me to ask, "How has (the absence of) sound in writing and rhetoric shaped Black women's identities and communication?" When I suggest "the absence of sound," I don't mean silence, not entirely, because we know silence is also a part of Black women's sonic rhetorics. What I am emphasizing here is the possibilities for theorizing types of sound as feeling, emotion, politic, or grammar especially when listening to, through, and with the body.

The sonic intersections of language and identity for Black women are especially important sites for conversation regardless of (in)formalities and disciplinary boundaries. Having spaces that engage in conversations of intersectional identities—even as they are formed through language, sound, image, and audience—are necessary for the growth and development of everyday folks, scholars, politicians, and knowledge-making disciplines more broadly. This engagement with the systems of *being* found in the everydayness of navigating one's multiple selves is embedded within Black women's generational sonic rhetorics and needs to be taken seriously. *From Blues to Beyoncé* focuses on Black women who use these variations of sound as vehicles for rhetorically distributing such generational teachings.

This work aims to challenge the normative literacy practices, the written and oral binaries, and the faux linearity of intellectual production actively working to excise particular bodies of knowledges, identities, and literacies. I bring those tensions, those years (and indeed those generations) of traumas, literacies, and knowledges with me, just as the opening image visualizes, into all spaces. The goal of this work is to continue recognizing Black women's generational sonic rhetoric that pushes discursive boundaries toward greater intertextual, interdisciplinary, and communal inclusivity. Answering these challenges with an excavation of sound aligns with Eric Darnell Pritchard's solution for erasure, which is "Historical rootedness." This solution "is a key ingredient in one's identity construction, affirmation, and overall sense of self" (104). Recognizing, calling attention to, and listing to the rhetorics reverberating across time, regardless of the format of the "text," strengthens Pritchard's approach for rupturing the erasures mentioned here and elsewhere. Sound can help "rewrite" narratives, amplify identities, and reinforce marginalized literacies.

Thankfully more and more scholars continue recognizing the benefits of bringing in popular culture and music, like hip-hop, into educational spaces, bridging the gap between a standard curriculum that does little to welcome diversity and inclusion with students' lived experiences and epistemologies. Several authors have written about hip-hop's relationship with feminism and language ideologies and as a pedagogy (Akom 2009; Alim and Smitherman 2012; Brown and Kwakye 2012; J. Chang 2005; Hill and Pretchaur 2013; Love 2012; Waters et al. 2019; McWhorter 2008; Morgan 2009; Pough 2004; Richardson 2006; Emdin 2010). These authors argue for hip-hop as a critically engaging teaching tool that can draw students into the classroom, creating spaces for active learning—particularly as it connects with students' ways of understanding their own being in the world. This can be said for all genres of Black music.

The emerging subdisciplines of sonic rhetoric, too, proves useful in aiding this bridge between identity and rhetoric as well as rupturing erasures of Black rhetorical agency. Taking up this area of conversation, I look to Samuel Perry's article examining "Strange Fruit" and Alexander Weheliye's *Habeus Viscus*—which focus on technologies, assemblages of violences, and Black feminist theories—to redirect the field's critiques of rhetoric, affect, sound, and ecology. Additionally, I rely on Gwendolyn Pough's (2005) rhetorical construction of "wrek" in relation to Brittney Cooper's (*Beyond Respectability* 2020) discussions of Black women's intellectual legacies as well as Angela Y. Davis's *Blues Legacies* to push against static critiques of class, consumer culture, and stereotyped personae for Black women in music. Their texts are foundational for many scholars, including myself, who explore intersectionality within public and sonic spheres. As the opening quote suggests, the *wrek* that Black women do and the intellectual labor they manifest claim agency and voice, document our existence, extend Black feminist legacies, navigate respectability politics, and command recognition by empowering themselves and each other in public, private, and sonic spheres, which disrupts solipsism "by bringing wreck" (Pough 86).

From a methodological standpoint, *From Blues to Beyoncé* understands genres and discourses of Black music as parallel to this robust scholarly engagement with Black women's rhetoric and intellectual histories. By mapping out the generational sonic rhetorics used by Black women, I reposition the way we read and use music, sound, and voice as rhetorical, educational models. This project bridges conversations of popular Black music, rhetoric, resistance, and Black feminist perspectives to extend and link agency, identity, and technologies with time and space. Furthermore, I address sonic rhetorics by bringing Black women's voices together and blurring disciplinary boundaries. Such an attempt reflects the current calls to move beyond traditional approaches to scholarship and the "historical erasure" that Pritchard highlights.

This project uses archival material, auto/biographies, oral narratives and interviews, critical discourse analysis, and rhetorical analysis to discuss ways Black women use sound, music, and voice as interrelated systems of transmission, as vehicles for distributing social justice pedagogies across time and space. Hence, autoethnography (Heewon Chang 2008; Adams et al, 2014) and critical autoethnography (Borloryn and Orbe 2014) add to this research's imperative by fostering dynamic understandings of transmission and rhetorical manipulation of voice as factors for interpreting sonorous methods of teaching, surviving, and liberating other Black women from psychological, spiritual, or physical abuse and/or oppression. More specifically, auto/ethnographic methods allow me to overtly emphasize intersectionality and identity politics' fluidity, rhetoric, and performance to make my argument. Autoethnography does not privilege traditional research and texts such as canonized writings. Instead, autoethnography looks to the ways culture interacts with bodies (be that individual or communal) and allows for that knowledge manifested in those relationship to become *the* text, theory, audience, and critique. Tony E. Adams, Stacy Holman Jones, and Carolyn Ellis surmise that "[a]lthough most texts produce some kind of knowledge—every advertisement, movie, theater production, or novel offers a window into and insight about society—autoethnographers *intentionally* use personal experiences to create *nuanced, complex,* and *comprehensive* accounts of cultural norms, experiences, and practices" (32–33). As a method, autoethnography "take[s] seriously the *epistemic* (claims to knowledge) and the *aesthetic* (practices of imaginative, creative, and artistic craft) characteristics. . . . [T]his means studying and practicing the methods and means for conducting *research*, as well as studying and practicing the mechanics and means for making *art* (e.g., poetry, fiction, performance, music, dance, painting, photography, film)" (Adams et al. 23). Additionally, autoethnography as a method allows the speaker/writer to use rhetoric as a means of "doing, sharing, and reading" their own embodied experiences, their own voice and visual representations of Blackness as cultural, personal texts that are (and can be) validated in public spheres (Chang 53). Thus, "autoethnography can also help transform researchers and readers (listeners) in the process," (53) making these Black women (music artists) teachers, rhetoricians, and philosophers.

For rhetoric and composition scholars, the sonic is a subfield; it signifies an underused area of research that broadens the complicated notions of and relationship with voice, materiality, and spatiality in which to cultivate a context of meaning (Hawk 2018; Rickert 2013). For some scholars in Black studies (or gender and sexuality studies) where the body holds prominence, the sonic is a metaphysical third space communicating alternate histories and identities performed through vibrations and resonance (Stoever 2016; Eidsheim 2019). I would also suggest some rhetoric, composition, and/or communication scholars like Karma Chávez (2018) would find their work aligned with this school of thought because of the overt intersectional framing and emphasis on embodiment. And for some artists, the sonic acts as an affective method meant to invoke critical listening and thinking (Campt 2017) through one's subjectivity. Here the sonic is a rhetoric that vibrates and resonates through listening and emotion. Sonic rhetoric is a way of reading the body, of reading materiality, and of reading reflections of identity across media through the many ways one interprets messages. It is a methodology that inhabits the in-betweenness of self-making and space-making be that on page, on stage, in the airwaves, or in the bedroom in front of the mirror as we twerk to Beyoncé's "Sorry." Sonic rhetoric is how our bodies digest and produce voice, volume, noise, and vibration as a means of communication, to say the least.

As such, I emphasize the intertextuality of Black women's generational sonic rhetoric, both past and present, to continue giving language to my own lived experiences and the experiences of other Black women and girls. Through these sonic mechanizations, we can understand Black women's sonic rhetoric as audible advice, or iterations of mentorship in sound, aimed at connecting and transmitting generational meaning, experiences, and lessons learned across time, space, and place. We can expand our understanding of Black women's contributions as rhetorical agents by discussing various ways Black women operationalize sound into action. We can recognize Black women's rhetorical innovation to retell our stories across media sounding out many methods for surviving, navigating, healing, and imagining ways forward.

The chapters presented here are intended to complicate the messy relationship of rhetoric, sound, and identity while simultaneously revisioning possibilities for understanding "the rhetor" as a multidimensional and holistic model. At the heart of this reimagining for rhetoric and composition are Black women: our narratives, our literacies, our rhetorics, our languages, and our technologies. As such, this work takes up Black women's rich history in the hopes of evoking more attention to the lineages left behind and still being produced today. Recovering Black feminist intellectual traditions like the ones unfolding within this book, surmises Patricia Hill Collins, calls for "[r]einterpreting existing works through new theoretical frameworks . . . . Reclaiming the Black feminist intellectual tradition also involves searching for its expression in alternative institutional locations and among women who are not commonly perceived as intellectuals" (14). She leaves the door open for a project like mine, suggesting that "[m]usicians, vocalists, poets, writers, and other artists constitute another group of Black women intellectuals who have aimed to interpret Black women's experiences." She adds, "Such women are typically thought of as nonintellectual and nonscholarly classifications that create a false dichotomy between scholarship and activism, between thinking and doing" (15–16). Suspending these socially constructed binaries offers possibilities for more critical examinations of Black women's contributions.

The first chapter, "Sonic Sharecropping," investigates the exploitative practices employed by recording labels. Interpreted as a vernacular, and often audible, space of knowledge-making, "sonic sharecropping" describes the limited professional mobility Black women music artists were often faced with. It parallels their experiences in the music industry with antiBlack practices of sharecropping, arguing these actions are similar to the post-emancipative exercise of legal economic "freedom" in the Jim Crow era. Through this concept, this chapter connects sharecropping's harmful, racist legacy to the continued exploitation of early Black women recording artists in emerging genres of music like blues, rhythm and blues, and jazz. With recent cases of producers selling artists' music, like Scooter Braun and Taylor Swift, or artists' selling their rights to their own music, like Bob Dylan, the concept of "sonic sharecropping" can be seen not only as alive and well but also as evolving. Both Dylan and Braun/Swift profited from these exorbitant but "fair"[2] sale prices, while Black women music artists historically have rarely been fairly paid for their work. Grounded by professional and life writing, this chapter exposes the audible arm of lingering oppressive colonial tactics that historically have been used to control and/or manipulate people of color's economic conditions.

Chapter 2, "Strange Fruit Sonic Rhetorics," examines the evolution of Billie Holiday's rendition of "Strange Fruit" into a rhetorical discourse resisting antiBlackness and how it is later used by two contemporary Black women musicians, Melissa Elliot and Janelle Monáe Robinson. This chapter establishes how "Strange Fruit" becomes translated across generations from a visual image created by sound to a figure of speech. Using the vocalized imaging of strange fruit, that is, hanged Black bodies, I comment on the ways sound forms a means of resistance. More specifically, this chapter describes how the vocalized form of strange fruit changes over time and becomes symbolic of "the changing same" represented by the continued, repurposed iterations of strange fruit as a concept. This repetition suggests that we are not in a post-racial society, but that racism *is* very much alive.

Chapter 3, takes a closer look at sound, identity, and time by theorizing their intersections as part of a larger move to write the self and (re)claim agency at the sonic level. Said another way, this chapter explores how Black women music artists make space in their performances to assert themselves as agents, which, I argue, is done by taking time. This taking of time can be seen in the composing of sounds meant to stretch and hold the attention of the listener, making them likelier to remember the performance, the message, and the speaker. Using grammar, duration, repetition, and paralexical phenomena as techniques for altering time, I emphasize the ways Black women sonically counter demoralizing notions and stereotypes of Black womanhood. In pursuing this argument, this chapter identifies ways language can be used as a method of survival to the point at which Black women become visible as independent agents.

Chapter 4 puts forth the concept of "sonic mentorship," which examines a process of collective, sonorous knowledge-making production. More specifically, this concept is centered on the audibility of advice—primarily the advice from older Black women (music artists)—as an important vernacular roadmap aiding (younger) generations' navigation of space and reality over time. Using autobiographies and record albums as life writing, I argue that experiences that are are translated into and from gossip and interludes are generationally operationalized by Black women as a means for making sense of the world. Ultimately this chapter aims to present Black women's use of voice as a multigenerational and multimedia composing process for social justice pedagogies.

Finally, "Reverb," the concluding chapter, takes a closer look at the repeating themes threaded through the work. Here, I theorize the impacts and potentialities of sound and the sonic as part of a Black feminist rhetorical tradition. In this way, I offer my final thoughts on a century of Black women's meaning-making through and with sound.

This book recognizes Black women's generational sonic rhetorics as an applicable, embodied portion of Black feminist and antiracist theory. Moreover, the threads of thought streaming through these chapters recognizes Black women's generational sonic rhetoric as communicable care reinforcing our ability to survive and thrive—from ensuring Black support networks flourish beyond normative social expectations, to connecting and identifying the many ways antiBlackness systematically mutates, to building a resistive language springing from our temporality, to translating antiBlackness across time and media to answer back with Black feminist interpretations of hope. This book acts as the bridge between genres, between generations, and between discourses to (re)focus conversations of Black women's rhetorical presence in sound. *From Blues to Beyoncé* sees the importance of connecting rhetorical models found in Black music, like the blues, to the rhetorical models found in self-writing to create a caring dialogue and vocabulary extending conversations and future research regarding rhetorical (sonic) agency. More broadly, *From Blues to Beyoncé* is a history of Black women's sound.

Last, this book is intended as a kind of liner note accompanying Black women (music artists') generational sonic rhetorics in the hopes of resonating with you on some personal level. What I've tried to communicate throughout these pages is the outstanding ability Black women (music artists) have to change our own realities—individually and communally. The Black women (music artists) invoked here demonstrate a small sample of what we've been able to do with and in sound. They represent the numerous possibilities still to research and argue for our liberation, survival, and healing. Black women's generational sonic rhetorics surpasses such confining borders; their work is cumulative, collaborative, and innovative.

1

Sonic Sharecropping

Okurrr

—Cardi B

Or is it just a reassertion of the record industry's plantation mentality, in which music makers are treated like sharecroppers to be paid what the companies want, when they get around to it?

—Ruth Brown (293)

Fertile Ground: Sound as Land + Labor

Black music, specifically in the American context, is a major factor in the formation of social life. However, the ability to control our own creativity, ingenuity, and public-facing identity largely rests in the hands of power brokers who are often outside our own communities and immediate discourses. In these types of negotiations, elites, executives, and gatekeepers assess our cultural cache, leveraging our popularity against our "talent," to charge and exploit our labor as they bank on large potential profit margins. This process of economic risk/reward not only has been practiced for generations, but also has seeped into other major fabrications of our daily lives, from recording industry practices to academic socialization.

This chapter theorizes exploitative practices employed by some recording labels, arguing that the historical antiBlack practice of sharecropping can also been seen within sonic labor practices and expectations.

Moreover, I contend that cultural appropriation is intimately tied to extralegal practices, such as the Petrillo Strikes and the RICO Act, ultimately informing sharecropping's racist legacy, which continues in gendered, exploitative iterations beyond agriculture. In recognizing sharecropping's permutations, we can better understand how antiBlack mindsets extend beyond singular instances. Racism is a peripatetic, converging ecology. Recognizing this mobilization across time, space, and medium affords us more critical interpretations and teachings regarding the many instances of exploitative harm directly impacting Black women recording artists' labor, creativity, and sonic style.

These demeaning practices are seen in moments where emerging genres of Black music—like blues, rhythm and blues, and jazz—take shape. Artist Ruth Brown provides telling descriptions of how "sonic sharecropping" processes were constructed and affected various aspects of daily survival. In doing so, she leaves behind pedagogical pathways for navigating antiBlack acts within the recording industry's all too-often attempted spirit murder[1] and co-optation; she provides one model of resistance to racism's permutation. Grounded by governmental policy as well as archival and biographical information, this chapter exposes oppressive colonial tactics and traditions historically used to control and/or manipulate people of color's economic conditions through inequitable remuneration of labor.

With this intersectional tapestry in mind, my aim in this chapter is to better understand mechanisms underlying systematic exploitation of Black folks. It is my hope that, in doing this, we can better recognize the transmission of antiBlack policies and processes—remaining vigilant against its attacks. As in other chapters of this work, I primarily focus on Black women's positioning within and navigation of this oppressive ecology. And, while I don't have answers regarding how to solve the many iterations of sharecropping built into our popular institutions, I can suggest that Black women's generational sonic rhetoric not only contributed to the dismantling (however minor) of some systemic, antiBlack structures but also provided instructive countermeasures for asserting agency in these harsh ecologies.

Developing a Sharecropping Praxis and Mentality

To get a fuller picture of what I am arguing here, I dive deeper into historical approaches to sharecropping. Sharecropping has been practiced for centuries in many cultures across the globe. Some societies may call it by a different name, like "share contract," "share farming," "tenant farming," and "landlord-tenant model," but the concept is still the same. In its basic form, sharecropping is an obligatory relationship between someone who "owns" and someone who cultivates the land. Sharecropping is most often discussed in economic, agricultural, or political terms.

From an economic perspective, sharecropping was a legal, semi-reciprocal form of exchange in which landowners supply plots of land to individuals, families, or working groups. In exchange for allowing people to settle on and cultivate the land for livelihood and potential economic independence, landowners would receive payment in the form of crops, goods, and supplemental monetary payment. The landowner(s) then sold these procured goods at higher prices on open markets and kept the proceeds. In Derek Gregory's *The Dictionary of Human Geography,* Miriam Well details this exchange process as usually "involve[ing] short-term contracts for the annual [agrarian] cycle of production of a specific crop in which crop raising is contracted out to labouring households, individuals or work gangs, who thereby take on the large part of economic risks of production" (681). More complex economic webs could also involve commissaries and third-party vendors to buy and sell essential items for the cultivation or exchange of commerce. Part of what made this practice unusually common, despite its being a fiscal commonsensical oxymoron, was its embedded hierarchy that offset seasonal risks of agricultural failures. The potential to accrue and/or maintain power through monetary exploitation surpassed the potential pitfalls of agricultural failure and uncertainty for land "owners," thus incentivizing this lopsided partnership.

The politics of this economic process involved distributing power based on fiscal expenditures and labor output. Debpriya Sen suggests that the landowner's ability to "sell his output at a higher price" socially translates to a perceived social hierarchy demonstrating "the superiority of sharecropping *over* fixed rental contracts" (182, emphasis added); thus, most of the power is placed in the contract holder's/landlord's hands. The owner of the goods can manipulate the marketplace (e.g., hoarding and/or transporting crops to more malleable markets) and receive maximum payment for the goods. This capitalistic process stands in opposition to the general process of sharecropping agreements where crop yield equates to fixed rental agreements—clearly providing the contract owner with the upper hand. This "superiority" is bolstered by the sharecropping contract's specifications constructed by landowners. Landlords "specifie[d] the shares for both parties, a rental transfer and a price at which he offers to buy the tenant's share of output. These are interlinked contracts that enable the landlord to interact with the tenant in two markets: land (through share and rent) and product (through his offer of price)" (Sen 182). The landowner, the one who safekeeps and amends the contract(s) at will, maintains the definitive authority or control over the tenant who depends on the contract for survival. As such, "The tenant's incentive is determined by (i) his share and (ii) the price he receives for his share, so the optimal level of incentive can be sustained by multiple combinations of these two variables" (Sen 182). On the surface, these contracts seem straightforward. However, these contracts don't often stipulate or acknowledge the vast network of intermediaries who have (or are given) more power, control, or autonomy over the sharecropper *because* of their social standing (e.g., ethnicity, class, national identity). This piecemealing of power between/within an agricultural-labor economy no longer represents equal distribution among the parties involved. Someone will be short-changed as those in power try to grab more "power."

As such, from a psychological standpoint, the "superiority" also manifests in the landowner's ability to exploit, manipulate, and control sharecroppers' behaviors. In the article "Altruism, Moral Hazard, and Sharecropping," Jiancai Pi notes that economic advisors and theorists such as Avishay Braverman and Joseph E. Stiglitz—who suggested that sharecropping is composed of interlocking systems (1982)—and Hallagan (1978)—who discusses the rhetorical risks involved with taking on sharecropping as a business venture—consider sharecropping as a far-reaching, intimate, and hierarchical transaction. Pi notes that "Braverman and Stiglitz (1982) further argue that under the share contract, the landlord can induce the tenet to behave in the way he/she likes through the interlinking contracts which are related to the land, labour, credit and product market" (qtd. in Pi 575). Pi also draws on Hallagan (1978), who asserts that "abstracts from the moral hazard considerations and shows that the share contract and the fixed rent contract can act as a screening device which is used to distinguish the tenets with different skills or abilities" (qtd. in Pi 575). Said another way, the landlords use the contract as a way for interviewing prospective tenants; if the prospective sharecropper seems too "resistive" (or add any other negative adjective used to stereotype Black folks here), then the landlord can reject the sharecropper or change the contract altogether. The contract owner thus threatens to withhold the possibility of survival from the sharecropper if they don't agree to acquiesce. These psychological aspects play into sharecropping's practice, which inherently creates conditions that favor oppressive and hierarchical structuring.

In a similar vein, Well adds, "[s]hare farming undermines the solidarity of the work force, increasing the landowner's ability to set the terms of the relationship [. . . . and] stratifies the work force into components with different prerogatives and obligations ("The Resurgence of Sharecropping" 19–20). Sharecropping can instill social hierarchies by pitting ideologies (i.e., political philosophies, human rights beliefs, etc.) against each other—often through manipulating economic conditions—so that multiple collaborating units prioritize different aspects and outcomes of the job at hand. As a result of this divided mentality (and respective individualistic prioritization), current working conditions either remain the same or deteriorate. In either instance, the faction in power stays in power because the subsets of workers are more concerned with their own group needs or requirements than with the betterment of the whole; this creates an internal stratification and diminishes the possibility for unionizing and enforcing equity on all levels.

As an economic motivation for landowner(s) to psychologically control laborers, sharecropping increases laissez-faire leadership. This hands-off management approach decreases supervisory expenditures by maximizing cheap, unregulated labor costs that can easily be manipulated (Well, "The Resurgence of Sharecropping" 19–20). Extending slavery's use of "the overseer," this method of surveillance—which is the threat of always being watched—encouraged sharecroppers to govern themselves in line with the landowner's expectations and directives. Simone Browne, author of *Dark Matters: On the Surveillance of Blackness*, provides a similar analysis by way of the Panopticon. Referencing Jeremy Bentham's eighteenth-century architectural blueprint, Browne describes this structure's initial purpose as "a model for workforce supervision" (33). She goes on to explain that "With this 'seeing machine' [that is, the self-surveillance structure], the unverified few could watch the many and 'the more constantly the persons to be inspected are under the eyes of the persons who should inspect them, the more perfectly will the purpose of the establishment have been attained.' This is control by design, where population management and the transmission of knowledge about the subject could . . . be achieved" (qtd. in Browne 33–34). In other words, sharecropping functioned within a minimum input-maximum output model that exploited marginalized folk's labor to do not only the work needed for cultivation but also the work of policing ourselves; doing this cut the number of expenditures the employer should have been responsible for, thus gaining additional funds for him-/herself.

However, one glaring presupposition stands tall in these few accounts of sharecropping. Embedded within this process is the overwhelming dependency on ethics, morals, and equity—or the lack thereof. There is an assumption that the landlord will be fair in purchasing the crops harvested on "his" land, is fair in renting out fertile plots for cultivation, and is ethical in "his" expectations of a "work"/life balance. These implied treatments were not always granted, as we know from historical accounts, particularly in the post–Civil War American South. What remains a continuous thread across different cultures' use of sharecropping is that this practice almost always "tend[s] to be associated with highly concentrated patterns of landownership and exploitive labour relations" (Well, *The History of Human Geography* 681). Exploitation remains a theme of antiBlack practices even as we move across time, space, and medium.

Southern State of Mind: Normative Applications of Sharecropping

Much of these discussions, from economic, political, or psychological discourses, largely contextualize this sharecropping praxis within a large-scale, community-based ecology rather than on individualistic levels. However, popular culture and literary scholarship contextualize sharecropping on a much more personal level. In the post–Civil War American South,[2] sharecropping was, as Raymond Gavins explains, "[a] post-bellum farming system that mirrored southern slavery"; it was a system that intentionally targeted

> far more black than white tenant farmers. Blacks accommodated it to survive, to escape gang work and the whip. They hoped to support themselves while protecting their women and children. Landlords and sharecroppers signed contracts for "halves." The landlord furnished the land, house, fuel, tools, work stock, feed for stock, seed, and half the fertilizer; he earned half the crop. The cropper supplied labor and half the fertilizer, earning half the crop. He also had to repay (at high interest) for food and supplies from the store, clearing little or nothing when he settled. Sharecropping fueled landlords' cheating as well as racial violence. (251)

With this in mind, Black authors, artists, activists, and scholars alike detail and define sharecropping in much bleaker personal contexts.

As Jerry Ward writes in *The Richard Wright Encyclopedia*, sharecropping in the American South dates "back to the Reconstruction period when the United States withdrew its troops from the South in 1877" (239). The vacuum created by government's absence after declaring the Civil War's end allowed for "southern states to re-enslave black people with systems of segregation and sharecropping" (Ward 239). Furthermore, white Southern landlords used sharecropping as

> an oppressive system of exploitation of unskilled labor in the South, especially black unskilled labor. It grew out of the social disorganization, agricultural disasters, and extreme poverty which southerners faced as a result of the Civil War. . . . Plantation commissaries were established to furnish supplies to tenants who bought these supplies on credit. This credit would be paid off at harvest time with crops raised by the sharecropper. . . . sharecropping] became a brutal form of economic exploitation amounting to forced labor of blacks and poor whites, condemning them to a mode of life which preserved many of the forms of slavery. Landowners paid so little for the crops raised and harvested by their tenant farmers that these people were forced into perennial debt and dependency upon plantation owners. Southern sharecroppers from the 1880s to the 1950s received some of the lowest wages and harshest working conditions of any American workers. (Ward 349)

Just as Ward mentioned, Joy DeGruy, author of *Post Traumatic Slave Syndrome: America's Legacy of Enduring Injury and Healing*, explains that landowners or merchants "charge[d] exorbitantly high interest rates, rates that made it impossible for families to pay off their debts. Other merchants would take advantage of the local sharecropper's illiteracy and simply create false billing statements," resulting, inevitably, in more debt, thus "be[ing] forced to remain on the farm to work in order to clear the debt" (83). Under the threat of re-enslavement or other extra-legal processes such as lynching or convict leasing, Black folks would start the cycle over again: borrowing money to till the land in hopes of a better yield to not only pay off the previous debt but also buy our way to freedom—eventually. This was our immediate "liberation" after a bloody Civil War: much of the same thing. As such, "Sharecropping and segregation, therefore, became interlocking structures of social, political, and economic domination which deprived African American people of the rights and opportunities of American life" (Ward 350).

In fact, remnants of sharecropping and convict leasing are still seen in contemporary times. Michelle Alexander reports that "Upon release from prison, people are typically saddled with large debt—financial shackles that hobble them as they struggle to build a new life. In this system of control, like the one that prevailed during Jim Crow, one's 'debt to society' often reflects the cost of imprisonment" (154). The contemporary system of agricultural sharecropping (Well, "The Resurgence of Sharecropping" 1984) also resonates in America's manufacturing of the prison-industrial complex. "Throughout the United States, newly released prisoners are required to make payments to a host of agencies, including probation departments, courts, and child-support enforcement offices," Alexander writes (154). Additionally, "[i]n some jurisdictions, ex-offenders are billed for drug testing and even for the drug treatment they are supposed to receive as a condition of parole . . . . Every state has its own rules and regulations governing their imposition (Alexander 154–55). Some of these fees that Alexander refers to include pre- and post-conviction fees like "jail book-in fees levied at the time of arrest, jail per-diems assessed to cover the cost of pretrial detention, public defender application fees . . . , and the bail investigation fee imposed when the court determines the likelihood of the accused appearing at trial," as well as report fees and fees associated with the cost of "caring" for convicts in "residential or work-release program[s]" (155). Similar to the earlier sharecropping intimidation practices, those in the position of power (i.e., the landlord and appointed authorities) exercise their power when convicts released from prison fail to pay their fee or "debt to society," resulting in possible "additional community control sanctions or a modification in the offender's sentence" (Alexander 155). In addition to these immediate fees, some states enforce what Alexander has called " 'poverty penalties'—piling on additional late fees, payment plan fees, and interest when individuals are unable to pay all their debts at once, often enriching private debt collectors in the process" (155). Even though " 'debtor's prison' is illegal in all states, many use the threat of probation or parole revocation as a debt-collection tool. In fact, in some jurisdictions, individuals may 'choose' to go to jail as a way to reduce their debt burdens, a practice that has been challenged as unconstitutional"

(Alexander 156). The relationship and evolution of sharecropping praxes has, indeed, seeped into many institutional frameworks. The recording industry is not exempt from such critique, as early practices show similar interactions and legacies. This history demonstrates an impossible trap for Black folks long in the making. The limited ways for resisting these processes meant that Black folks had to find other ways for cultivating freedom, survival, and liberation.

Now, I realize these descriptions and definitions laid out in the paragraphs above are taken from a particular imperial or colonial logic. To "own" land (or bodies, as we understand the Southern logic behind enslavement) is to side with a particular epistemology grounded in colonization and early settler ideologies. As Anthony Pagden explained, early British (and to some degree French) settlers in North and South America "legitimize[d] their settlements in terms of one or another variant on the Roman Law argument known as *res nullius*. This maintained that all 'empty things,' which included unoccupied lands, remained the common property of all mankind until they were put to some, generally agricultural, use. The first person to use the land in this way became its owner" (76). This political, philosophical, and utilitarian theorization of power or superiority extended to occupants of the land as well. If inhabitants were not using the land "appropriately" or in a manner that helped to manifest the potentiality of life, then the inhabitants became susceptible to colonization, enslavement, and/or conversion.

The influential eighteenth-century work of Emeric de Vattel took up a particular iteration of this Roman law in his writing, which became a model for arguments in favor of colonization: "the cultivation of the land . . . is not simply improvement; for [Vattel] . . . a crucial part of what it is to be human is the drive to actualize nature's potentiality, an obligation 'imposed upon man by nature' . . . . They fail 'in their duty to themselves' as men, . . . since it clearly constitutes a violation of the law of nature, makes them less than human" (Pagden 79). Of course, these imperial ideologies are incredibly problematic, both in retrospect and by today's measures, but unpacking the interconnectedness of these antiBlack practices and logics demonstrates how deep and interconnected racism is to numerous popular institutions. Taken together, Black bodies have been classified as unimportant and less than human, some*thing* to control, especially as white settler logic has mapped the idea of *res nullius* onto our bodies.

Coining a Phrase

There are other insidious ways sharecropping's evolution has manifested. In March 2019, singer/rapper/actress Belcalis Marlenis Almánzar, better known as Cardi B, attempted to trademark a vernacular revision of "okay" suggesting that her signature trill of the tongue, high-pitched tonal inflection, and drawn-out ending of "okurrr" is a distinguishable sonic lexicon[3] specific to her identity or public persona. A *Billboard* article reported that her petition to trademark this word's revision intended "to cover 'clothing, namely, T-shirts, sweatshirts, hooded sweatshirts, pants, shorts, jackets, footwear, headgear, namely hats and caps, blouses, bodysuits, dresses, jumpsuits, leggings, shirts, sweaters, undergarments' using both 3 R and 2 R versions of the phrase" (Kaufman). While the petition primarily covers material ephemera, many people wondered if this move also extended to the daily utterance or digital use of the phrase. But how could one know the difference between "okurr," "okurrr," or "okurrrrr," for instance, without seeing it spelled out on a screen or in print or timing how long the note had been held? How can one translate a phrase based on sound, repetition, and its (hang)time? Does taxing the use of the word do much to change or separate the sociocultural context of the term from its phonetic meaning? Cardi B's petition asks us to critically think about how sound can be made profitable and how she could maintain control of her material and sonic "crops." Indeed, this example leads us to rethink what "coining a phrase" may actually mean. As such, this scene highlights messy relationships between language, identity, and power as they filter through lenses of labor, race, gender, and class, as well as nationality, space, and/or medium.

According to the United States Patent and Trademark Office (USPTO), "[a] trademark is a word, phrase, symbol, and/or design that identifies and distinguishes the source of the goods of one party from those of others" ("What Is a Trademark?"). In addition to protecting Cardi B from other people copying or using her sonic identity without her permission, this move to trademark a specific pronunciation of "okay" potentially meant that she could make money anytime someone was documented using her revision of the term, giving her exclusive rights to the word. In other words, it would have allowed her to charge folks who assumed her voice or asked for her labor as they specifically requested she perform this word. Trademarking "okurrr" was, potentially, a way to capitalize mainstream's cultural appropriation of her public persona and bilingual identity.

As public awareness of her petition grew, a wave of backlash began to surface, attacking Cardi B for her grossly capitalistic move. *ET Canada* critiqued Cardi B's live Instagram post where she expressed her motivation and frustration at the recent public resentment criticizing her attempt of commercializing her language use. In her post, she said:

> Y'all hoes is mad because I [tried to] trademark "okurrr"?! Let me tell you somethin'. Every single time I go to these corporate meetings these folks be like [in a "white" voice] "Oh my God, can we just please hear you say 'okurrr.' [in Black language] Every time I go to a TV show: "hey, hey, can you teach me how to say 'okurrr'?" "Hey, hey, hey." Every time I go and do a commercial: "hey can you finish it off with 'okurrr'?" You think I ain't gonna profit off this shit?! Bitch! White folks do it all the mutha fuckin' time! So you wanna be mad at me cuz I wanna get some mutha fuckin' money?! Huh! [quick laugh] Let me tell ya somethin', while I'm still here, I'ma secure all the fuckin bags. ("Cardi B Defends Trademarking 'Okurrr,'" 0:00–0:32)

Even though various publics lashed out in response to Cardi B's move, she does bring up a valid point about the inequitable expectations and assumptions of non-white, particularly Black, women's "free" labor (be that physical, social, emotional, or, in this case, sonic and linguistic). With this exchange, she illuminates the antiBlack historical trend (often permeated by misogynoir[4]) of name calling that positions Black women as mammies and/or as gold-diggers—separating Black women's bodies from our lived identities, motivations, epistemologies, and labor. However, Black feminists often use intersectionality to bring these spheres together as overlapping aspects of our everyday life. Her explicit attempted trademark and response to critics interrupt a long-standing and perceived adherence to respectability politics for Black women; she challenges public musings of how far Black women's agency can be stretched on the intersectional playing field. Once this lexicon becomes embedded within popular culture, it is hard to fault Cardi B's attempt at profiteering from the word, particularly because of its swift uptake in memes, merchandise, TV shows, and commercials. Marginalized people's work so often gets co-opted and makes a profit for someone other than the people who created it.

This public consumption and appropriation were especially evident in a 2019 Superbowl commercial for Pepsi ("Okurrr | Pepsi 30") in which the rapper made an appearance. In the beginning of the ad, a customer, sitting at a booth in what appears to be an updated nostalgic Americana diner, asks the waitress for a Coke. The waitress, pulling out her notepad from the front pocket of her white apron, responds: "Is Pepsi okay?" The next scene frames Cardi B (with long, straight blonde hair and dressed in a nude-colored, bedazzled corset and matching denim jacket and short denim cutoffs), who whips her head around, looking back at the waitress and customer, and asks in disbelief: "Did you just ask, 'Is Pepsi okurrr'?!" Stunned, the waitress responds with "Excuse me?!?" Cardi B then fills her in: "Of course Pepsi is 'okurrr'!" The baffled waitress directs her question at her customer in a hushed voice and asks him to translate: "Is she saying 'okay?,'" to which Cardi B interrupts and clarifies: "No, no, no. okurrrrrrrr."

Following this exchange, nearby spectators join in and try to mimic the singer/rapper/actress's lexicon. These spectators-turned-participants, mainly consisting of middle-aged and older white men and women, try their hands at rolling their tongues like Cardi B. After the camera shows a handful of white folks' botched attempts at this specific pronunciation, the camera pans to one queer Black body in minimal drag who tries to help the confused white people with their pronunciation, saying, "Like this: 'okurrrrrrrrr.'" Following the quick tutorial, we follow the camera's gaze, allowing us to view more everyday people trying to replicate this specific wording and, in effect, imitate Cardi B. One segment of this reaction even shows two pigeons cooing on the windowsill outside the diner, looking in on their human counterparts, emphasizing both the word's sound and motion of the neck needed for some to produce a semi-respectable reproduction of the rolled "r" in their vocal "okurrr."

Nearing the end of the commercial, the hodgepodge of (mis)pronunciations from spectator-participants is abruptly truncated by a slurping sound; we see the original customer (who asked for a Coke) sucking up the last drops of his Pepsi while conveniently standing near a soda-dispensing machine with the Pepsi logo in clear sight. The customer looks up to a now-silent room and asks "What?! I wanted a Pepsi, okurrr." Satisfied with the ultimate outcome, Cardi B gets the last word on the matter: "Now that's what I'm talkin' about, oww!" As we watch the last scene of the commercial, where Cardi B drinks an ice-cold Pepsi from a full glass that has the soft drink's logo perfectly placed for the viewer's eyes to read with ease, we hear Cardi B's hit single "I Like It" play in the background ("Okurrr | Pepsi 30").

This now-ubiquitous popular culture terminology proved to be a primary reason for denying Cardi B the trademark. Ultimately, her application was rejected by the USPTO because "okurrr" is seen as a "slogan or term that does not function as a trademark," meaning the term does not "indicate the source of [Cardi B's] goods and/or services," nor does it "identify and distinguish them from others," essentially arguing that "the applied-for mark is a commonplace term, message, or expression widely used by a variety of sources that merely conveys an ordinary, familiar, well-recognized concept or sentiment." The trademark office went on to add that "[t]his term or expression is commonly used in the drag community and by celebrities as an alternate way of saying 'OK' or 'something that is said to affirm when someone is being put in their place' " (qtd. in Kaufman). The trademark denial adds fuel to arguments regarding who owns language and debates of the term's origins. The dramatized lexical performance, that is, the holding of the rolled "r" for an extended amount of time, can signal support for and/or critique of playful semantics. This sonic performance can also document the singer's agency through Black grammar and queer time, as a later chapter suggests. Furthermore, this performance also prompts larger conversations regarding how common language appropriation in sonic, digital, and physical spaces impacts many marginalized people's livelihood, making us think about this ecology more critically.

So how do we continue the conversation that Cardi B started? Better yet, how we can use Cardi B's prosodic[5] application of Black grammar[6] and time to further investigate Black women's sonic and rhetorical methods of agency-making? How is Cardi B's legal battle situated in a longer history of devaluing Black women's labor? Answers to these questions can be found by taking a closer look at the sociohistorical context of Black women's (sonic) rhetoric *as part of* the labor we are asked and expected to do.

Resonance of (Sonic) Labor

Juxtaposing sharecropping's discourse with the recording industry's development and early treatment of its artists is not a far stretch for the imagination. With this sociocultural-sociohistorical context in mind, I situate my argument within these lineages highlighting the kinds of tensions Black women's sounds and voices confront. Sonically reorienting sharecropping's definition allows us to clearly see the abstract and intersectional relationships between "ownership" and "labor." In this sensorial iteration, the cultivated land becomes the curated body (including its embedded acoustics), and the profit comes not from crops but the artists' ephemeral and sonic material. This residual auditory identity is used by managers and audiences alike as a base substance for cultural appropriation and public exhibition of Black bodies (i.e., the contracted artists). As such, "sonic sharecropping" parallels this sociohistorical antiBlack practice—even as traditional sharecropping becomes "unlawful"—as it relies on similar exploitative methods targeting marginalized populations to create and enrich profit for a group of people already in positions of power. Said in another way, sonic sharecropping invokes the same exploitative process for Black folks as agricultural sharecropping did in the post–Civil War era; thus, the liberal[7] "color-blind" economic gain—regardless of the "crop"—was still reinforcing similar social hierarchies positioning white cis fe/males as gatekeepers and wielders of power at the expense of Black bodies' labor, voice, hope, and existence.

Sonic sharecropping extended explicit antiBlack practices, spinning webs of (social) debt for Black (women) music artists in the form of social caché and entertainment. Early recording company practices abused (and, for some, continue abusing) Black bodies' laboring and skill for the company's own profit. Even as Black music artists, especially Black women, found ways to survive and collect some monetary support for survival (as we see with Cardi B's attempted trademark), recording practices, legally binding contracts, public opinion/respectability politics, and government policy pressured Black artists to continue working themselves into pauper's graves with very little recourse.

This chapter interprets sonic sharecropping as a vernacular, and often audible, racist practice that Black women (music artists) frequently confront—sometimes with their activism, their sound or voice, their performance, and/or their mentorship. Their moments of autonomy, negotiation, and resistance reflect ways Black women music artists push back on the recording industry's attempt at "ownership" of their public and sonic identity. It is in these moments, where Black women speak back to these oppressive expectations, we can see their generational sonic rhetorics extend into metaphysical spaces of knowledge-making, knowledge-mobilization, and negotiation. These are moments that Browne defines as "dark sousveillance," which "plots imaginaries that are oppositional and that are hopeful for another way of being. Dark sousveillance is a site of critique, as it speaks back to black epistemologies of contending with antiblack surveillance, where the tools of social control in plantation surveillance . . . were appropriated, co-opted, repurposed, and challenged in order to facilitate survival and escape" (21). Black women's sonic resistance as it is described here can be thought, in part, as a social method for resistance, survival, and social health. As such, Black women's generational contributions of sonic rhetorics supplement strategies for survival and resistance, often resulting in coalitional network building and subversion of normative expectations.

Tensions with Technology and the Early Days of the Industry: Unionizing Sound + Twentieth-Century Legislative Affairs

The Atlantic Recording Corporation, commonly known as Atlantic Records, was founded in 1947 by Ahmet Ertegun, "the little Turkish Prince,[8]" and Herbert "Herb" Charles Abramson. Although Ertegun was a music mogul by the time of his death in 2006, he was not always the picture of success—though he was always privileged. Born to Hayrünnisa and Munir Ertegun,[9] Ahmet Ertegun enjoyed a privileged upbringing.

As a result of his father's passing and his choice to stay in the United States for college, the Turkish government granted him a $100 monthly allowance. Even though this subsidized paycheck was more than many working-class family salaries, Ertegun still fell on hard times. Some family friends offered him help in terms of extra funds, job opportunities, and rent-free accommodations in New York City. Free housing and a monthly allowance were nothing to downplay, but even with these entitlements, it was not enough for Ertegun to live the artistic lifestyle he envisioned for himself. To make ends meet during this transitional stage, he sold off his vast record collection and became an expert at swindling money from his affluent connections.

As he grew older, he visited musical acts in Black city centers like Harlem, Philadelphia, Houston, Atlanta, and Annapolis—surrounding himself with Black music as often as he wanted. While he was in college, Ertegun decided to take his love of music more seriously, turning his passion for Black music into his profession. Having navigated the elite social circles from his time in DC, Ertegun was already familiar with what the recording industry appeared to be. According to Robert Greenfield, author of *The Last Sultan: The Life and Times of Ahmet Ertegun*, Ertegun remarked that

> all these guys who had these independent record companies . . . were all a bunch of third-rate crooks. They were jukebox operators or they had nightclubs in black sections or whatever. Anyway, they were all like very rough-and-tumble guys who didn't know much about music. I figured, "If they could make it, I certainly can. I know much more than they do." I knew much more about what black people bought in record shops than any of these people. I knew who the musicians were. I knew the singers. And I knew who was buying what and what to make. (110)

Armed with connections and gusto, Ertegun decided to capitalize on his panache for appropriating Black culture. His experience at Howard University and his frequent visits to clubs in DC and New York, for instance, led him to believe he had a deep understanding of Black life in America. Ertegun said he felt like he "knew what black life was like . . . . I felt I knew what black music was . . . . I felt I knew what black roots were—gospel music and blues from the Delta that went to Chicago and Texas blues that went to the West Coast. In loving America, I felt I knew more about America than the average American knew about it" (Greenfield 110). Rather than rely on education to fulfill his notion of the "American dream," Ertegun depended on his vision of Black music to make a career for himself.

    Eventually, Ertegun and best friend, Herb Abramson, founded Atlantic Records in 1947. Abramson "brought more than just a shared interest in black roots music and hands-on experience in actually making records to the venture" (Greenfield 119). Abramson also provided the clout on which the American Federation of Musicians (AFM)[10] granted Ertegun and Abramson license to become a recording company. Abramson also brought in some of the first artists to record hits for the fledgling Atlantic Records. All they needed was the financial backing and a hit record to really solidify the company as a legitimate competitor in the new recording industry. As Ertegun recalls, " 'I turned to my dentist, Dr. Vahdi Sabit, who actually fell for the line I was peddling . . . , 'If we could only sell one record to each record shop . . .' He turned out to be a gambler and mortgaged his house in order to put up the $10,000 that we needed" (Greenfield 127). Soon after, a contract was drawn up and formally recognized Abramson, Ertegun, and Sabit as partners. The original agreement between the partners stipulated Abramson and Ertegun be paid "$40 a week for expenses in return for expending thirty . . . hours a week in such endeavors" (Greenfield 124). This pay scale positioned them for capitalistic gain and exploitation. Their $40 weekly paycheck was more than the recording artists' pay—even though Atlantic was perceived as being a fair employer in terms of pay equity. Additionally, the original contract specified that each year "all parties would receive an equal bonus from one half of the company's net profits with the other half to be distributed in accordance to the shares they owned" (Greenfield 124). As we will come to know, these yearly profits were primarily generated by Ertegun and Abramson's exploitation of Black musicians' current conditions and Black music artist's desperate search for economic stability and survival.

Surviving the Music (Industry)

Many of the recording artists in the early twentieth century belonged to the AFM, which encompassed both the United States and Canada. This union was founded in 1896, and, by 1906, this union "organized 424 locals [i.e., chapters] and 45,000 musicians in US and Canada. Virtually all instrumental musicians in the US were union members" ("History" 7). This rapid growth in union members added to its bargaining power across nations in its effort to formalize fair pay for musicians. "By 1910," as AFM history states, "the AFM had developed greater control over its business and extended its interests further than any other union in the American Federation of Labor. . . . Its structure provided a fair degree of local autonomy and yet was sufficiently centralized to harness the collective power that came from representing professional musicians across the country" (7–8). As the unionization of music artists gained traction, political and governmental action regarding fair pay and technology use were scrutinized.

According to AFM's 125-year review of its history, "[o]ne of the AFM's primary missions has always been to not just ensure musicians are paid for the work they perform, but that their creations are protected and not exploited for use by others. As technologies change, the AFM has had to adapt with new priorities and agreements" ("125 Musicians Staying Stronger Together" par. 10). However, what the union failed to compensate for and adapt to was the inequitable distribution and appropriation of labor systematically devaluing Black folks' work. Since the 20% Cabaret Tax in 1918, the AFM has pushed back on the tensions of technology, specifically in relation to how society implements technological advances as means for sculpting, curating, and capitalizing on the sounds informing popular culture and influencing the ways musicians earn their livelihood. James Petrillo, a labor leader in the 1940s, urged members of the AFM to take a more active stance regarding the rise in artists' unemployment, particularly because the increased use of technology to record, market, and use sound beyond the initial performance greatly impacted how musicians could get paid royalties. Petrillo called for two strikes (1942, 1947) against record companies, ultimately forcing them to (back)pay artists for their labor. In 1944, "Petrillo created a system" called the Music Performance Trust "where [the] industry contributed royalties from record sales into a fund to employ musicians for admission-free, live, public performances." This fund began distributing these payments in 1947, and the second ban on recording companies ensured this trust's longevity ("125 Years" par. 21, 22) making the AFM's collective bargaining unit a particularly effective strategy for change. This aggressive union organizing directly impacted the big break that Atlantic needed to initiate successive profits.

Commonly known as the "Petrillo Strikes," these strikes were largely standoffs between the union (and its members) and the recording industry. These companies initially would/could not agree to the terms regarding royalty payments on recorded performances ("The Recording Ban of 1942" par. 1). Entertainment institutions (like casinos or speakeasies and social nightclubs), who once relied on musicians' live performances to draw in patrons, have now opted to operationalize the relatively free or cheap recordings of their former musical acts instead of employing and fairly paying the artists themselves—cutting out overhead from their expenses and putting musicians out of work. To combat this technological shift, Petrillo eventually "instituted a total ban on AFM members participating in any recording session for commercial sale." This greatly affected artists who recorded for companies like Capital, Decca, Atlantic, and so forth. As a result, "[r]ecording companies feverishly stockpiled recordings in the weeks leading up to the ban, and combed through back-catalogs for potential hits" ("The Recording Ban of 1942 par. 1).

On a larger, international scale, the results of the Petrillo Strikes changed the relationship between the "owner" of the sound and the "laborer" who created sound. Tim Anderson argues that these events should be more critically reflected on. "[T]hese struggles need to be understood as organized moments of critical intervention and protest to the construction of a new, dominant economy of music production that would be based on recordings rather than the production of musical performances" (232). Anderson goes on to explain that "these strikes were involved in a struggle over the terms, forms, and goals of popular musical production in the United States. The end result of this struggle constructed an industrial logic of repeatable use values that are vital to the modern-day employment of all media and entertainment technologies" (232). While the tensions between the recording industries and the union rose, "a great number of musicians devoted more time to radio, cementing the importance of the medium. Conversly [sic], many musicians could not find work and smaller-format groups prevailed in post-war years with the decline of big-bands and the rise of vocalists and small jazz combos" (The Recording Ban of 1942" par. 2). However, as was just noted, this shift in medium and types of sonic labor did not impact all musicians equally.

At the time of Atlantic's founding and early recording adventures, the AFM was deeply invested in these strikes. Ertegun recalls that social climate while describing the resultant exchange that helped build the company:

> the major companies would be doing a lot of recording in Europe and we couldn't afford to do that, "Europe" turned out to be New Jersey because you could go there and record anybody you wanted because the local [i.e., the AFM chapter] wasn't sending anybody to check up. The guys who were used to making scale would come up and say, "Hey, listen, we're willing to record nonunion. . . . Don't let anybody know and we'll do it for $25 a session." Suddenly, with the strike on, the price went down. All the musicians were scuffling for work. (Greenfield 126)

For Abramson and Ertegun, the artists' willingness to set aside union regulations and camaraderie was their golden ticket that went into building their own sonic plantation. Music artists, particularly Black music artists, struggled to survive as they received $25 dollars for their work while Ertegun and Abramson received $40 a week. Recording music, regardless of the sociopolitical nature of the regulatory policies suggested, was one essential method for Black folks to make a living. Abramson and Ertegun exploited this unfair, inequitable economic-labor deficit relationship.

Ertegun even got advice from his brother, who also started a small jazz record label in Los Angeles. In their epistolary exchange, the Ertegun brothers discussed ways to expand the new company's profits, capitalizing on their record-pressing abilities and artists' desperation for income: "Nesuhi counseled Ahmet not to bring out his records too fast so they would have 'time to be properly exploited'" (Greenfield 128). It's clear from Atlantic's early stages that profiting from Black culture via music was the main goal of this company.

As the Story Goes

What is often not described in the historical accounts of Atlantic's empire or Ertegun's life story is how Atlantic, like other recording labels, built its legacy and buying power on the backs of burgeoning popular Black music genres like blues, jazz, and especially R&B. While the recording industry was in its infancy, Atlantic Records built its empire by steadily signing Black artists and producing their albums. Some of the most well-known artists contributing to Atlantic's success included Led Belly, Big Joe Turner, Ray Charles, Sarah Vaughan, Mary Lou Williams, and Ruth Brown. It was often regarded as one of the top record labels for Black music and Black music artists. As Ruth Brown recalls, "When I joined the company in '48 they were ranked twenty-fifth in the R-and-B field; by '51, and from then on, Atlantic was the undisputed number-one label" (131), and that, from Brown's view, was due in large part to her own sonic style and labor. In fact, in her biography, *Miss Rhythm: The Autobiography of Ruth Brown, Rhythm and Blues Legend*, written with Andrew Yule, Brown points out that "[s]ome people to this day call Atlantic 'The House that Ruth Brown built,' and even if this is an exaggeration, few would deny that I contributed a solid portion of the foundation as well as quite a few of the actual bricks" (64). Brown was the most prolific and best-selling artist Atlantic had during its early tenure. There is no question that Brown's success did, indeed, build Atlantic.

As the story goes, the company's first hit came from Stick McGhee's "Drinkin' Wine, Spo-Dee-O-Dee." Originally a drinking song popularized by Black military units, this song was first produced by J. Mayo Williams, the head of the "race music" department at Decca Records, and became a hit in New Orleans, Louisiana. Ironically, even though the song had been wildly popular in the South, it was still a relatively rare find, and record stores were desperate to locate more copies. Ertegun caught wind of this conundrum and set out to find a way to re-create and manufacture this record under his new company, hopefully making a profit on the sales. He originally called up Brownie McGhee asking him to cover Stick's song, but Brownie rejected that offer and told Ertegun Stick was his brother: Brownie handed Stick the phone. Ertegun asked Stick if he signed the rights to his song to anyone at Decca. Greenfield writes that he "replied, 'No man, I never signed anything. They gave me $75 and a couple of hot dogs.' Ahmet promptly offered him $500 to cut the song for Atlantic" (144). The record was re-produced[11] and released in 1949 under the Atlantic label. Some music historians suggest that McGhee's record sold 400,000 copies and earned him $10 dollars for his labor; however, Greenfield cites Ertegun as saying "[w]e sold at the time, I would say, 700,000 copies of 'Drinkin' Wine Spo-Dee-O-Dee,' and the bootleggers sold a million," and McGhee was paid $500, not $10 (145). This single went to number two on the jukebox chart, number 26 on the pop chart, and then entered the best sellers chart for twenty-three weeks (Greenfield 145). What is clear is that Atlantic profited more from its first hit than what McGhee was actually paid to record it—either $10,[12] $500, or $75 and some street food. Atlantic had its first hit, and that rush created a lifelong addiction for Ertegun, who did whatever he could to keep generating best-selling songs (and profit) for the company.

Because of this new-found success, Atlantic was able to capitalize on the moment by signing new artists and recording more than three times the number of songs they had in previous years—jump-starting this record label's exponential growth. Soon after its initial prosperous accomplishment, Atlantic tried to cut a deal with Columbia Records to help cover production costs, specifically manufacturing and distribution costs. This deal would have paid Atlantic a 3% royalty[13] on every copy sold. However, because Ertegun was supposedly paying 5% in artists' royalties, which was more than Columbia executives, the deal fell through (Wade and Picardie 35–36; Brown 179).

For decades, Atlantic Records and Ertegun publicly insisted that their interactions with artists had been grounded in fair compensation; they took pride in their cultivated industrial ethos, which depended on the perception of treating their artists fairly. However, thanks to Black women's activism—specifically Ruth Brown's tenacity and testimony—Atlantic Records was eventually forced to face the music. Correspondence, business documents, and legal proceedings eventually showed Atlantic as often defaulting on artists' earned compensation and building its plantation on unpaid or partially compensated labor, not unlike the early practices of sharecropping discussed above.

Black Feminist Activism: Resisting Sonic Sharecropping for Generations

After making their first big hit with "Drinkin' Wine Spo-Dee-O-Dee," Abramson and Ertegun scoured as many Black acts to subsequently sign and record as they could. They hoped to ride the waves of Stick McGhee's relative success. According to Greenfield, "Both Ahmet and Herb Abramson knew the next step in building Atlantic was to find, sign, and then develop an artist who would give the label staying power in the marketplace." He adds, "Much like the motion picture industry in Hollywood, the record business had always been all about stars and the best way to ensure a label's enduring success was to have as many of them under contract as possible" (149). While searching for new acts, Abramson and Ertegun received an urgent telegraph message pointing them toward an "undiscovered" singer: Ruth Brown.

Ruth Alston Weston, professionally known as Ruth Brown, was born in Portsmouth, Virginia, on January 12, 1928. Her mother, Martha, was a "farmgirl from Macon, North Carolina" (8). Her father, Leonard, worked multiple jobs as a laborer to provide for their family of seven. Her mother and her grandmother, Delia, both farmed land to help ends meet. In fact, "Granny Delia," born to formerly enslaved Emily Baker, was a sharecropper for most of her life. She often asked for her children's and grandchildren's help to harvest crops each summer. While I am not going to rewrite Brown's biography here, I do want to point out this personal connection to American history in making my point. Brown's history is intimately tied to the history of sharecropping as I've outlined above, which makes her testimony especially rich and compelling. Brown had firsthand experience with how exploitation influenced one's quality of life.

While Brown was performing in a Washington, DC, club owned by Blanche Calloway called Crystal Cavern, Abramson and Ertegun scouted her. Brown found herself reliant on Calloway for a living, having recently been fired from her previous gig. When Calloway advised Brown to sign with Atlantic, Brown verbally committed without hesitation. For Brown, this new relationship with Atlantic Records was a way to do what she loved: perform *and* make a living. However, because Brown dropped out of school early and got her taste of fame at a young age, she naively saw the relationship with Abramson and Ertegun as a genuine friendship in addition to an opportunity. "Why had I accepted the conditions if I didn't like them?" Brown asked in *Miss Rhythm*. "It was an unwillingness to let folks higher up get even a hint of that last school report card, admitting the limit of my education. So many of the black groups and singers who catapulted to fame in the fifties, I explained, came out of the backwoods and were delighted to sign any piece of paper that was shoved in front of them" (144). What's more is that Ertegun knew about Brown's naivete and still peddled his terms for a contract. Neshui validated this mindset, writing in a letter to his brother that "*She'd never received a recording offer before, she was very young, she said fine, great, and they made a deal right there and then in a small club in Washington*" (qtd. in Greenfield 148–49, emphasis original). Ertegun and Abramson depended on Brown's "illiteracy" to contractually bind her to the industry and manipulate her into being a sonic "cash crop."

Before she physically signed the contract, however, Calloway managed to convince the owner of the Apollo Theater in Harlem to offer Brown a supporting role in Billie Holiday's upcoming show. On the way to the Apollo, Brown and a few of her entourage were in a horrible car accident, leaving her with limited mobility in her leg and a hefty hospital bill, which Atlantic covered. While recovering from the accident in the hospital, Abramson and Ertegun showed up with gifts in one hand and a contract in the other. While this sign of collegiality is indeed thoughtful, it also demonstrates the thin line recording executives inefficiently balanced: demanding production while dismissing bodily limitations as well as the overall health of the performer. By the time Brown signed the contract, she was already indebted to Atlantic records for settling her hospital bill. From that moment on, Brown's efforts to survive were always in the context of repayment. This contract exploited Brown just as sharecropping exploited her ancestors; after all, the landowner, the one who controls and amends the contract(s) at will, maintains the definitive authority or control over the tenant who depends on the contract for survival. It wasn't until much later that Brown exposed the full extent of this problematic practice that supported the very foundation of this new audible profession. This is the backdrop for many early Black music artists who were being signed to new record labels.

Brown only began questioning these problematic moments and memories later on in her career. Brown describes her reaction to the contract: "[C]aught up in the euphoria of having a contract to sign at all, I had taken no advice beyond a quick word with Blanche before signing with Atlantic. Ahmet had a great pitch that settled any question . . . . Sure sounded good to me, although I knew I was starting at the bottom as far as advances were concerned . . . . I also understood that I was responsible for certain production costs" (Brown 70). The excitement of signing a contract soon became lackluster. Without genuine advice or legal counsel, the hidden costs of sonic laboring[14] came into sharp focus. "Leaving school at fifteen," Brown notes, "Lord knows I was no rocket scientist, but there were people like Big Joe Turner, next door to illiterate, lining up like lambs to the slaughter. Only corporations had access to lawyers in those days . . . . And besides, we *trusted* these contracts and the people who drew them up" (179).

On top of that, Brown's managerial representation was often transferred from one manager to another without her knowledge. Most of these interactions were strictly business (not to better Brown's conditions but more so to increase the share of profit for the company and manager). Because of this commonplace interpersonal exchange, Brown's trust in Ertegun and Abramson was understandably misguided. Even though she knew she would be responsible for some costs, she wasn't prepared to cover fruitless, implied expenses not communicated to her. Not only did Brown pay for managerial expenses such as salary, but she was also fiscally responsible for paying other expenses like transportation, lodging, venue rental, and promotion of both herself and the bands she played with. These costs came out of her advances and/or her share of the profit from the show's ticket sales or admission costs. As Brown describes:

> I had paid no attention to such mundane but all-important matters as transportation, leaving them all to my booking agency, . . . and I paid their price, which was steep. They had several mini-busses they called suburbans, made to hold up to twelve people, which they allowed you to rent to take your musicians and the rest of your entourage on the road. You were provided with a driver, and a sign on the side saying who you were. If your group of eight or ten made $1,000 a night, a lot of money back then, $350 came right off the top for the suburban and driver. We practically lived in that darn

thing when we were on the road and I had to pay for everything—wages, accommodation, meals—and still hope to clear something at the end of it all. (Brown 67)

Even though she used all-encompassing event services from one company, she was also being taxed by multiple managers who arranged the shows in the first place. "What did it mean?" Brown wrote in her biography, adding, "[o]nly that every time I had sung my heart out on the back of a tobacco truck, suffering slings and arrows while making far from outrageous fortune, the boss men in New York, not content with giving handouts instead of proper royalty accounting on my records, had systematically been collecting their pound of flesh from the road as well" (302). The multiple institutions Brown paid for reflects similar procedural expectations that built sharecropping: the farmer (already in debt from last year's crop production) is forced to go to the commissary to borrow feed, seed, and equipment and pay back the landowner from the skimpy earnings s/he was able to hold onto.

While this frustrated her, she also understood that this transaction was also unfair to Blanche: "Who do I blame? Blanche, for surrendering two-thirds to Herb and Ahmet of the ten per cent I paid her? . . . I tell myself she had to play along, for who would voluntarily accept one-third of her due?" (Brown 302–3; qtd. in Greenfield 163–64). Resenting Calloway's attempt at survival wasn't going to address the root of the issue:[15] the recording industry (just like other economic and political systems) was set up to profit white men.

Without much protection from the record company and very little legal protection built into early Black music artists' contracts, and already in their debt, the live performance shows Brown took on were essential to her survival (and many of her band members' survival as well). During her career, she was "[p]aid about $70 to record a side, the highest fee Ruth Brown ever received for a session at Atlantic was $250. . . . Like all musicians during this era, Brown made her real money by performing, earning as much as $750 a night on the road" (Greenfield 161–62). These kinds of performances also, unfortunately, often piled on additional risk: "there were many times when the promoters ran off with the ticket money, leaving us high and dry. We had no clauses in our contracts saying we had to be paid before we performed, or even at the intermission, so we were wide open for such abuse. When it happened it was considered just too bad and I had to make it up to everybody" (Brown 67). As a result, "despite my continuing chart success," Brown states, "I had to ask every time I needed cash. Any real money I made came from touring, and I was always out there promoting the records. Back then any record by a black artist needed every ounce of help it could get. The expression 'R-and-B chart' was another way in the late forties and early fifties to list 'race and black' as well as 'rhythm and blues' record" (Brown 70). Thus, segregation, Jim Crow legislation, and racist ideologies limited Brown's professional mobility.

STARTING THE CYCLE (OVER)

For the two Atlantic executives, the relationship was less about kinship and more about profit. As Abramson later recalled, "Ahmet and I not only wanted to sign her up, which we did, but also have control of her career and try to build her" (Greenfield 154). *Miss Rhythm* describes the ways in which early recording industry practices tried to coax out particular sounds, or a kind of voice, from Black (women) music artists. Ertegun and Abramson strongly encouraged Brown to sing the blues rather than the ballads *she* wanted to sing. Once producers found and fine-tuned their ideas of the "right" kind of Black sonic identity, they profited from their systematic commodification and branding of Black bodies, sound, and culture. These procedural manipulations and controlling of the body were customary for early recording industry practices. These actions surveilled and regulated Black mobility within public and economic spheres. Simone Browne points out that capitalist practice of branding has a deep and racist history: "Branding was a practice through which enslaved people were signified as commodities to be bought, sold, traded" (93). Browne adds that branding "mak[es] blackness visible as commodity and therefore sellable [;] branding was a dehumanizing process of classifying people into groupings, producing new racial identities that were tied to a system of exploitation" (94). For recording purposes (as well as for live performances to some extent), intentionally augmenting Black women's voices by controlling the genre, recording or performance locations, and imitation of style—were practices that classified, branded, and pigeonholed Blackness. Like the plantation and sharecropping systems discussed in this chapter and elsewhere, restricting sonic identity in these ways harkens back to older racist methods: "the restriction of mobility . . . served as an exercise of power" (Browne 53). As such, this process highlights the antiBlack mechanization of sound as a means for limiting Black mobility; it also ensures the maintenance or upholding of colonial power structures within recording company practices as they reinforce a prepackaging of Blackness through this sonic, discursive commodification.

Additionally, Ertegun reflected on their decades-long relationship and mentioned that "Ruth Brown was kind of a shitty singer but she had good rhythm and she thought of herself as a pop singer. The reason I signed her up was that she sang this song 'So Long' imitating the way Little Miss Cornshucks used to sing it. I couldn't find Miss Cornshucks, who had sort of disappeared, but Ruth Brown must have heard her singing that song and she would imitate her" (Greenfield 154; Brown 234–35). This forced engineering of a particular sonorous identity through imitation was intimately tied to and dependent on what Alexander Weheliye defines as *habeas viscus* or racializing assemblages of Blackness (2014), which makes visible the manufacturing of profit through bodily exploitation and segmentation. Here, Brown's voice becomes separated from her whole self and can be replaced with another disembodied (Black) voice. While the rhetorical process of imitation can be an effective maneuver for survival, imitation can also be used in insidious and problematic ways, as we see here.

As an antiBlack function, imitation can reduce Black identities into a monolithic construction where one form of Blackness can be exchanged for or collapsed into another. This process of making Blackness interchangeable, or assembling Blackness, to use Weheliye's words, has been addressed and theorized as "Black fungibility" by Hortense Spillers and others. Shannon Winnubst, author of "The Many Lives of Fungibility: Anti-Blackness in Neoliberal Times," draws from Spillers's work, noting that fungibility is a "mechanism that produces ontological singularity" that is the very basis of an imperial logic for commodification (104). Winnubst clarifies, "To be fungible, in both its economic and legal meanings, is to have all distinctive characteristics and content hollowed-out. . . . In economic terms, fungibility refers to those goods and products on the market that are substitutable for one another" (104). Thus, "[i]t is this precise abstraction of living, human bodies into quantities of commerce that enacts an ontological transformation" that exchanges human-ness for profit (Winnubst 105).

As such, Ertegun and Abramson's directive of imitation led Brown to produce a similar sonic identity to Little Miss Cornshucks's instead of encouraging and cultivating her own sonic style. Ruth Brown's generated voice was operationalized by Ertegun and Abramson as a capitalist exploit for profit. Instead of putting resources toward rehabilitating or fairly paying Little Miss Cornshucks, Atlantic opted for the easier and more profitable route of re-creating their own version of her with Brown. It was "an era when nearly all independent record company owners treated their artists like hired help who could be easily replaced," Greenfield writes (158). Ertegun and Abramson applied this antiBlack practice of Black fungibility to Brown as they mechanized her voice as a racist, capitalist technology that privileged commodification over representation.

The recording companies depended on imitation and genre control to not only make Black performers (both as public personae and their voice or sound) interchangeable, but also mechanize these branding systems as a means for appropriation, further growing their profit margins. Exploiting Black women music artists by emphasizing the malleability of their sonic identity diminishes Black bodies' human-ness and agency in exchange for capital via the audiences' ease of consumption. Instead of simply exaggerating racist tropes and stereotypes to create content, white singers during this time blatantly stole Black music and repackaged it as their own—doing away with the minstrel theatrics but amplifying the shameless cultural appropriation for profit and continued social exclusion. Brown explains:

> throughout my biggest hit-making period I was forced to stand by as white singers like Georgia Gibbs and Patti Page duplicated my records note for note and were able to plug them on top television shows like *The Ed Sullivan Show*, to which I had no access. . . . My label mate and good friend LaVern Baker, who joined Atlantic in '53, suffered the same fate on her original of "Tweedle Dee"—another note-for-note copy by Her Nibs Miss Gibbs. There was no pretense, either, that they were anything but duplicates. Mercury actually called up Tommy Dowd on the day they were cutting "Tweedle Dee" and said, "Look, we got the same arrangement, musicians and tempo, we might as well have the same sound engineer too." (71)

And, because the entertainment industrial ecology was dominated by white businessmen baptized by solipsism, many of these popular white performers were rewarded for "their original" hits. This recognition often translated to more money, more popularity, more opportunities, more freedom—in sum, a greater validation of their contribution to American life and culture. As Vattel's imperial reasoning would have us believe, these white duplicates used the "land" "appropriately" and rationalized this theft as "acceptable." This intersectional imbalance was exemplified by "Oh, What a Dream," originally composed for Brown but popularized by Page: "The record was barely on the streets when the inevitable happened. You guessed it, a Patti Page duplicate on Mercury . . . . Page made Billboard's mainstream Top Forty; I settled for the upper reaches of the R-and-B chart. It would be nice to report that my original had crossed over to the white chart. Instead, the reverse happened. 'The Singing Rage' crossed over to the black R-and-B list!" (97–98). As a result, "the bulk of the sales creamed off" (98). Brown theorizes that "the reason so few discs by black artists crossed over to Billboard's mainstream chart was simple: it was compiled from white-owned radio stations playlists featuring music by white artists, with our list confined to stations catering to black" (Brown 70). She would be right.

These early interactions between artists, executives, radio station executives, and radio deejays (not to mention television hosts and other media broadcasting corporations) resemble the imbalanced, systematic sharecropping ecology mentioned earlier. Even though Black music artists were responsible for the labor and creativity that manufactured popular culture, the flow of power and money came from the top-down and right into the hands of those who did much less of the legwork. This unequal distribution of compensation happened to many Black music artists. As Brown notes, "It was tough enough coming up with hit sounds, therefore doubly galling to see them stolen from under our noses. Few seem to stop and question the morality of this, least of all the publishers, to whom it was a case of the more the merrier. LaVern for one did, protesting to her congressman over her treatment at Mercury's hands, but then as now, there was no copyright protection on arrangements" (71). This unfair distribution also lined the pockets of the company. "[I]n the same year that Atlantic, with its black originals," Brown writes, it "was declared the 'most-covered label' in the U.S. . . . I would have termed it 'most-duplicated,' for my gripe would never be with the legitimate covers, or subsequent versions like Cliff Richard's, but with bare-faced duplicates, with no artistic merit whatsoever" (98). With Atlantic's credibility building, Abramson and Ertegun stockpiled social caché on which to continue roping more Black artists into contracts and starting the cycle over.

"In the Worlds of Business, Politics, and Entertainment": The Affordances of the RICO Act

Brown's peak production years were the decade between the 1950s and 1960s, but after that, Brown was hard-pressed to find a job to support her two children. She found work as a hairstylist, a bus driver, and later as a temporary teacher for Head Start. She took any and all work she could find. From the 60s to the early 80s, Brown also found work on Broadway and off-Broadway plays and even appeared in a few television shows. But these jobs were sporadic and kept her moving from one place to the other, making it somewhat difficult to provide a stable home, repay loans, and stabilize her marriage. The lack of equitable pay for her sonic labor and identity greatly affected her day-to-day existence. Brown did everything she could to keep a roof over her family's head, surviving by any means necessary. She describes a low point during this time:

> It did not take long before debts of all kinds had piled up, and it soon got to the point where I was seriously wondering if I could ever cope. . . . The boys knew they were living through rough times, and there were days when they had to count their lunch money in pennies, or go collect a can of kerosene to heat the house. When the lights were turned off that first winter because I was unable to pay the electricity bill, I found a metal tray, say about forty Pepsi-Cola bottles on it and stuffed tallow candles in every one. That gave us light, together with a certain amount of heat. (140–41)

This was a turning point for Brown, and she eventually reached out to Atlantic, asking for another advance. "Things got so bad that I sat down one night and wrote a ten-page letter to Ahmet," Brown writes. "I hesitated to write what I did, for I laid myself naked. It was a declaration of desperation, pleading, begging for help. I still insisted I was not asking for anything I was not entitled to, but I was in a bad way, I needed money to pay my grocery, fuel and rent bills, I was having a hard time, I'd even pay it back if I had to. Ahmet responded by sending me a check for $1,000" (142). Even though this check helped temporarily alleviate some strain, it was still not something she believed she should have to do. She believed she deserved more after working so hard to build that company with her own sonic labor. Brown proclaimed, "During the fifties I had a total of thirteen Top Ten R-and-B hits . . . certified by Atlantic to Billboard as million-sellers. . . . Through all this I had to ask, like I was begging for a handout, for every advance on royalties beyond the flat contract sum"; however, when she received that check from Ertegun, she "knew it was over" (131). This would be the last advance Brown received from Atlantic until the 1990s; she launched a legal campaign against Atlantic for years of unfair accounting and fought for her fair share of royalty payments.

We know from Brown's biography that she was suspicious of the company's accounting before she even parted ways with Atlantic. She credits Bobby Darin for raising her alarms. While making his switch from Atlantic to Capitol Records, Darin peeked at not only his account records but Brown's accounts as well. When Darin told Brown to "push a little harder," Brown responded, "I didn't know whether to laugh or cry. All I'd ever had over the years were advances to keep me going, combined with either blank stares or cries of, 'Hey, don't push it. Taking our expenses into account, you're in the red'" (128–29). Repeatedly threatening Brown with retaliation and increasing her debt ensured Brown's complacency and complicity for the time being.

Atlantic's continued threat is a rhetorical tactic we've seen before in plantation overseers and sharecropping's contract negotiations. These threats of surveillance highlight part of Alexander's argument regarding the "threat of probation or parole" or additional jail time as a means for extorting more money from convicts—knowing that through debt institutions can force maximum labor output (156). In part, this is what Browne describes as a "racialized surveillance" practice. Browne references Kevin Haggerty and Richard Ericson's "surveillant assemblage" theory, writing that "the surveillant assemblage see the observed human body 'broken down by being abstracted from its territorial setting' and then reassembled elsewhere (a credit reporting database, for example) to then serve as virtual 'data doubles,' and also as sites of comparison.'" Browne also adds, "Racializing surveillance is a technology of social control where practice, policies, and performances concern the production of norms pertaining to race and exercise a 'power to define what is in or out of place'" (qtd. in Browne 16). Moreover, "'racializing surveillance' signals those moments when enactments of surveillance reify boundaries, borders, and bodies along racial lines, and where the outcome is often discriminatory treatment of those who are negatively racialized by such surveillance" (16). Atlantic operatives used this repeated intimidation tactic to ultimately enforce Brown to "control" herself by quashing hope of ever getting the financial freedom she was entitled to and instead replace that hope with fear. Connecting these kinds of colonizing practices closely ties sharecropping to early recording practices. Atlantic employed similar tactics of aggressive rhetoric and intimidation toward the person with less power, in this case Brown. However, instead of eliciting more money from Brown as current judicial practices aim to do from convicts, Atlantic uses this method as a means for protecting its company interests, namely its own profit and public-facing ethos.

After that $1,000 response from Ertegun, and still having trouble making ends meet, Brown's friend advised her to look into legal representation and fight for royalty (re)payments, hoping a more substantial payout would be the end result. Brown flew through lawyers trying to work her case pro bono, but they quickly dropped her case at the first sign of resistance from Atlantic, which doubled down on its intimidation rhetoric. Eventually Brown connected with Howell Beagle, a corporate lawyer specializing in mergers and acquisitions who also happened to be a Ruth Brown fan. Beagle became her primary lawyer in 1983. During her first meeting with Beagle, Brown relayed her experiences with Atlantic and told him what they'd told her: she was in debt to Atlantic, explaining,

> Well, the original agreement had called for a flat payment up front for every side I recorded, starting at $69. That sum was against royalties, which were calculated at a straight five percent of sales . . . . The snag was that those royalties commenced only when Atlantic's production costs were recovered, for I was responsible for both the musician's fees and arrangements. . . . On top of that there was a ten percent allowance for breakages. Understandable in the days of shellac, it was less easy to comprehend as we moved into vinyl. What none of us understood was that cutting . . . did not mean their guaranteed release. If only one side out of every three cuts was released, that one side was loaded with the expenses incurred for all three sessions. . . . The computation of those expenses, of course, was entirely in the hands of those in charge, and was never spelled out. . . . Those old "session costs," according to the royalty report I'd gotten out of Atlantic, far outweighed what they claimed I'd earned in over twenty years. Would you believe those earnings amounted to $785 domestic and foreign combined? Specifically, $354 at home, $431 abroad." (179)

Beagle was in disbelief. He responded to her testimony by saying, "They say *you owe them* money? And the total sales of your stuff both home and abroad amounts to just *seven hundred bucks over twenty years*? (179). Having bought a few of Brown's records himself, Beagle instinctively knew something was wrong. He asked Brown to collect any and everything she had with Atlantic's name; he began working the case.

The first decision about how to proceed was crucially important. The right approach for putting pressure on Atlantic's (later Time-Warner's) lawyers boiled down to either charging them with malpractice or defaulting on moral obligations; the former would be easier to settle and thus easier to sidestep, while the latter had higher risk and greater reward. Beagle and Brown chose the latter. She describes Beagle's approach: "Instead [Beagle's] strategy was to begin with low-level information-gathering approaches, then to choose his battles, utilizing his various contacts in the worlds of business, politics, and entertainment. . . . If a legalistic approach was out, the concentration had to be on the moral policy issues. Warner, in short, had to be persuaded they had a real PR problem on their hands" (187–88). Beagle was in communication with the company for months, and Brown took every opportunity she could get to publicly shame Atlantic. Their relentlessness paid off.

Beagle eventually got access to Atlantic's accounts in 1984 after months of correspondence and veiled, reactive threats from Atlantic's lawyers. After hours investigating their records, Beagle finds the lynchpin, which, ironically, was provided by their own business communication. "[Beagle] was immediately aware that a wealth of material was missing, not least any record of sales from my best-selling period, . . . it was a relatively innocent-looking handwritten scrawl spread across a copy of the typed royalty statement I'd been sent in 1983 that made him sit up and take notice," Brown writes. "The first message read, 'We did not go back to pick up royalties earned between 1960 and 1971 on foreign. *We had no way to check*'" (194–95). The introduction to and the evolution of computers drastically altered the way businesses did their record keeping. This abrupt, major technological transition affected the company's ability to archive and translate some of their oldest contracts and record keeping, which included Brown's accounts. "Atlantic, it seemed, had routinely failed to record my foreign sales throughout the sixties . . . . Despite this, they had furnished the statement showing royalties for the period as $431"—an arbitrary number. She continued, "[t]he second message was, if anything, even more damning: 'We didn't post information to deleted accounts when we were on the manual system.' [. . . . this] proved conclusively not only that there was an inherent flaw in their system, a gaping hole with eleven years' missing data, but that they had been fully aware of it and sent out intentionally false royalty statements" (194–95). This written admission was exactly what Beagle needed to build the case against Atlantic.

Beagle and Brown met for dinner a few nights after he found this evidence. At the table, Beagle laid out his strategy for defeating Atlantic:

> "It's called RICO . . . . It's an act that allows individual plaintiffs to sue corporations privately. If you win you get triple damages, together with your attorney's fees—if, that is, you can prove activity of the type organized crime gets involved in . . . larceny, extortion—and mail fraud. It's not necessary to prove mob links, only that crimes frequently *associated* with the mob have been committed. . . . If we can prove that Atlantic *knowingly* sent out incorrect information through the U.S. mail—and I believe we have that proof in the form of those scribbled messages—we have a clear case of mail fraud. And every time we can get them to send more royalty reports, it's a repeat offense." (195–96)

The United States Department of Justice describes the Racketeer Influenced and Corrupt Organizations Act, better known as the RICO Act, as being "unlawful for anyone employed by or associated with any enterprise engaged in, or the activities of which affect, interstate or foreign commerce, to conduct or participate, directly or indirectly, in the conduct of such enterprise's affairs through a pattern of racketeering activity or collection of unlawful debt" (United States, Department of Justice par. 1). More specifically, to prove a violation of this law, one must prove five coalescing actions:

1. the enterprise is real
2. the enterprise's business conflicts with interstate commerce
3. the defendant was, at one time, employed by the enterprise
4. the defendant acted in a manner complementary to racketeering

5. the defendant exhibited racketeering-esq activity two or more times

Additionally, the U.S. government defines this repetitive pattern, as it is associated with RICO, as: "require[ing] at least two acts . . . committed within ten years of each other . . . . The government must show that the racketeering predicates are related, and that they amount to or pose a threat of continued criminal activity. . . . Racketeering predicates are related if they have the same or similar purposes, results, participants, victims, or methods of commission, or otherwise are interrelated by distinguishing characteristics and are not isolated events" (United States, Department of Justice par. 4). Broadly speaking, the RICO Act, passed by the U.S. Congress in 1970, attempts to combat and prosecute entities who operationalize methods that are like patterns of organized crime, or, put simply, forms of racketeering. This law primarily covers acts like mail fraud; extortion; illegal acquisition of enterprises; murder; and/or trafficking (Schultz).

As Brown and Beagle built their case against Atlantic, Beagle connected with Gerald "Gerry" Bursey, the accountant at Atlantic for twenty-five years. Bursey gave Beagle the real "smoking gun" and the last piece of crucial evidence to bring this case home: "Atlantic had converted all their old acts to their new computer system, mixing up in old and new artists willy-nilly regardless of the enormous differentials in royalty rates," Brown explains. "Unlike our old five percent top, current artists rates, typically twelve to fifteen percent and up, had been negotiated to stand current practices, such as: getting paid only half-rate on foreign earnings; treating ten percent of sales as 'free goods'; charging twelve percent for packaging; bearing the costs of 'remastering, remixing and editing'" (232; 243). She thought aloud, "How did Atlantic justify lumping their old artists in with this?" and answered, "Oh, it was impossible to keep two systems running side by side, the wisdom ran, so it had to be only one way. The *new* way . . . . [Howell said,] 'They've been stacking all the charges of a *modern* contract against an *ancient* five percent royalty'" (232; 243). Additionally, "Gerry confirmed that Atlantic had been automatically charging back as a recording cost the contributions it made to artists' pension funds. That was a flagrant violation of federal law as well as union contracts" under the Taft Hartley Act (232; 243).

While this damning information was uncovered, Brown, at the same time, testified on Capitol Hill in July 1986. At this time lobbyists tried to excise crucial traits of the RICO Act that would inevitably make the law defunct if not relatively harmless. Brown joined other activists, such as Rev. Jesse Jackson, to urge Congress to keep RICO intact. Brown recounts her testimony: " 'I'd like to have this opportunity to speak today instead of sing.' And that's exactly what I did, for forty-five solid uninterrupted minutes. RICO was the only affordable way I had to sue Atlantic, to gain justice not only for myself but for dozens of black performers who struggled to push what was once called 'race music' into mainstream American rhythm and blues, and its descendant, rock 'n' roll." She continues:

> I ticked off a long list of artists, alive and dead, and stated that Atlantic and other companies too were guilty of cheating people like Clyde McPhatter, Joe Turner, Frankie Lymon, Dee Clark, Etta James, LaVern Baker, Brook Benton, Dinah Washington, the Clovers, the Drifters, the Platters, the Five Keys and the Moonglows. I pointed out that many of these artists had given a great deal to their music and gotten very little in return. Now their survivors couldn't afford to take on the might of record corporations. Without RICO, I added, neither could I. A black woman living in a single-room apartment in Harlem versus the corporate might of Warner?
>
> Even today, I told them, Atlantic was selling my records in Europe and around the world and not paying me a dime on the grounds of 'unrecovered costs.' I'd seen it in Japan and I'd been in Paris in the spring, I explained, and there they were again—Ruth Brown records still selling a quarter of a century after Atlantic and I had parted company, and yielding me not one thin dime. How could it be? Was that justice? Was that American justice? Surely we have moved away from plantation days when we took what the boss massa handed out? Or sharecropping with its accompanying debt peonage? (209–10).

We see, in Brown's case, Atlantic violating all five of these points outlining the RICO Act. This clearly identifies Atlantic—during its early years at the very least—as being akin to organized crime and mechanizing extra-legal practices to continue harming Black folks. Even Atlantic's "oversight" or surveillance of accounting was informed by sharecropping's antiBlack legacies. As Brown noted, "some referred to Atlantic's old ways of dealing with their black acts as 'plantation accounting'" (267). Without government intervention, unionization, and testimony, antiBlack methodologies would be even more prevalent than they are today. These extra-legal practices and justifications are often employed to systematically eradicate Black folks as well as other non-white minorities. A prime way of resisting these practices, particularly for Black women, has been to operationalize sound and voice—to implement a sonic rhetoric—even if it is just to tell our stories and experiences.

The end of this legal battle, which arguably started in 1983, was nearing its end. Beagle and Warner reached a compromising agreement in 1988. "All of our 'debts,' our session costs, would be wiped out. In exchange for that, as well as for the setting up of the Rhythm and Blues Foundation—capable of awarding grants to both Atlantic and non-Atlantic artists—the backdated repayment would be for only eighteen years, from 1988 to 1970." In addition, "$250,000 had been set aside for payment to the initial seven artists and their estates, and Atlantic had agreed to begin immediately to conduct the same limited audits on behalf of twenty-eight additional pioneer artists who'd recorded for the label in the fifties and sixties" (263). While this settlement didn't come close to making the kinds of reparations it could've made, this was still a better result than the $30,000 buyout that some of the other artists took in the early stages of the legal battle or the last $1,000 check Brown received from Atlantic decades earlier.

Financial payback was indeed a priority of this case, but Brown's activism went a long way toward ensuring recording industries would be held accountable (at least to some degree) for their role in sonic sharecropping. Brown remarked, "Atlantic had tried to deny the very existence of the people who'd made them worth $17 million plus what Warner/Seven Arts had paid . . . . The company hadn't produced these records in a vacuum . . . . Their sounds had soared from the throats of real people, artists who had suffered for their art, who had been dirt poor." She added, "Token recognition is one thing, but you can't take that to the bank, it don't buy no groceries. Ahmet hadn't settled for token recognition when he'd sold his company in 1967. So why should we?" (268).

Black women are often faced with questions of agency and authority: Whose side of the story is believed and/or given more power? We know that Black women's experiences are less likely to be held up against white male testimonies, so why is it hard to accept that these same problematic relationships play out in the recording industry and around our vocal labor? This antiBlack phenomenon becomes not only visible but exacerbated when we overlap the sociohistorical frame of sharecropping with early recording practices. Thus, Ruth Brown's testimony is important for countering other manifestations of antiBlack, misogynoir discourses. Brown's biography and numerous public appearances provide clear evidence against Atlantic's ethics, resisting sonic sharecropping and shining light on early recording practices that extend and update racist rhetorical tactics.

In so many words, Brown's testimony and biography describe Abramson and Ertegun as enforcing sonic sharecropping. They drew up the contract, settled the terms of her labor, and directed the kinds of labor she was expected to churn out all under the guise of fair sonic discursive expectations that the whole system reenforced. They were "owners" of the land who bought and sold her goods (i.e., records) or crops (performances, name, etc.) at a fraction of the cost and then sold them at market value, making their own profit from her sonic labor and identity. Additionally, the exploitation of Brown's voice and sonic identity align with the earlier description of Vattel's *res nullius* application as an argument for colonization. As Abramson and Ertegun saw it, Brown did not know how to use her "land" "appropriately," at least not in the way that the marketplace dictated. This interstitial situation offered Abramson and Ertegun an excuse for oppression and exploitation. As a result, they cultivated Brown as a blues/R&B singer, instead of the balladeer she wanted to be, maximizing profit and expanding their sonic landscape by leasing out more Black labor. The cycle, indeed, continues.

"Securing All the Bags"

Remembering the scene with Cardi B, and having been reoriented to an expanded definition of sharecropping that includes voice and sound, we can reinterpret "coining a phrase" within a much more nuanced etymology. "Coining a phrase" for Black women music artists, like Cardi B and Ruth Brown, is an attempt to push back on sonic sharecropping's extended, generational reach. Calling out unfair labor practices, including how executives capitalize on Black women's voice-as-labor, challenges publics to take stock of ongoing, insidious, and racist colonizing webs. Cardi B's attempt at "securing all the bags," especially through governmental pathways, is one method for protection, survival, and agency that has been used for generations to help navigate unfair societal expectations and force notions of citizenship, equality, and equity into the limelight.

As we've read in this chapter, this lopsided economic return is most readily integrated in white music artists' cultural appropriation of Black music discourses and even our language. This cultural appropriation extends to verbatim copying of music, like Brown's accusations toward Patti Page and Georgia Gibbs. These Black women music artists are not alone in drawing attention to or publicly addressing imbalanced labor practices that Black women (music artists) are often faced with. These displays of resistance are one of many methods for survival Black women employ. These are two case studies within a long history of Black women fighting to be heard, to be listened to, to be compensated for the sound and the labor of their voice. In fact, the lineage of examples from Black women demonstrating fiscal disadvantages has been well documented, as we read here.

It has long been argued that Black music isn't really for Black listeners. Primary audiences, that is, the group of listeners with a substantial chunk of buying power, have largely been composed of white listeners: from white, rebellious teens to the avant-garde, to the nostalgic "Boomers," the activists, the purists, and the critics. When a large listening base rarely has similar sociocultural histories that frame our sonic spheres, miscommunication and poor representation are inevitable. As I discuss in a later chapter, intercultural communication is fraught with potential moments of miscommunication that can lead to (social) death. H. Samy Alim notes, "These misunderstandings usually occur not because the languages have different syntactic structures, but because they have different rules of language use" (51). For Black folks in the early days of the recording industry, the rules of language were survival; however, the rules that recording industries played by were exploitation—a practice stemming from racist plantation logics. Thus, the trail of money does not flow freely from the audiences' hands into performers' pockets. The flow of money and power filter through recording companies and their outsourced co-operatives (i.e., deejays, producers, promoters, etc.) before artists see their share of the profits. And with the evolution of technology, Black women music artists like Brown and Cardi B have adapted and found new ways to ensure they have the option to "secure all the bags," be that from filing suit or trademarking catchphrases. White, middle-class America's purchasing power was/is an extension of multi-billion-dollar recording industries like Time Warner and RCA, which have undoubtedly operationalized and sculpted inequitable policies that manipulate Black recording artists generation after generation. These solipsistic practices of cultural appropriation and capitalistic greed remain central to the development of Black music genres like blues, R&B, and hip-hop.

Hopefully these practices continue changing for the better—especially as more Black artists own and operate their own recording houses (e.g., Wondaland and ROC Nation)—and further solidify the generational contributions of Black women's voices in the development of the industry and sound more broadly. As we've read here, and as the other chapters in this book suggest, Black women's sonic rhetorics can communicate ways in which our agency carves out power for ourselves, demonstrates our knowledge-making, and validates our sonic rhetorics as a valuable commodity—whether that be on the stage, page, or podium.

2

"Strange Fruit" Sonic Rhetorics

Southern trees bear a strange fruit

—Abel Meeropol, "Bitter Fruit"

Maybe this year will be the year

—Billie Holiday, *Lady Sings the Blues*

Whether written or performed, the anticipation of change (for the better) weighs heavily in the hearts and minds of people, particularly people of color. The "changing same," originally postulated by Amiri Baraka (formerly LeRoi Jones), signals Black folks' constant and repetitive search for freedom, which is often foiled by continued white supremacist acts (1998). Baraka suggests that "the device of [Black folks] asking for this freedom remains a device for asking if the actual is not achieved" (197). Therefore, the search for freedom cannot be found solely in the asking for freedom, but there must be other ways of producing freedom. For Baraka, the mere asking for freedom will never actually give us freedom; rather, we must manifest and organize freedom(s)—even if they are subversive—to survive and liberate ourselves and communities over time. We must act, dream, or reimagine ways out of oppressive structures and epistemologies because our continued, generational calls for freedom(s) have not yet been fully realized. Hence, this tension of anticipation, this push and pull of hope and doubt, is the "changing same" in which we so often find ourselves battling.

Alternatively, Nathaniel Mackey reinterprets Baraka's "changing same" another way. Mackey suggests that the changing same is a tension between "changes in the black stance and situation" and the continued belief in "the threat of dilution, cooptation or amalgamation [of Black life and culture] by the dominant white culture" which ultimately becomes represented as "a kind of 'unmoved mover' at the root of black America's transformations" (360). In this way, Blackness becomes a type of measurement in which to assess the social, political, and cultural progress of the nation. All in all, the changing same is a signification of Black folks' recognition of a potential stalemate between the push for freedom and the pushback from dominant culture; it is the recognition of how the hegemony resists and reacts to Black folks' calls for equity and liberation.

This understanding of the changing same is so prevalent in our everyday that the changing same has become a motif in which authors, artists, public intellectuals, teachers, activists, parents, and more have named, explained, remixed, and extended. Across media and genres, the changing same has been so readily acknowledged that it has become solidified in our psyche. The lasting impression of the changing same illustrates time and time again that racism, along with many other types of oppression, continues finding ways to inhibit "progress," namely by persistent practices of marginalization and/or (socially) killing non-white bodies. To emphasize this impression, this chapter's opening quote from Billie Holiday speaks to the many ways Black folks deal(t) with this tension: with skepticism and hope. The lasting physical and psychological traumas, passed on from generation to generation, leave marks so deep that this pendulum of social (ex)change marred by the mixture of pain and hope often surfaces in popular culture as practices of catharsis, rememory, and community-building.

As one might expect, the changing same can be readily identified in Black music—one of the many methods Black folks "ask" for freedom(s). A prime example of this changing same rhetoric embedded within Black music discourses can be found in one of the most recognizable American protest songs of the twentieth century: Billie Holiday's recording of "Strange Fruit." As this particular song reverberates across generations and genres, it continues being cited, signified, and remixed, explicitly and metonymically naming issues of antiBlack violence. Since its debut, "Strange Fruit" has the haunting power to conjure up the histories of generational traumas—including racism and resulting antiBlack acts like lynching—in the United States. Holiday's guttural, poetic, and honest performance vocalizes the (in)calculable emotions accompanying the changing same, contributing to its staying power within popular culture, memory, and imagination. In this way, "Strange Fruit," known for its moving and illustrative depictions of lynched Black bodies, embodies the frustration of the changing same for generations and signals the importance of Black women's use of music as a sonic rhetoric.

Today, you can go to YouTube, search for Billie Holiday's "Strange Fruit" recording, and scroll through a long list of listeners—from various ages and countries—who felt compelled to comment on or respond to Holiday's sound. Many of them acknowledge the timeliness of the song even though decades have passed since the release of her album *Fine and Mellow*, which includes this track. Some of these listeners identify the "dark" tone of her voice and "honest" lyrics as qualities appropriate for today's sociopolitical and cultural climate—a delicate balance between despair, pain, and hope invested in the belief that a change will come. Some of the online audiences wield the commenting space on YouTube as a digital bulletin board, posting names of the Black women, men, children, and gender-nonconforming individuals slain by agents of systemic injustice; some listeners post names of Black women blues and soul artists who gave their life and livelihood to the music, hoping it would lead toward change, progress, and liberation for the next generation.

Such material and archivable ephemera, like recordings, sonically and visually resist oppressive conditions and realities. Even more contemporarily, music videos are transforming the past sounds of the changing same into visual and sensorial experiences for their twenty-first century audiences—fine-tuning the changing same into a sonic rhetoric complete with visual storylines. By using rhetorical theory as an analytical framework, this chapter specifically examines the evolution of "Strange Fruit" sonic[1] rhetorics. I investigate how Billie Holiday's rendition of a song turned into a broader rhetorical discourse and generational social justice movement resisting antiBlackness. This intersection of sound and sonic legacy is ultimately where this chapter lies, untangling the rhetorical evolution of the sound and the sonic as a Black feminist rhetorical move toward freedom(s). Viewing this intersection as an ongoing legacy within and between communities allows us to tease out how sound became and becomes the sonic; it outlines a means for Black women to teach generations about survival and liberation. I hope tracing this exchange of "Strange Fruit" documents ongoing conversations about change, progress, survival (or lack thereof), and the struggle for humanity and citizenship on which Black folks have been insisting for centuries. Said another way, this chapter argues that sound can be operationalized as a sonic rhetoric to insinuate topics regarding change and liberation.

To do this, I first build on Ersula Ore's analysis of lynching to emphasize its ecology as a discourse, one that is in conversation with the changing same. I use this as a backdrop for Black women music artists' response to the changing same in their work, sonically and visually resisting normative expectations or conditions of Blackness. Then I consider the historical and rhetorical imprint of Holiday's "Strange Fruit." This song's history and infamous performance detail important information for how sound can act as a rhetorical resistance to antiBlack violences; it also demonstrates how Black women's sonic rhetoric can alter collective memories and change the course of popular culture. Next, I emphasize the rhetorical function and generational relationship of this sonic evolution by focusing on two contemporary Black women musicians, Melissa ("Missy") Elliott and Janelle Monáe Robinson ("Janelle Monáe"), who extend the "Strange Fruit" sonic rhetoric by repurposing its sonic and visual discourse. This juxtaposition allows me to trace how "Strange Fruit" reverberates across genre and generation. I maintain that the visual and sonic representations of lynching discourses, affectively positioned within Holiday's recording, serves as a foothold for the continued employment of Black women's generational sonic rhetoric.

A Changing Same Is a Past Not Yet Past

It is difficult to believe that such violent, antiBlack measures maintain(ed) prominence in contemporary times.[2] However, when one takes a closer look at lynching practices, it is unsurprising that these demonstrative acts of citizenship unfortunately were tolerated. In fact, Ore, author of *Lynching, Violence, Rhetoric and American Identity,* suggests that lynching not only was an intentional act designating America as a "white" space, but also symbolized a methodological process of citizen-making, both on individual and communal levels (2019). The correlation between continued antiBlack violence in the United States and centuries-old attempts at maintaining white supremacist ideologies is a foundation of American politics, culture, and identity. Ore argues that "the logic, discourse, and practice of American lynching have been adapted in the twenty-first century in ways that sustain a democratic project predicated upon the circumscription and eradication of black life" (7–8). The changing same for Ore, then, is not necessarily focused on the process of creating and reimagining Blackness and Black freedom(s) through art or music, as Baraka pointed toward. Instead, it is focuses on how variations of anti-Blackness in the United States continue supporting ways of minimizing Black life through community acts, policies, institutions, and ideologies. It is in this recognition of a continued lynching discourse evolution in the United States, or what is designated here as "lynching(s)," that I ground this discussion of "Strange Fruit" sonic rhetorics. What becomes evident in discussing both iterations of the changing same—that is, music/art and the politics of citizenship—is that Black folks continue to call for change and justice as part of our moves for liberation. While the medium or genre may change, the substance of the messages is tied to a much larger and older conversation.

To further nuance its discourse, lynching(s)[3] can include multidimensional definitions such as an antiBlack "material practice and a rhetorical performance" or an act that aligns with "an ideological belief regarding black inferiority, white superiority, and the need to keep blacks in their racially prescribed place" (Ore 16). As a discursive sentiment, "Lynching was a form of social control that maintained the racial status quo through its denial of due process of law" (Ore 19). Drawing from Jesse Carr, Ore describes a prime attribute of this pervasive and insidious literacy as "involv[ing] the strategic use of language and symbols" to supplant newly granted citizenship with divisive and violent acts on presumed "others," marking these bodies as "black beast rapist, black brute, black thug, threatening Negro," which validated such harsh ostracization of Black folks (qtd. in Ore 8).

These problematic descriptors and rationales for lynching are readily seen in Ida B. Wells's anti-lynching pamphlets. In her introduction to *Southern Horrors and Other Writings: The Anti-Lynching Campaign of Ida B. Wells, 1892–1900*, Jacqueline Jones Royster presents lynching as being "in the company of other acts of mob violence, as a multilayered aspect of American history, with dimensions related to political and economic power as well as to race and gender control" ("Preface" vii). In sum, lynching as a discourse—past and present—can encompass physically, emotionally, and symbolically violent or traumatic actions intent on asserting whiteness, at the expense of Black freedom(s), as a dominant measure or practice. To be clear, I'm not trying to devalue or separate the grotesque act of lynching from its very specific cultural etymology.

Lynching is intimately tied with and to Black life (in the United States) and is explicitly oriented toward terrorizing Black folk. To imply that a lynching discourse can be thrust on other cultural groups' sociopolitical contexts, nation-making process, and/or historical navigation of society or space would be inaccurate. I do, however, intend to suggest that lynching can be understood as a discourse community.[4] A lynching discourse has been used as a precursor for procuring white citizenship and has rhetorically applied language and symbols for devaluing Black folks' humanity, even when the symbol is something as simple as "a look."

The always-present connection between the white gaze's reduction of Black bodies and the assertion of white citizenship points toward the many ways the changing same remains present, particularly as this gaze continues objectifying the body. Indeed, the white gaze's presumed assemblage of Blackness often served as the foundation for harmful, essentialist stereotypes, like "the black beast rapist" or the "licentious female," and as a way for authorizing lynching in the United States, particularly during the late nineteenth and early twentieth centuries. Lynch mobs often propagated lynching discourses by using these stereotypes, especially in relation to Black men, as a scapegoat for purging Black folks from communities; it was a way of preserving and/or defending white female respectability, which also symbolized the young (white) Republic.

Although the victims of this lynching discourse were overwhelmingly Black men, Black women and children were not excluded from such heinous acts. Royster highlights that Wells's inclusion of Black women as victims of lynching destabilizes the idea that lynching was reserved solely for Black men. She writes, "Wells also documented that several lynching victims were not men, the assumed predators of rape, but women and children" (29). In fact, Well's 1892 record of lynching showed five women hanged for arson, rape, being kin to a "suspect" Black man, for possibly poisoning a well, and for an "unknown offense" (qtd. in Royster 82–87). To further highlight this rampant violence accompanying such blatant antiBlack behavior, I draw on Wells's descriptions of Black women's situatedness within a lynching discourse here in detail. I think it important to provide full descriptions of these accounts because we have seen similar rationalizations extend to how listeners may have heard and seen Black women music artists' voice, music, and the body as responses to this lynching discourse. Wells recounts the lynching of Mildrey Brown in her *Southern Horrors: Lynch Law in All Its Phases* and later describes it in her *A Red Record*: "So great is Southern hate and prejudice, they legally (?)

[sic] hung poor little thirteen-year old Mildrey Brown at Columbia S.C., Oct. 7th, on the circumstantial evidence that she poisoned a white infant. If her guilt had been proven unmistakably, had she been white, Mildrey Brown would never have been hung" (Royster 71). The same vehement outcome was applied to family and friends when certain targeted Black folk (often Black males) eluded the "law." Some Black women and girls were lynched because their close relation to Black men—be that a fictive or familial kinship. These "citizens" perceived close relationships with Black men as an opportunity for harboring secrets and thus harming the established way (or quality) of life. Wells details this by writing, "In the case of the boy and girl . . . , their father, named Hastings, was accused of the murder of a white man; his fourteen-year-old daughter and sixteen-year-old son were hanged and their bodies filled with bullets, then the father was also lynched" (87). Similarly:

> Five persons, Benjamin Jackson, his wife Mahala Jackson, his mother-in-law, Lou Carter, Rufus Bigly, were lynched near Quincy, Miss., the charge against them being suspicion of well poisoning. . . . The matter came up for judicial investigation, but as might have been expected, the white people concluded it was unnecessary to wait the results of the investigation—that it was preferable to hang the accused first and try him afterward. . . . Against the wife and mother-in-law of the unfortunate man there was not the slightest evidence and the coroner's jury was fair enough to give them liberty. They were declared innocent and returned to their homes. But this did not protect the women from the demands of the Christian white people of that section of the country. . . . The hanging of one victim on an unproven charge did not begin to satisfy the mob in its bloodthirsty demands and the result was that even after the women had been discharged, they were at once taken in charge by a mob, which hung them by the neck until they were dead. (111–12)

In addition, Wells exposed the Southern white majorities' call of chivalry and decorum, which intended to serve justice in the name of white gallantry; she articulately deconstructed this cloaked excuse of preserving women's honor as a rationale for operationalizing lynching(s). Wells's attention to the assumed sexual guilt, or the unsubstantiated belief that Black women and girls were naturally more promiscuous than their white counterparts, exposed a common method for punishing Black women and girls when lynching did not or could not occur. This pervasive excuse for racial and sexual violence indicates the great lengths taken to denounce or govern Blackness, often through means of controlling gender and sexuality. Wells points to this double standard in both quantitative and qualitative data and condemns the baseless provocations of widespread lynching(s) particularly as a gendered, raced, and classed antiBlack act. She writes, "In Baltimore, Maryland, a gang of white ruffians assaulted a respectable colored girl who was out walking with a young man of her own race. They held her escort and outraged [i.e., sexually assaulted if not raped] the girl. It was a deed dastardly enough to arouse Southern blood, which gives its horror of rape as excuse for lawlessness, but she was a colored woman. The case went to the courts and [the "white ruffians"] were acquitted" (128). Similarly, "In Nashville, Tennessee, there was a white man, Pat Hanifan, who outraged a little colored girl, and from the physical injuries received she was ruined for life. He was jailed for six months, discharged, and is now detective in that city." Also, in Nashville, some months later, "a white man outraged a colored girl in a drug store. He was arrested and released on bail at the trial" (129). Wells proclaimed, "At the very moment when these civilized whites were announcing their determination 'to protect their wives and daughters,' . . . a white man was in the same jail for raping eight-year-old Maggie Reese, a colored girl. He was not harmed. . . . The outrage upon helpless childhood needed no avenging in this case; she was black" (129). While the latest iteration of a pro-lynching argument[5] relied on centering the raced and gendered bodies of white women, it clearly did not extend to Black women and girls, especially those who tried to experience freedom(s) and citizenship for themselves.

    Wells also discussed the lynching(s) of a family driven into paranoia by continued white psychological terrorism, having previously experienced the forced sacrifice of their land to satisfy a white man's demand for money. She retells this story: "The woman began to cry and said, 'You intend to kill us to get our money.' [The small white mob of about fifteen men] told her to hush (she was heavy with child and had a child at her breast) as they intended to give her a nice present. . . . A few minutes after, the shooting began." After the white mob had murdered the Black father, expecting mother, and baby and gravely wounded the son, one of the shooters took off the mother's "stockings and took $220 in currency that she had hid there" (90). The sheriff's office responded to public inquiries about this case by acknowledging the culprits were still in the area but that no charges had been carried out because no one was talking about it (91). Thus, the lynching discourse did not just exemplify desperate measures taken to maintain a racially constructed social and economic order, as Ore and others note, or only attack Black males. Lynching(s) worked across gender, race, and class and across the physical and psychological bounds to assert a rejection of Black bodies as a standard, thus degrading Black identity into "other," "devious," or "bad" *things* unworthy of protection, freedom(s), or citizenship.

Like many of us, Billie Holiday understood this reality of the South and the changing same all too well. One February night in 1937, Holiday received a call from a veteran's hospital in Dallas, Texas. She got word of her father's passing from someone who was trying to clean out their morgue. Later, she found out that her father had pneumonia, but, for Holiday, that wasn't what killed him. In *Lady Sings the Blues*, Holiday writes, "And it wasn't the pneumonia that killed him, it was Dallas, Texas. That's where he was and where he walked around, going from hospital to hospital trying to get help. But none of them would even so much as take his temperature or take him in. That's the way it was." She continued explaining, "Pop finally found a veteran's hospital, and because he had been in the Army, had ruined his lungs and had records to prove it, they finally let him in the Jim Crow ward down there. . . . All they could do for him was give him a bed to die in and notify his next of kin" (77–78). Black folks, whether veterans, musicians, men, women, or children, were consistently considered "less than" the "civilized" white mob, and were treated accordingly. Holiday saw this and felt this; she used it to shape her music and sound.

Thus, this changing same was not new for Holiday, having experienced a hypervisual public life and the exploitation of her own labor and body for others' personal gain. She wrote, "It wasn't long before I was one of the highest-paid slaves around. I was making a thousand a week—but I had about as much freedom as a field hand in Virginia a hundred years before" (121). As her popularity grew, she became more of a target for the newly formed Federal Narcotics Bureau. Her managers and even police repeatedly planted drugs on her, for which she was charged and sent to prison; her biography also details the insidious ways the legal and health care systems purposely introduced drugs into her system to either prove she was guilty of drug use/abuse or to make her more compliable for legal extradition and punishment. Thus, when Holiday sang the blues, she *sang* the blues: she knew what she was saying with her voice and her body. Her sound created a soundscape[6] because many of her performances were more than entertainment; they were her personal calls for freedom(s). "The whole basis of my singing is feeling," she wrote (160), and listeners can hear that evidence in "Strange Fruit."

When discussing the early performances of her infamous song "Strange Fruit," she describes how important that song was for her to sing and for pushing her career forward. Holiday writes, "["Strange Fruit"] still depresses me every time I sing it, though. It reminds me of how Pop died. But, I have to keep singing it, not only because people ask for it but because twenty years after Pop died the things that killed him are still happening" (95). The lynching discourse Ore pointed out can readily be translated into a sonic rhetoric provoking calls and memories of the changing same. In the next section I detail the history behind "Strange Fruit," which is essential for developing a "Strange Fruit" sonic rhetoric and for understanding how the sonic can be used as a measure of resistance.

A Piece of "Strange Fruit" History

As we have read, and as some of us have experienced firsthand, the American South has a long and storied past. Many people view the South as an extremely violent and racist place, particularly when recalling America's history with lynching. This regional identity is so widely speculated as accurate that it has been emblazoned in song and story. While some of this true, as evidenced by Wells's works, the South is not the only place (in America) harboring such vehement antiBlack pasts. Marion, Indiana, was the sight of one such heinous, but unfortunately common, lynching of two Black teenagers and the brutal beating of a third. J. Thomas Shipp (age nineteen), Abram S. Smith (age seventeen), and James Cameron (age sixteen) were accused of murdering Claude Deeter, a white man, and raping Deeter's white girlfriend one August evening in 1930. It was this speculation of rape, as opposed to the murder, that made the newly formed mob seethe with anger and indulge in delusions of justice. These three youths were initially thrown into jail by the town's sheriff but were soon handed over to the unruly mob outside. A crowd of more than one thousand spectators, including women and children, demanded that Shipp, Smith,

"Strange Fruit" Sonic Rhetorics | 65

and Cameron be released and turned over to them so they could expend a "just" punishment. Unsurprisingly, the mob got what they asked for: these three young men. This pack of citizens violently beat Shipp, Smith, and Cameron, tearing at their clothes, drawing blood—all while cheering and gawking at this "democratic" American act.

As the violence persisted and the night grew longer, the boisterous mob carried out their lynching (re)quest reserved for these three teenagers. Although their fate seemed to be sealed, an unidentified participant within the mob suggested Cameron's release, saying that Cameron (the youngest of the accused at sixteen years of age) was not involved with the rape of the young white woman. The mob released him but not before he was brutally beaten. Shipp and Smith were not as "lucky"; they were hanged and then hanged again. One video details this very public act of civic engagement: "[The mob] broke into the jail and took Thomas Shipp out of his cell first. They beat him; they spit on him; they mocked him; they killed him before they even got out of the jail. And then they slung a rope over a tree and lynched him even though he was already dead" ("Strange Fruit—The Story Behind the 'Song of the Century'" 3:47–4:06). The night's activities were far from over. "Then, [the mob] went back in for Abe dragging him a block and a half to the courthouse square. Abe was alive all the way to the courthouse where there was a maple tree and another noose that was tied around his neck" ("Strange Fruit—The Story Behind the 'Song of the Century'" 4:42–4:34). Smith, after already having been attacked and displaced by the angry mass, saw what awaited him. "People who were there that day said that as they were lifting [Smith] up he reached for the rope; he tried to hold it away from his neck, so [the mob] lowered him down and broke his arms" and proceeded committing this "great" American act ("Strange Fruit—The Story Behind the 'Song of the Century'" 4:35–4:53). This event, this "community-building" activity, marked a beginning of a particular collective, sonic remembrance. This documented lynching, along with Holiday's experiences, eventually became one of many influences for one of the most iconic songs of the twentieth century: "Strange Fruit."

Lawrence Beitler, a local photographer, captured this lynching on the night of August 7, 1930, and remade the spectacle and white gaze by reprinting the image. His initial proliferation of the photograph continues the American practice of visually propagating a "racial terrorism" and exploiting Black bodies for communal and personal (often financial) means. Ore notes that "Lynching photographs functioned as visual topoi of white supremacy's tie to the legally codified script of white racial terrorism. As such, these photographs served as a repository of civil life in that they offered citizens across the color line a *visual vocabulary* for the 'deep rules' of democracy" (83–84, emphasis added).

Beitler's photograph shows the stark contrast between the two types of citizenship-belonging—that is, the ever-present two Americas: a "democratic" (white) America and an "othered" (non-white) America. This visually reproduced grammar of citizen-making shows Shipp's and Smith's hanging bodies, bruised and bloody, in torn and soiled clothes. The hoard of white onlookers gaze at the bodies and stare directly at the camera lens. Men, women, and teenagers—some who look no older than Shipp and Smith—gape at the two young men they helped bring to "justice" just hours earlier. This lynching photograph's lingering presence extends the very real antiBlack violence because this image is "a form of political iconography that inculcates citizens to the practice of white democracy by way of modeling anti-Black violence as a customary, natural, and revered practice of white civic identity" (Ore 55–56). Even though photos were taken, and the lynching occurred in a very public manner, this antiBlack measure was never prosecuted: no witnesses were willing to talk or convict a member of their *own* community, just as Wells explained in the case of Hamp Biscoe and his wife, the expecting mother.

Beitler's positioning of the large growth as a prominent character in the visual narrative sets the scene of this "pastoral" image. A large tree offsets the framing of the picture, skewing the lynching slightly to the right. This woody growth also serves as a measuring stick, providing an invisible axis running both horizontally and vertically. The branches and leaves of the tree stretch across the top border of the image, and some blurred leaves protruding from the branches indicate movement, perhaps a slight summer breeze. The serenity of the maple tree is disturbed by the performance below and the heavy weight of the tensions it bears witness to. The two hanging Black bodies burden the single, sturdy branch supporting Shipp and Smith, who are draped and positioned against the dark night sky. The image of the perceived "Black beasts" settles in the middle horizon of the photograph. Displaying Shipp's and Smith's bodies in such a prominent way, with only themselves to hold the gaze of the consumer, suggests that Beitler rhetorically curated this frame.

Although Shipp and Smith do occupy some central aspect of this snapshot, they are one-third of the image's central focus. The camera is positioned far away so as not to closely examine their bodies. However, it does document evidence of such brutal antiBlack acts by clearly showing trails of blood staining their torn clothes; the large, welted scratch marks on their skin; and the glistening areas around their mouths where fresh blood reflects the bright light of the camera flash. Even in this black-and-white photo, one can make out the discoloration of their clothes from being dragged on the ground and viciously attacked. But who knows what details are missed by Beitler's choice to position their bodies in the distance?

For some of us, this image reverberates on a deep, internal level, creating significant feelings of fear, horror, sadness, anger, and loss—feelings that grew out of past generational traumas. For others, this image may simply echo common societal practices or expectations. Beitler's curation of the image may fall into the latter. When analyzing his lynching photograph, we can surmise a positionality that may uphold discursive, racist practices. He frames an objective posture, aligning the scene and figures as contrasting realities, potentially resounding the colonial, white supremacist logics of the day. This unobstructed display of still and "quiet" Black bodies without remorse is an attempt at visually documenting the lynching, as if one were cataloging any number of happenings. But, as Ore surmises, "Lynching photographs were, thus, staged depictions of white refinement that frame anti-Black violence as the work of the 'leading' and 'best citizens' of the community" (59). Thus, the unembellished bodies of Shipp and Smith not only hint at the disregard of Black life, but also may divulge of a feeling of comfort for Beitler, as he is among peers. His positionality and privilege to capture this moment work as an extension of the historic, rhetorical "convict photograph"[7] genre that Tina Campt discusses by seamlessly invoking a white gaze method of "objective" display, which creates a visual depiction of affect and power.

Campt, author of *Listening to Images*, draws from John Tagg's and Allan Sekula's historical critique of convict photos, asserting that this kind of photo was used because it produced " 'images whose truth was guaranteed" and was recognized "as a 'perfect and faithful record.' " Photography was especially important for exercising a particular kind of situated white citizenship. "As [Sekula] famously argued, the camera was an instrumental tool brought to bear on the documents that furnished irrefutable evidence of what came to be defined as the 'criminal body' " (qtd. in Campt 76). Thus, lynching photos, like Beitler's, attempted documenting the outcomes of such antiBlack violence as a kind of legal and justified normalcy for a "respectable white citizenry" (Ore 58–59). These kinds of images tell a particular story by emphasizing the dominant, white-voiced, white-gazed narrative ensuring that Black folks' calls for freedom(s) remain silent in physical, visual, and audible forms and across geographic and material spaces. By surrounding Shipp and Smith with nothing, Beitler artistically suggests that there is little to take stock of, no other voice to be heard, that there is nothing else to the story could communicate; by proportioning the image as he does, Beitler captures the prioritized outcome of the "good" citizenry protecting its women and community rather than amplifying anti-lynching calls, which Wells, Abel Meeropol, and others later subverted.

In Beitler's photo, what is given the most attention is the white mob occupying the last third of the image. Rather than giving priority to Shipp's and Smith's lynched bodies, Beitler captures the crowd's lively presence, making sure to ensnare these details and focus on the antagonistic community. This most crowded, perhaps most detailed, section of the photo reflects the all-white spectators/participants firmly planted on the ground. Two older white men are leisurely smoking cigars, signifying an enjoyment, a satisfaction, an admiration of their vigilante justice. To the left, two white teenagers smile and hold hands, as if this spectacle also doubles as their "date night." This particular white female is holding the hand of her significant other while, oppositely, also holding a small tree branch with three jutting leaves, a small token of this night to remember. But what is most telling of this once seemingly apolitical, a-rhetorical image is one white man with a small moustache covering his upper lip who is situated in the bottom center of the photograph. Rather than foregrounding Shipp and Smith, Beitler used their bodies to center this domineering spectator/participant who points back at the two young men while simultaneously staring defiantly at the photographer. He dares other Black men, women, and children to attempt—or perhaps ask for—the same freedom(s) and quality of life afforded to white American citizens.

While Beitler's photo captured the joyous and almost righteous faces of the white mob, it also captured a visual interpretation of the lynching discourse that Holiday and Wells responded to—that is, the transmission of a defiant point warning those who try to go against these "ordinary habits" of white citizenship, a cautious warning for those who live while being Black. *There* is the strange fruit that drops down from the maple tree. Ore mentions that "if the lynching spectacle demonstrated the practices of civic life during post emancipation America, then the lynching photograph, by way of its resonance as an irrefutable representation of 'the real,' ideologically naturalized lynching as an esteemed practice of white citizenship" (Ore 57). Said another way, these spectators who documented their citizenship by immortalizing lynching(s) in film, practice, and circulation of the expectations, (re)claimed and (re)announced Shipp's and Smith's Black bodies as threats to the "American" way of life.

For almost two weeks, Beitler worked on making copies of the photograph to sell as souvenirs or to other interested parties. The photograph sold thousands of copies, making its statement as a postcard image and as a visual in New York magazines. Once in circulation, this image, this documentation of "strange fruit," jump-started a documented rhetorical evolution of "Strange Fruit" sonic rhetorics. More specifically, the act of listening to images (either still or in motion) became incorporated into embodied knowledges. Its transmission of the changing same surfaced as an embodied rhetorical method, which Black women like Holiday employed for communicating lived experiences and teaching other generations about survival and liberation. Campt argues that images, particularly photographs, can act "as conduits of an unlikely interplay between the vernacular and the state" by resonating low sonic frequencies (5). In other words, the images on display and in circulation across media and time act as a way of signifying, communicating, documenting, and testifying such deep emotions transpiring behind the vocal timbre of words and phrases, and even actions; that is, a "Strange Fruit" sonic rhetoric. Campt suggests that listening to these images is "attending to the quiet but resonant frequencies of images" and allowing the possibility for the visuals to permit a methodological focus on the "sonic and haptic frequencies and on the grammar of black fugitivity," which can uncover "the expressiveness of quiet, the generative, dimensions of stasis, and the quotidian reclamations of interiority, dignity, and refusal marshaled by black subjects in their persistent striving for futurity" (11). Beitler's lynching ephemera can be seen as a proponent of the very form Campt speaks against, while Holiday's sound in "Strange Fruit" can be heard as the opposite: his photo *is* the state-sanctioned way of life, whereas Holiday's vocality is a generative dimension of change. Beitler attempts to locate a stillness that deciphers lynching as commonplace; however, what eventually becomes Holiday's audible imperative vocally documents the danger imposed on Blackness by resonating as the vernacular in response to his visual conversation with the "state."

The Other History

Before Holiday could translate the lynching(s) into the sonic, Abel Meeropol,[8] better known by his pseudonym, Lewis Allen, had to translate the image into words. Meeropol saw Beitler's photograph and was reportedly traumatized by the image: "the photograph 'haunted' him 'for days,'" writes National Public Radio's Elizabeth Blair ("The Strange Story of the Man Behind 'Strange Fruit'"). Meeropol—a Communist Party member, a teacher, an activist, a novice composer, and a writer—is credited with writing the original lyrics of "Strange Fruit," which is an adaptation of his 1937 poem "Bitter Fruit." His poem was originally published in *The New York Teacher*, a local union magazine (Nancy Baker 25, 45). After publishing the poem, Meeropol and his wife set the stanzas to music and debuted the song to the Café Society owner. Soon after hearing this early work, Billie Holiday was quickly tapped to record it in April 1939. Holiday remembers this pivotal moment:

> It was during my stint at Café Society that a song was born which became my personal protest—"Strange Fruit." The germ of the song was in a poem written by Lewis Allen.... When he showed me that poem, I dug it right off. It seemed to spell out all the things that had killed Pop.... [Allen] suggested that Sonny White, who had been my accompanist, and I turn it into music. So the three of us got together and did the job in about three weeks. I also got a wonderful assist from Danny Mendelsohn, another writer who had done arrangements for me. He helped me with arranging the song and rehearsing it patiently. I worked like the devil on it because I was never sure I could put it across or that I could get across to a plush night-club audience the things that it meant to me. (94)

The song "Strange Fruit" quickly became a very public symbolic, sonic, resistive icon of the anti-lynching and civil rights movements (Baker 45, 52). However, although Holiday's recording of the song is widely identifiable, what is less discussed is the stress Holiday endured to make that recording happen and the emotional cost of vocalizing the changing same. Holiday's recording label at the time, Decca-Records (now Columbia Records), refused to give permission that would have allowed Holiday to record "Strange Fruit" under their label. By this time, she "was making thirty-five hundred dollars a week, but I didn't have a nickel in my pocket" (177). Like Ruth Brown, much of Holiday's wages came from performances rather than recordings and were usually tied up with her agents. Thus, recording "Strange Fruit" was a risk too great for the company, which put profits above Holiday's personal mission. The company ultimately released her for a time, allowing her to do a one-time recording of the song. She recorded the song amid much personal and professional distress with Milt Gabler, who owned a record shop, and Commodore Records, a small independent label.

Having already connected to this song on a deeply personal level, and already acutely aware of how her voice was perceived, Holiday pushed through and used her voice to demand attention and change. She understood that performing this song was essential for teaching her audience about the changing same; she knew the kinds of physical demands required of performing this song and still invested in its transmission as a sonic rhetoric. Holiday states, "I finished a set with 'Strange Fruit' and headed, as usual, for the bathroom. I always do. When I sing it, it affects me so much I get sick. It takes all the strength out of me" (95). She used her experiences and embodied knowledge to shape her vocals and plug into the audience's ability to receive messages. Emory Pretchauer would call this "edutainment,"[9] the moment when listening becomes learning. There were very few shows where Holiday did not perform "Strange Fruit." In fact, the only time Holiday did not perform this song was when a (most likely) white woman requested it with the misconception that the song was describing Black bodies' sensuality. Holiday mentions that, "One night in Los Angeles a bitch stood right up in the club where I was singing and said, 'Billie, why don't you sing that sexy song you're so famous for? You know, the one about naked bodies swinging in the trees.' Needless to say, I didn't" (95). It is a surprise that Holiday continued performing this song after being confronted with such a gross misunderstanding of the lyrics and the physical toll it took on her, but it is telling of the kind of person Holiday was: a bold Black feminist teacher who did what she could to survive and help others who knew where she was coming from.

During another performance of "Strange Fruit," Holiday describes the performance where she was really feeling the song's message, where she was hyper-aware of the power within her voice. She mentions, "When I came to the final phrase of the lyrics I was in the angriest and strongest voice I had been in for months. My piano player was in the same kind of form. When I said '. . . for the sun to rot,' and then a piano punctuation,

'. . . for the wind to suck,' I pounced on those words like they had never been hit before." She goes on describing the audience's reaction: "I was flailing the audience, but the applause was like nothing I'd ever heard" (96). As a result, her use of voice and sound often persuades audiences to resist common antiBlack acts like segregation practices and lynching. The extent of "Strange Fruit"—in its many iterations of signified titles, sampled sound bites, and remixed visual iconography—knows no bounds, as its legacy continues standing in as a loud, resonating marker for collective change.

Examining her legacy and the lasting sociocultural impact of "Strange Fruit," Angela Davis compels us to (re)consider the song as a sonic rhetoric:

> When Billie Holiday was offered the poem, it seems as if she found her raison d'être; she found her reason for being. . . . I think that her decision to foreground "Strange Fruit" in her work gave her love songs a richly textured historical meaning. Now you may know that Columbia refused to record "Strange Fruit." [Columbia] said "they won't buy it in the South; we'll be boycotted; it's too inflammatory," but Lady Day persisted . . . I don't know if she could have foreseen the catalytic role that her song would play in rejuvenating a tradition of protest and resistance and African American and American traditions of popular music and culture, but I think that "Strange Fruit" is perhaps *the* most influential and most profound example and a continuing site of the intersection of music and radical social consciousness. ("Angela Davis introduces Billie Holiday's 'Strange Fruit'" 1:10–4:35)

Indeed, her perseverance and commitment to anti-lynching did pay off. "Strange Fruit" was added to the Grammy Hall of Fame in 1978, and in 1999 Holiday's recording of the song was named "Song of the 20th Century" by *Time* Magazine ("The Best of the Century"). This is how we see "strange fruit" as a sonic visual.

While this is all good, and it seems like Holiday's story ends here, this is not true. Some of you may be wondering: how can this process of turning sound into a sonic rhetoric be seen in other contemporary Black women music artists' sound-work? If the changing same is still prevalent, then how has this manifestation of "Strange Fruit" sonic rhetoric not been used more often in current Black feminist pedagogies and practices? How is the sonic a rhetorical process of meaning-making? In the next section, I emphasize the rhetorical function and generational relationship of the sonic rhetoric that is "strange fruit" by closely reading a scene from Melissa ("Missy") Elliott's music video "I'm Better" and scenes from Janelle Monáe Robinson's *Dirty Computer*. In doing this, we trace how "Strange Fruit" can reverberate across time and genre.

Evolution of "Strange Fruit" Sonic Rhetorics

Following the release of "Pep Rally" in 2015, Elliott's "I'm Better" music video teased audiences that a soon-to-be-released album, *Iconology*, would indeed be dropping. This newest, and long-awaited, extended play (EP) album was issued on August 23, 2019. Elliott describes her mindset regarding her recent album to Amazon Music's interview channel on YouTube, *Rap Rotation*, asserting that making albums is as much about the visual interpretation of the lyrics as it is about the sound of the songs. Elliott notes that "when I create the records . . . I don't just make a hot record. It's not about that for me. *It's about saying things that visually I can do*. So, when people hear the record, that's the first think that they think of" ("Missy Elliott Discusses Her Album 'Iconology'" 00:04-01:12, emphasis added). For Elliott, it is not uncommon for Afrofuturistic themes of outer space/"alien," "otherworldly" environments, or alternative realities to be present and represent a backdrop for her lyrics. Her songs frequently implement rhythmic and repetitive sounds, drawing in listeners and urging them to dance. At the surface level, Elliott's songs attempt to persuade her audience to indulge in the pleasures of sound. On a deeper level, her music may signal a more subversive message. Like Holiday, Elliott's visual representations of her sound often point toward the many ways Black culture learns from itself and builds on its past. When her playful beats, repetitive percussive sounds, or deep booms of the bass become coupled with her extraordinary visions of reality, an augmented sonic message of generational rhetorics is transmitted. Elliott's songs become a vernacular space that sonically and visually resists oppressive conditions bent on diminishing Blackness. Elliott's "I'm Better" music video is a good example of this.

Directed by Elliott and Dave Meyers, "I'm Better" opens with Lamb rapping the hook, making it known that [I/he/she/we] "started from the bottom." This popular hip-hop phrase signifies the grit,[10] determination, and hard work necessary to not only survive in the world but also gather individual and collective strength (be that physical, emotional, spiritual, or some combination thereof). It signifies a level of agency needed to thrive in the world one navigates. This turn of phrase flips the often referenced "bootstraps"[11] motif by shifting audiences' attention and subverting the emphasis away from the (white) protagonist's moral missteps of boyhood and adolescence. Instead, in the context of Black music, this turn of phrase gives credence to imaginative inventions of hope as a means of survival that is often spawned out of said missteps. This orientation of the phrase inherently recognizes the constraints of systematic oppressions and the intersectional knowledge-making required to put oneself in a space other than "the bottom." That is to say, this literacy is specifically grounded in the cultural influence of hip-hop and Black culture; it shifts the focus from a nationalistic, sexist, and capitalistic adherence to a particular kind of "success" afforded to (white) citizenry to an intercultural, intersectional experience of survival that resists a single-axis understanding of the "American dream."

When one invokes this semantic idiom, they begin outlining a personal narrative about how they "git free" and/or how they made something of themselves.[12] As a Black literacy practice, the personal narrative also "acknowledge[s] the burdens" of one's lived experiences and reconciles the everyday events with our journeys of/for self-making. Rhea Estelle Lathan notes that "acknowledging the burden operates from the premise that admitting a hardship requires making meaning through a process of access, evaluation, acceptance, and communication located within a historical continuum in which practitioners eagerly participate" (32). Meaning, in order to know that one has left, or "come up," one has to also know where they came *from*. Moreover, this phrase invokes a generational understanding of position. Therefore, this recognition of a past signifies social, spatial, and historical relationships; it recognizes starting points as being largely entwined with previous generations' navigation of the changing same. Hence, the navigation of the changing same can be seen and heard as part of this sonic rhetoric.

This phrase, "started from the bottom," testifies to the generational lessons handed down by way of storytelling or other embodied markers; these lessons teach younger generations how to "git free" by lyrically describing personalized versions of events leading to a pathway of "success" and survival. When you send a call to the audience, telling someone about where you (individually and collectively) come from, the anticipated response from the listener(s) is an eager "how?!" to which the caller diligently replies with a story about how they got there. As a rhetorical tool, the naming of the many ways that s/he/they/larger Black collective is "better"—including the testifyin' of their own personal journey—allows the artist(s) to set the scene for a collaborative, multilayered experience or coming to consciousness. This dynamic narration between the image of "success" and the lyrics, in this instance, serves as a sonic and visual creative space for learning about survival and the possibilities for healing and resisting.

At the same time, Elliott (and Lamb) give homage to the past through their subversive use of imagery and performance. The narrative of how one is "better" along with images that challenge problematic civic constructions of Blackness displays an oxymoronic, perhaps dystopic, reality. In other words, the lyrics and visual elements of this music video are jarring but, as a couple, they create a way of seeing both America's problematic and violent history as well as its potential for progress, equality, and liberation. This video's emphasis on choreography and visual aesthetics is classic sonic style for "Missy." In reintroducing her style to new audiences, she invites a collaborative envisioning for a Black future, one that also embraces and learns from the past. Thus, Elliott's representation of Black life in America grounds this song's vernacular literacy, calling on audiences to engage in and think through their passive or active consumption of Blackness.

The lyrics of "I'm Better" detail how confident Elliott is in her sexuality, her body politic, and her economic status all the while the backdrop—the images and aesthetics of the video—tells a historical narrative and reflects cultural tensions resonating from the changing same. The visuals (in)formed by these dancers' outfits, additionally, collide with the message of Elliott's song, which is one of "success" and progress. This contrast, I surmise, was done to suggest that change, progress, memory, vision, hope, and pain are all interrelated. In effect, the sonic and the visual are juxtaposed with each other, which allows one to recount a violent past and embrace feelings of hope or comfort. While there is much to discuss in this video, I choose to focus on the opening scenes because they most explicitly (albeit in a reverberating way) reference a "Strange Fruit" sonic rhetoric.

During the prelude and introduction to the chorus, we see a combination of scenes. Some of the stage is occupied by dancers, and at other times it's occupied by Lamb and/or Elliott along with the performers. With the first beat we see Elliott enveloped by shadows formed by a spotlight hanging from above. Then the illumination of the faceless dancers' outfits in the background quickly brightens up the space. The ensemble of the dancers in these opening scenes is telling. They are dressed in cropped black hoodies; nude-colored leotards that have small black symbols equally spaced across the entirety of the suit; thigh-high, shiny, black boots; and opaque face shields that hide their faces and wrap around a large portion of their heads. This shield seems to be connected to a helmet-like structure that is covered by the hood of the hoodie. Along with the spotlight, the shield manufactures its own source of light, randomly flashing a warm white glow for a brief moment, which is synchronized to the irregular, singular sonic pulses of the intro. These helmets don't flash for all dancers at once; rather, random, individual shields are selectively lit like the recurring pop of corn kernels attuned to the strange, high-pitched funky sci-fi beats. In a space where bright, cool white and intense infrared backlighting are constant, these enhanced "faces" become the primary method of illumination in a darkened room.

Additionally, what the message of this ensemble foretells (or perhaps what this outfit calls us to remember) is in the combination of these items. The boots, the shield, and the helmets summon flashbacks of police rioting gear used to suppress factions of unrest and even older histories of lynch mobs. In modern American history, images of police riot gear have been tied to moments of protest during the Civil Rights era as well as current #BlackLifeMatters protests. More recently, US cities like New York and Los Angeles have spent billions purchasing military surplus to supply their local police departments with protection, like riot gear, while they quell demonstrators; this gear includes "riot shields, gas masks, stun guns, specialized shotguns for shooting tear gas, and other items" (Mankarious & Willingham). While the advancement of technology has given law enforcement more dangerous weapons to suppress citizens, the purpose and rhetoric behind validating such substantial charges and abuse of power reflects similar substantiations that validated lynching, namely positioning rioters (often people of color) as unruly and criminal. Many "defended [police] tactics by pointing to sporadic looting, vandalism and projectiles thrown at them" for incurring the cost and use of the gear (Mankarious and Willingham). I doubt this generational similarity of extra-legal antiBlackness is lost on Elliott.

Moreover, the dancers' ensemble invokes the changing same and the hope of change with the weight of the symbolic hoodie. Nicole Fleetwood, author of *On Racial Icons: Blackness and the Public Imagination*, argues that the image of the hoodie, originally circulated in response to the lack of prosecution for the racialized murder of Trayvon Martin by George Zimmerman in 2012, symbolized a generational link to earlier photo-based evidence of Black life. She writes: "these photo-based protests signal generational and racial shifts among many black and non-black protestors. Masses of protestors imagine and (temporarily) identify with blackness in ways that are not through minstrelsy, slumming, or parody. Instead, one could argue that these images symbolically demonstrate an identification with racial isolation, profiling, and forms of abject suffering associated with certain groups of blacks and other vulnerable populations in this country and elsewhere" (20). The imagery provoked by this opening scene in the music video thus connects past and current iterations of Black methods of resistance, be that by protest, images, language, or art. Elliott flips the meaning of the riot gear by emphasizing the rhetorical agency accompanying the subversion of power and survival through fashion. The disassembled uniform no longer acts as a symbol or image of extra-legal oppression. Instead, they emphasize the body as a cultural site of meaning-making; Elliott's dancers rock a Black fashion of liberation. Where the riot gear once served to "protect" a particular kind of citizenry—like the lynch mob—in Elliott's video, it serves as a stand-in for a Black reclamation of rhetorical agency.

To extend this analysis further, the illumination of the dancers' shield serves as a sonic and visual metaphor for reading the generational rhetorics of such an ongoing process that protects these offenders—that is, whiteness. Similar to the "Strange Fruit" lynching photograph, the majority of Black faces are out of focus or nonexistent, which is the case in this scene. The shields' flashing lights directs us, as listeners and viewers, to see the "whiteness" while contemplating being "better," to see what was once (or more realistically, what remains) a systemic invisibility as the instigator to Black folk's struggle. Thus, the shields' white lights may symbolically signify the recurring ability to hide behind the privileges and traces of whiteness which translates into a lack of persecution. As we have seen, read, and heard—more times than we would like to admit—there are many instances of killings, lynching(s), and violences committed by police and everyday citizens who are rarely treated as equal to Black and non-white citizens. We have generations of proof for this changing same. White spectators/participants-deemed-citizens were not questioned or convicted of Shipp and Smith's lynching, for example, because they were able to hide behind the presumed safety net of whiteness. For the white faces of the spectator/participants of the past, a level of comfort could be found in knowing that their particular kind of citizenship put them above the law; or, perhaps it is more accurate to say they may have found comfort in knowing their acts favoring the preservation of whiteness shored up a process that keep Blackness outside the law: marking Blackness as "alien," "not human," or "other" unworthy of being protected by law. Having the agency and technology to turn "off" the lights, Elliott can signal that change will come. In other words, the technology in fashion and the proclamation of a "better" position asserts that liberation is on the horizon. Indeed, these opening images provide an ominous and contrasting environment when set against the braggadocio of Lamb's and Elliott's lyrics.

Elliott's video capitalizes on the dynamic possibilities of performance and new technologies to assert subversive uses of the body as a site of resistance against the changing same's likelihood. Particularly in "I'm Better," the choreography of the opening scenes serves as a primary point of reference for retelling a "strange fruit" narrative. Similar to how Holiday's vocal resonance of "Strange Fruit" conjured a scene of "Black bodies swinging" in listeners' minds, a choreographed dance of performers hanging from (presumably silk) ropes welcomes listeners into the soundscape, luring us deeper into the song, the visual, and the experience of Black life for Elliott.

Reminiscent of Beitler's lynching photograph and other illustrated depictions of lynching for public consumption, we are confronted with similar graphic "strange fruits." There is a simple framing of hanging bodies in a sparsely occupied and trichromatic room that draws our memories back to the message and history of "Strange Fruit." Using hanging Black bodies in the video as part of the performance and aesthetic encourages audiences to not only register the violent history but also recognize the many creative ways Black folks survived and gained liberation and/or freedom(s), that is, through fashion, art, storytelling, writing, teaching, dreaming, and imagining. Bettina Love calls this survival rhetoric "freedom dreaming." According to Love, freedom dreaming is "a relentless task for people on the margins of society. . . . Their art makes them visible and makes clear their intentions for love, peace, liberation, and joy." Furthermore, freedom dreaming is "dreams grounded in a critique of injustice. These dreams are not whimsical, unattainable daydreams, they are critical and imaginative dreams of collective resistance" (101) and a space for teaching resistance (102). While we hear the fruitions of this dream in Elliott's lyrics, we also visually see the challenges to this dream and ways Black folks have resisted (social) deaths and lynching(s).

In this particular use of the beginning backdrop, we see a small number of supporting performers hang, swing, and dance their way across the stage. Whereas Beitler's photo emphasized the crowd of citizens, Elliott's "I'm Better" strips away the "justified" spectator/participant and moves the agency onto the bodies stage-center. While Beitler's photo shows a degrading "quiet stillness" of Shipp and Smith, Elliott's dancers embrace movement, emphasizing vivacity and longevity. They individually place body parts in opposition to the downward pull of gravity: arms are suspended in midair, toes are pointed straight up, hands are flexed directing fingers (and gazes) to the sky. "I'm Better" sonically and visually inverts the reverberation of lynching iconography to call it into question as a past not yet past.

This imagery speaks as loud as words, transmitting "Strange Fruit" sonic rhetorics as a visual and sonic frequency across generations, genres, and media. Incorporating lynching iconography, be that phantasmal or

Figure 2.1. Screenshot from Elliott's "I'm Better" music video to illustrate reinvention of lynching. *Source*: Elliott, Missy, "I'm Better (feat. Lamb)," YouTube, uploaded by Missy Elliot. 26 Jan 2017. https://www.youtube.com/watch?v=TwyPsUd9LAk

subversive, draws a firm connection across time, validating the presence of the changing same in its many forms. Thus, Elliott not only recognizes the importance of Holiday as a performer and activist, but also repurposes and updates Holiday's sonic rhetoric, continuing a resistive form of teaching agency and social justice while promoting Black art, Black rhetoric, and Black literacies as a way forward. As a more contemporary, digital, and subversive interpretation of antiBlackness, Elliott's implementation of "Strange Fruit" sonic rhetorics visually emphasizes the contortion of "strange fruit." By doing this, she gets the audiences "hearing the hurt," which, for Eric King Watts (2012), is the agitation of voice as a theoretical frame for understanding Black bodies/Blackness through affective, ephemeral, and descriptive materials. In effect, Elliot vocalizes hope as progress, survival, and liberatory rhetoric while connecting measurements of freedom(s) to the evolution of the changing same—that is, facing the technological and discursive evolution of "strange fruits."

Thus, key to Elliott's "Strange Fruit" sonic rhetoric inheritance, then, is her ability to collapse images and lyrics to present a critical antiracist dialogue. While her lyrics paint a picture of a capable, self-loving Black feminist—complete with braggadocio and signifyin'—her music video displays the push-pull of a communal Black identity and the (limited) progress of gaining freedoms once promised. She issues a foretelling of citizenship by proclaiming "I *am* better" against the backdrop of lynching(s), which causes viewers to pause and ask, "Better than *what*?" Better than *who*?" Elliott's "I'm Better" music video asks audiences and listeners to critically reflect on what it means to be "better." Her single provides insights into how Black women can navigate this metonymic, mixed-media evolution of resistance, healing, survival, and liberation. But she is not alone in this techno-driven postulation of Black rhetorical agency vis-à-vis citizenship. Janelle Monáe Robinson is another contemporary Black woman music artist who repurposes Holiday's "Strange Fruit" sonic rhetorics.

Unchaining the Melody, or "Jim Crow Jesus . . . Rose Again"

Continuing a similar storytelling tradition that combines the sonic and the visual, Janelle Monáe uses technology, sound, and narrative to describe current conditions of Black and non-normative folks. Her recent work attempts to provide a solution to the changing same, and that is empathy and education. As with "I'm Better," this next close reading focuses on a few scenes form *Dirty Computer* to point toward the many ways contemporary Black women (music artists) still engage with Holiday's "Strange Fruit" as a sonic rhetoric.

In her latest studio album, released on April 27, 2018,—in collaboration between Wondaland Records, Bad Boy Records, and Atlantic Records—Janelle Monáe opens up discussions about embracing the spectrum of Blackness as she documents the android rebellion through music, iconography, and dialogue. More specifically, Monáe's recent speculative film and album critiques inherited antiBlack sentiments and speculates about Black futurity. At its center, *Dirty Computer* plays out an audible and visual augmented reality conveying how the beauty of Black life, Black culture, Black language, and Black history can survive. From small acts of resistance such as memory, gathering, celebration, love, pleasure, joy, and fashion to larger subversions like entrepreneurship, (time) travel, im/migration, home/ownership, environmental preservation or cultivation, and education, Monáe's soundscape plots a path for liberation even as organized, extra-legal methods of Black (social) death continue—dystopic reality or not.

Moreover, Monáe's "emotion picture,[13]" *Dirty Computer*, sonically and visually disrupts and resists privileging normativity and respectability. Instead, Monáe uses the reality of her alter ego—Cindi Mayweather, an "arch-android" who signifies as a mediator between worlds, realities, and possibilities—to assert the necessity of embracing oneself. In an interview for the 2014 Grammys, Monáe describes who Mayweather is: "there has to be a mediator between the two, uh, between the have-nots and the haves, between the oppressed and the oppressor. Cindi Mayweather is that; she is the mediator . . . she is the heart" ("Janelle Monáe—Who Is Cindi Mayweather?" 0:04-0:44). This resonance of the heart drives the epic escalation of Mayweather's protagonist journey as well as Monáe's own sonic rhetoric. This message of love is particularly geared toward marginalized identities such as Black and Brown queer folks, as Monáe makes explicit the past methods of gender and sexual violence accompanying lynching(s).

Much like Elliott, Monáe centers Afrofuturistic tenets of imagination, technology, and Afrodiasporic culture in her narration and performance. Her creation of the sonic visual, then, is ultimately a call for empathy, for heart, for a reckoning with the range of feelings that are integrated with Black experiences. This call is one that shifts citizen-making from violence, power, and aggression to kindness, solidarity, and care, asserting that the foundation of a just humanity lies at, or in, the heart.

In a Q&A session following the release of this project, Monáe describes *Dirty Computer* as her "love letter to all dirty computers," ushering in the idea of leading from a space of love rather than hate. Thus, her techno-narrative is a means of showing listeners how to work through all the media and technologies that spotlight (and perhaps continue) Black (social) death rather than Black joy. She provides a roadmap for navigating emotions as a generative process:

> When I turn on the news, to reading the newspaper, to even this most recent election, umm, I felt a deeper responsibility to telling *my* story before it was erased. Um, I think that there is an erasure, erasure of of us. And if we don't tell our story, then it won't get told; if we don't show us we won't get shown. And, literally, you know, if you just think about what that means, um to see these images of of us as Black women as as [pause] um, you know as [pause] minorities, you know, more times than no[t] they're negative. There's something really sad that's happening; there's some police stop that happens; two of us are in Starbucks, and because we *are* Black, we get escorted out. . . . It's a lot . . . people need to get educated about. And I really wanted to start with empathy. ("YouTube Presents" 9:42–10:46)

Thus, *Dirty Computer* intentionally unsettles the notion that there is one "right" way to be, that there is one "acceptable" kind of (Black) person. Because, after all, "it is only a matter of time." Her digital and audible narrative of resistance, survival, and liberation illustrates a dystopic reality that is, in actuality, not so dystopic. Monáe's augmented world-building goes one step further than Elliott's, but both have similar calls to action. By coalescing the sonic and the visual resistance to the changing same, *Dirty Computer* argues for an awakening and advocates for a celebration of the color spectrum as a first step toward recognizing (Black) humanity.

Led by the heart, Monáe's performance and storytelling show us how to listen to the stories and histories of marginalized people surviving. That is, with sight, sound, *and* feeling. Like Holiday before her, Monáe lets sound guide the narration and feelings of being Black (in America). In the beginning of the film, Monáe's voice-over dictates that "They started calling us 'computers.' People began vanishing, and 'the cleaning' began. You were 'dirty' if you look different. You were 'dirty' if you refused to live the way they dictated. You were 'dirty' if you showed any form of opposition at all. And if you *were* dirty, it was only a matter of time" (0:00-0:28). Moreover, if we read Monáe's sonic techno-narrative through a "Strange Fruit" sonic rhetoric lens, then we recognize how language becomes a site of powerfully pathetic rhetoric that can last for generations and influence how we interpret situations. In this contemporary rendition, then, "dirty" becomes the metonymic substitution for "strange," and "computer" morphs into the stand-in for "fruit." Both phrases reiterate how Black, or non-normative, bodies have been constructed as being outside the margins and thus suspect to deviation, a point at which the white savior/citizen feels compelled to rectify, clean, or discard.

A "dirty computer" is a metaphor for the disenfranchised, "non-normative" peoples. For Monáe, like Holiday before her, language and sound are intentionally used to resist and counter generationally produced negative stereotypes attempting to maintain various forms of oppression. Monáe, like Elliott and Holiday, uses her sonority and visual imagination to disturb these unjust realities for the audience. This audible reclamation of existence shows us that even as systems control, surveil, and attempt to reprogram our being or life/style, people of African descent, and other marginalized populations more broadly, resist such fungibility in many ways. This lexical substitution only adds to the generative bridges formed by Black women's generational sonic rhetorics, strengthening the sonic as sites of critical reimagination and possibility.

In *Dirty Computer*, Monáe's storytelling reaches back and connects our histories with our present. Her use of sankofarration[14] implores us, as an audience, to listen to and visualize a past not yet past. As evidence of the changing same, Monáe plots out sequential events that resonate and haunt American (and other colonial) psyches because of ongoing, rationalized acts of genocide and conversion. For instance, the "cleaners'" process of erasing "computers" is eerily reminiscent to what Wells described in her lynching accounts. For Wells, lynching usually followed a progression of blame and accusation, custody of Black bodies, hanging, then "shooting bullets into the *lifeless* bodies" (52, emphasis added). For Monáe, her vivid "cleansing" process illustrates similar antiBlack conventions. The "cleaning" process is carried out by, first, capturing the "dirty computer"; second, the "cleaners" (two white men) shoot the "nevermind," which is a thick, white gas, like bullets at the non-normative body in detention; and, then, further restraints for the Black body are used to erase the memories of the past and reprogram the "computer" before releasing a "clean" version of the appropriate (read normative) body back into a society.

One stark difference between these generational processes of recurring antiBlackness is the possibility of survival. For Wells, in the nineteenth and twentieth centuries, documenting the violent actions of lynch mobs and angry citizens proved to be an important form of validating the existence of Black life because these antiBlack acts often resulted in the extinguishment of Blackness. There were few cases of lynching survivors who could rejoin society like James Cameron of Indiana. If, on the slim chance these victims were "lucky" enough to survive attempted lynching, these bodies were often scarred by the trauma and at times carried that trauma into communities or passed it onto younger generations. Later in the twentieth and twenty-first centuries, as lynching evolved into a discourse involving many kinds of antiBlack acts, the possibility of surviving lynching(s) became more complex; it is a paradox we still grapple with: which death is "better"? What we can coax out of this temporal juxtaposition of process, however, is the importance of recognizing survival in many forms, be that as a lasting legacy or physical, immediate presence. Our modes of survival are inherently resisting antiBlackness. Monáe's process updates what Wells brought to light years earlier, but her alteration also allows us to focus on hope that a change will come.

While it is important to note that the process of lynching communicates excessiveness for both Wells and Monáe, in that both descriptions detail steps taken for overkilling Black bodies, Monáe audibly and visually subverts lynching iconography in *Dirty Computer*. Additionally, she addresses the intersections of gender and sexuality with systemic medical malpractice—a topic constantly lurking in the background of conversations regarding the ways systems play into the organized executions of non-normative "citizens." In doing this, she repositions her body and affirms it as a site of cultural meaning. While literally hanging upside-down, Monáe performs her song "Take a Byte."

What becomes uncovered when her lyrics clash with the images is, again, the intentional critique of racial, gendered and sexual mistreatment. In this song, Monáe sings about temptation and pleasure while having us watch Black bodies be drained. This symbolic sonic visual can represent the ongoing treatment of Black (queer and/or trans) women as "promiscuous," "alien," "other," and/or "superhuman." Historically, these common myths often resulted in problematic public speculation that Black bodies feel no pain—a predecessor to the "strong Black women"

Figure 2.2. Screenshot from Monáe's "Take a Byte" in *Dirty Computer* to illustrate a reinvention of lynching. *Source*: Robinson, Janelle Monáe. *Dirty Computer* [Emotion Picture]. YouTube, uploaded by Janelle Monáe. 27 April 2019. https://www.youtube.com/watch?v=jdH2Sy-BlNE

trope. Rather than referring to "the Tin Man," Monáe's android shows us how the system is draining our very life essence. In "Take a Byte," Monáe's visuals go so far as to tie this mistreatment into America's past practice of unethically experimenting on and exploiting Black folk in the name of scientific advancement. We see her color being drained from her body as she hangs upside-down wrapped in neon-colored rope. After being drained, we see scientists who presumably are running tests on her "abnormal" or "unclean" byte.[15] It is here that Monáe urges us to listen with our hearts. She urges us to acknowledge pleasure and desire not just as part of an identity but also as part of a larger method for resisting systemic oppression á la normativity. In doing this, Monáe visually engages with an inverted, sonic storytelling that reinforces messages of liberation.

From this interpretation, we can see how the past can guide current Black women music artists' sonic activism in yet another form. As such, Monáe's neo–anti-lynching campaign challenges normalized generational traumas seen in our everyday life as Wells did generations before. However, Monáe's attention to the intersectional impact of lynching(s) is one way that "strange fruit" has evolved as a sonic rhetoric. In this way, *Dirty Computer* calls on listeners and viewers to engage with intersectionality as a means for creating compassion, empathy, and a way forward. Afrofuturist scholar Boni Wozolek asserts that dialogues formed by works like *Dirty Computer* are imbued with "the feminist lens, particularly within the traditional roots of the African American intellectual tradition, [and] avoid these pitfalls of identity politics by honoring the messy nature of being and knowing with an understanding that one's being is significant as it is resonant to her experiences" (13). Monáe's "emotion picture" is thus an audible act of a visual sonic rebellion, a proclamation of human-ness, agency, and hope for Black bodies, and non-dominant cultures and communities alike. Monáe's *Dirty Computer* is engaging with a legacy of Black women intellectuals who use sound and visuals to resist, survive, liberate, and even heal. Thus, this work continues conversations of freedom(s) by offering listeners an allegorical Black rhetorical literacy narrative foreshadowing what could happen if we continue appeasing the stalemate of "progress," that is, the changing same. *Dirty Computer* communicates a fantastical (and at times subversive) message prompting listeners and viewers to reimagine a future derived from collective histories.

"Strange Fruit" Sonic Rhetorics

Even though the visual soundscapes Elliott and Monáe create are compelling, the sonority of this resistive legacy is rich and part of a larger history. In tracing these audible disruptions back to Billie Holiday's rendition of "Strange Fruit," we can see how voice plays an important rhetorical function. Because vocality is a key factor in this chapter's understanding of how sound can function as a rhetoric, I think it prudent to address how I recognize the potentialities of voice as simultaneously audible, visual modes of communication. More importantly, I think it necessary to ground voice as part of conversations that give weight to the idea that the body is a powerful source of meaning-making. After all, Jennifer Lynn

Stoever, author of *The Sonic Color Line: Race & The Cultural Politics of Listening*, suggests that "listening has greatly impacted how bodies are categorized according to racial hierarchies and how raced subjects imagine themselves and negotiated a thoroughly racialized society" (14). With this line of thinking, it is hard to untangle sound from the self. The misrecognition of such profound intersectional and embodied meaning-making is at stake when Black women's generational sonic rhetorics are dismissed or devalued. My concern in this chapter, then, is tracing Black women's generational resistance through the visuals created by their sound, starting with Holiday's "Strange Fruit." Her distinct voice and manipulation of sound to better transmit a defiance of the changing same still the echo in the public's (re)memory. Her continued presence as a sonic icon is a haunting reminder of the many ways rhetorical calls for freedom(s) can be engaged and the many vernacular spaces where Black feminist teachings of survival and liberation and healing can be found. This is so much so that "Strange Fruit," I argue, acts as a foothold for younger generations to continue and build on calls for justice.

Like Monáe's use of Cindi Mayweather, Holiday's voice represented a self-portrait, a moving, persuasive, aural captioning of Black life. For Holiday, her self-portrait was tied to intersectional understandings of how her body was able to move in space, through lenses of gender, sexuality, class, ethnicity, and race. By the time she was fifteen, Holiday made a promise of survival to herself; she "was through turning tricks as a call girl" and "wasn't going to be anybody's damn maid" (35), so she searched for work as a dancer to keep her mother and herself from being evicted. She describes her first job getting booked as a singer after having lied her way into the audition as a dancer: "I had been singing all my life, but I enjoyed it too much to think I could make any real money at it. Besides, those were the days of the Cotton Club and all those glamour pusses who didn't do nothing but look pretty, shake a little, and take money off tables." Once the owner realized she was no dancer, Holiday caught a break and was asked to sing. She "asked [the piano player] to play 'Trav'lin' All Alone.' That came closer than anything to the way I felt. And some of it must have come across. The whole joint quieted down. If someone had dropped a pin, it would have sounded like a bomb. When I finished, everybody in the joint was crying in their beer, and I picked up thirty-eight bucks off the floor" (37–38). Since then, people have been trying to figure out the style of Holiday's voice or fit her sound into a prefabricated genre. But Holiday's sound is as unique as her fingerprint.

Even though Holiday was aware of the persuasive power behind her voice, she was acutely attuned to how her sound and body functioned within a racist society. Her recording of "Strange Fruit" is iconic, but this song's status has as much to do with her "unique" voice as it does with the positioning of her Black body that personified the lyrics. Rhetorically, her voice captivated public imaginations and intervened in antiBlack movements like lynching. In the case of "Strange Fruit," Holiday lends her voice to visually and audibly confronting widespread racism—even when these racist practices crept into the managing of her career. In her biography, she described Ralph Cooper and Frank Schiffman's conversation about her vocal style: "'You never heard singing so slow, so lazy, with such a drawl,' [Cooper] told him. But he still couldn't put any label on me. . . . 'It ain't the blues,' was all Cooper could tell him. 'I don't know what it is, but you got to hear her'" (43). Prescribing traits like "lazy" to Holiday's often disembodied Black voice amplifies the codified expectations of how Black women, as well as how Black music in general, is predicted to "sound"; anything outside those boundaries are, indeed, strange fruit. However, by permeating her sound with her identity and experiences, Holiday interrupted largely white audiences' ideas of Blackness and, relationally, Black voice. She sonically, and sometimes visually, inserted her Black body, history, and experience into the center of the performance, forcing such white audiences to reckon with the visual and "sonic color line"—to use Stover's phrase.

Said another way, Holiday makes real the ruptures between American "citizens" by audibly (re)presenting "strange fruit" in the flesh. And, from what we have seen from her successors, Elliott and Monáe, this method of asserting Blackness into audible spaces is a method that continues to be effective in challenging outdated norms. More importantly, what we can take away from this continued rhetorical method is the generative tensions yielded by visual soundscapes when confronting problematic, largely racist, ideas of Blackness; Black voice defies white listeners' presumptions of Blackness—be that physically or categorically—even when public consumption hypersexualizes or marginalizes their bodies. For many white audiences, Black (sonic) bodies like Holiday, Elliott, and Monáe become outliers, quirky, inconvenient oddities primed for dismissal (because of rare exceptionalism) or use/abuse (because of their ability to become the precedent). Because Holiday's voice is uncategorical, some listeners relied on the same harmful stereotypes seen in Wells's editorials to reinscribe Holiday's Blackness, personhood, and sound as "other"—something we also see in more contemporary Black music artists too. This kind of missed listening of Holiday's voice flattens her sound to a one-dimensional act as opposed to carrying on as a multidimensional and generational sonic rhetorician.

Moreover, Billie Holiday connected the social histories of a lynching discourse to the personal, physical traumas of a past not yet past for many of her listeners. She used the pain and pleasure from her personal life to shape her voice's tone and texture. In doing this, her sound aurally painted pictures of Black life in America and mimicked the push-pull of emotions felt by many at any given moment. She connected to her audiences on a deep and meaningful frequency. "The audience loved the way she sang her voice," noted poet Alexis de Veaux, "Patterns of dark embroidered textures / Gabardine and silk / Danced along the vocal scales with / hypnotic ease / Low notes / were mysterious midnight sounds / moonlight and smoky Harlem joints / Or tenor and alto saxophones crying / Or the mystical African moan / of oboes and balofones" (27). Similarly, Farah Jasmine Griffin describes Holiday's voice as having a particular sonic rhetoric, namely being able to convey "Death. Pain. Sadness" (12–13). Her long "drawl" and deep melodramatic tones in "Strange Fruit" echoed the low ache and creak of the tree branch weighed down by Black bodies swaying in the wind. The crisp break of a long-held note mimicked and accentuated a truncated end of the line, the branch's protesting groan of too much weight being placed on its arm. Snapped. "Technically," Griffin asserts, "she possessed the ability to bend notes exquisitely and she had an impeccable rhythmic sense: here she pushes tempo, there she delays the entrance of a phase. And she does so without ever losing momentum" (17). Even though the visual documentation of the lynching discourse spurred the poem-turned-song, it is hard to parse out what this song meant to Holiday (and Black folks more generally) from why this song exists. This relationship between sound and the body isn't lost on listeners or contemporary Black women (music artists). As Holiday notes, "If you find a tune and it's got something to do with you, you don't have to evolve anything. You just feel it, and when you sing it other people can feel it too. With me, it's got nothing to do with working or arranging or rehearsing. Give me a song I can feel, and it's never work" (43).

Rather than passively performing a song, Holiday used her identity to (in)form traditional features of voice (like duration, speed, tone, volume, pitch, and breath), effectively moving listeners to a more active engagement. Her voice connected what she heard to what she felt. As evidence, Holiday believed sound, including voice, was part of one's identity, noting, "Everyone's got to be different. You can't copy anybody and end up with anything. If you copy, it means you're working without any real feeling. And without feeling, whatever you do amounts to nothing" (53). Like Monáe's call of freedom, Holiday relies on sound and image to move us forward toward change. As a result, Holiday's voice (along with Elliott's style and Monáe's vision) symbolized the long durée of Black America, audibly representing the changing same.

Sonic as Rhetoric

I describe Holiday's voice in detail here to emphasize her sonority as an embodied, intersectional network of rhetorics, specifically ekphrasis and metonymy, that used visuals to sound experience; meaning Holiday was acutely aware of how sound can be used to invoke deep sensations. Again, we hear this rhetorical relationship in the lingering of notes and profound emotion in "Strange Fruit," which audibly describes a visual depiction of lynching(s), something that Samuel Perry defines as "ekphrasis." Some scholars, like Perry, have excavated the audience's emotive responses when listening to "Strange Fruit," validating that, at the very least, Holiday's performance of the song is moving. The ekphrastic quality found in Holiday's resonance ensures the longevity of "Strange Fruit" as a sonic rhetoric because of Holiday's ability to use sound for tapping into people's (specifically Black folks') generational relationship with the changing same and calling for change more broadly.

In his contemporary rendering of ekphrasis, Perry contextualizes Billie Holiday's musical interpretation of the poem with this emotive capability in mind. He suggests that "Ekphrasis provides a lens for critics to examine" how the rhetor uses "layered representations containing both discursive and visual elements to produce persuasive appeals." This use of sound creating visuals, in turn, causes the audience to partake in a critical "reflection about the way an audience sees and interprets a particular scene" (451). More specifically, Holiday's ekphrastic implementation "creates a space in which the performer . . . and audience create an image together that serves to condemn the practice of lynching" (Perry 449). In fact, this rhetorical method results in "'expos[ing] the social structure of representation as an activity and a relationship of power/knowledge/

desire-representation as something done to something, with something, by someone for someone" (qtd. in Perry 452). The visual image sung by Holiday proves to be persuasive, as its sonic rhetoric becomes a generational symbol for antiracism. By infusing Holiday's feelings, experiences, and voice into the interpretation of the recorded poem, the emotive, ekphrastic appeal cultivated a collective response to the song and social reality of life in America (and later, beyond), evolving the song into a sonic rhetoric.

The same can be said of Elliott's "I'm Better" and Monáe's *Dirty Computer*. Monáe's "emotion picture," for instance, layers the Afrofuturistic visuals with her audible resistance to the changing same. By the end of the film/album, audiences are drawn into this other word while also critically reflecting on their own reality. *Dirty Computer* ultimately becomes a space in which to co-create an opposition to oppression by embracing community and reflecting on emotions and experiences. Similarly, Elliott's music video implements discursive sentiments of the changing same to frame the musical message of progress and success. Elliot thus subverts common visual tropes as a way to critically question our social structures.

What makes ekphrasis a useful rhetoric in this increasingly digital reality is its emphasis on description to move an audience, particularly because the root of ekphrasis is its "clarity and vividness," asserts Frank J. D'Angelo (445). Even as part of an outmoded rhetorical convention, ekphrasis can address attempts of accurately portraying an artist's re-creation of something, some place, or someone that is truthful and honest (443). The resonance of Holiday's tone, speed, and pronunciation, for example, presented a "clear and vivid" aural painting of Meeropol's lynching poem and of Beitler's lynching photograph; she sonically expanded these multidimensional artistic sensibilities into the haptic realities of/for the listeners. For "Strange Fruit," Holiday's voice and body provided such a nuanced layer of meaning to the poem for her audiences that listeners like Lillian Smith[16] have gone on to generate similar scenes of resistance invoking additional calls for social justice. Likewise, Elliott and Monáe are models of how to use imagination and performance as a revolutionary and liberatory (sonic) tactic.

In this way, ekphrasis points us toward how sound can be used as a model of instruction, particularly in the ways we interpret art as part of the composing process. D'Angelo, for example, mentions this historical use of rhetorical pedagogy accounted for and counted as "a rhetorical strategy" that used "a rhetorical prose description of a work of art" as a way for "narrative to set the scene and to describe persons and events" (440). This means that ekphrasis as a rhetoric acknowledges art—regardless of whether the art is in written, visual, or audible form—as a pedagogical tool (D'Angelo 443). Holiday's performing of her own survival tactics seeps through her vocalization of "Strange Fruit" just as Elliott testifies her being and while Monáe creates an augmented reality—all creating teachable texts in their wake. All of these artistically driven conceptions of Blackness serve as teaching tools for how to survive. By sounding out the changing same and sharing the lessons learned, Holiday's, Elliott's, and Monáe's sonic visuals become models for antiracist listeners to build on and engage with long after the performance is made public or is over. As such, "Strange Fruit," and Black music more generally, can be a vehicle for transmitting multidimensional teachings of freedom(s), of carrying out resistance to antiBlack acts, and of promoting methods of surviving across generations.

While we have seen "Strange Fruit" taken up through the frame of ekphrasis, it is important to also note how metonym adds another layer of rhetorical meaning to how sound empowers the body and informs visual and sonic recognitions of the changing same. I layer metonymy onto ekphrasis because of its explicit, duplicitous nature of emphasizing a both/and strategy of understanding, which is helpful for recognizing how these two contemporary Black women artists signify, or revise, "strange fruit" as part of a sonic rhetoric legacy.

Like the Black rhetorical practice of signifyin(g), metonymy highlights the flexibility of language. Within this chapter's analysis, I lean on metonym to see and hear how artists represent the changing same and lynching discourses. In other words, the lasting impact of Holiday's sonic rhetoric can influence how contemporary Black women music artists and activists use sound to visually push against antiBlackness and connect resonant struggles to similar moments of the past—making "Strange Fruit" a *generational* sonic rhetoric.

For rhetoric and composition scholars, the conversation of metonymy usually positions Kenneth Burke, Diana Fuss, and Krista Ratcliffe, to name a few, as foundational reference points for debate. In "Four Master Tropes," Kenneth Burke defines metonymy as having a "basic 'strategy,'" which is "to convey some incorporeal or intangible state in terms of the corporeal or tangible" (424). For example, Burke uses the vernacular phrase "to speak of 'the heart'" as a stand-in or "reduction" of the meaning 'to communicate one's emotions' (424). "Strange Fruit" has morphed into vernacular language and rhetoric in a similar way.

From a theoretical stance, Holiday's rendition of this song works as an example of metonymy in two ways. First, in a traditional sense, "Strange Fruit" has the ability of turning the figurative into literal, meaning that Holiday empowers the lyrics by performing and embodying the poem and ultimately giving a more nuanced rhetorical life to the audible image. Once Holiday records and performs "Strange Fruit," the (in) corporeal topic of citizen-making becomes an artistic and material sonic documentation (i.e., the record of the performance, performance posters, albums, ticket stubs, and photographs, etc.) of such oppressive antiBlack acts. Her sonic rhetoric reveals and connects what was once unimaginable for some (white) audiences—a lynching discourse—to a very real and tangible example of the lasting pain caused by presiding racist realities.

Second, Holiday's sonic rhetoric can also be understood as a *reverse metonym* in that it also (potentially) turns the literal back into the figurative, qualifying "Strange Fruit" as a subversive Black feminist sonic rhetoric. Contradictorily to the traditional use, which is often employed by white gazes, Holiday's effective and moving "Strange Fruit" performance can also be understood through a conceptual—and perhaps ephemeral—lens, more often than not employed by non-white gazes. In addition to making lynching(s) real for white audiences, Holiday conveys Black and Brown communities' literal, philosophical, and embodied knowledge of generational traumas through a melodious allegory. Ultimately, "Strange Fruit," for many Black folks, artistically represents the hegemonic (de) valuation of Black life through song and story; her sonority captures the emotive and generational responses of Black folk who continuously press up against the lasting ramifications of unjust, extra-legal antiBlack practices. Because of the unfortunate familiarity regarding the changing same and Holiday's accuracy of communicating such deep emotions, the song "Strange Fruit" has over time evolved into the vernacular construction of "strange fruit." Represented here in lower case, "strange fruit" is often employed as a stand-in for antiBlack violences, especially when referring to lynching(s). To use Burke's phrasing here, "to speak of" "Strange Fruit," the song, is to recognize its sonic meaning as lynched Black bodies and the respective anti-lynching campaigns, but "to speak of" the vernacular "strange fruit" is to recognize its transformative meaning as a "stand-in" for the lynching discourse and the many ways Black bodies continue to be oppressed. Thus, the sonic recording has taken on new lives over the generations, signifying not just hanged black bodies but also acknowledging numerous ways Black people are (being) killed by solipsistic ideologies and antiBlack acts.

Both working definitions of metonym, however, invoke listening as a crucial task for contextualizing sound within a broader ecology of identity. Pointing to this relationship reiterates Stoever's conceptualization of the "sonic color line." That is, sound and its rhetorical effectiveness are intimately tied to the visual interpretations of the sound-maker, which inherently brings along the social and historical baggage of race, gender, and power (2016). Similarly, through the process of rhetorical listening, as Krista Ratcliffe suggests, "metonym foregrounds resemblances based on juxtaposed associations, thus foregrounding both commonalities *and* differences" (68). The embodied experiences Holiday brings to the table through her unique voice and performances of "Strange Fruit" opens pathways for listeners, protégés, and successors like Elliott and Monáe to repurpose earlier calls for justice into subversive, contemporary, and even digital forms of social justice. By doing so, these Black women music artists highlight the commonality of the changing same while also reinterpreting how antiBlack violences have mutated in more recent times. What remains constant through this temporal juxtaposition, however, is how sound is often also a rhetorical aspect of identity.

Furthermore, Ratcliffe posits that metonymy can provide a productive interpretation of identity that coalesces identification, nonidentification, and disidentification with others' positioning and interpretation of identity. This is to say that Holiday's identity as a Black woman plays a key role reverberating "Strange Fruit" across audiences and generations because she experienced these lynching discourses firsthand and reads these experiences through an intersectional frame. The loss, grief, anger, despair, and hope (among other emotions) accompanying Holiday's sound (and Black audiences' experiences with lynching[s] broadly) can be understood as being so intense, so deep, so strong that these emotions cannot be described accurately when a name of the emotion alone is attached to the feeling. Although naming is an extremely important rhetorical pillar of Black rhetoric, the direct, plain naming of emotion can sometimes fall short of communicating its rhetorical gravitas when attempting to accurately convey the weight of a situation—rhetorical or otherwise. Thus, the musical accompaniment of Holiday's intonated words, for example, coveys a weightier representation of the deep level of understanding attached to conditions of Blackness, particularly within the confines of the American citizen-making process. As an Afrofuturistic rendition of their Black feminist sonic rhetoric, Elliott and Monáe visually and sonically implement this form of resistance, survival, and liberation by employing embodied knowledges and literacies, continuing the communication of lessons learned from their predecessors.

It's Not Over

It is not a stretch to say that Holiday's sonic rhetoric continues to serve as a generative epicenter of resistance, survival, and liberation. One could even argue that Holiday's unapologetically Black protest song is a frontrunner for other contemporary Black women musicians today. I am specifically thinking about influence of Beyoncé's Super Bowl halftime show that (controversially) introduced audiences, listeners, and spectators to a more recent Black history with her Black Panther–inspired performance of "Formation." It is also something of note to point out that in *Dirty Computer*, Janelle Monáe also draws on Black Panther and Pan-African movements to inform "Django Jane"—perhaps this global nod to African heritage is another area to be examined at a later date or by other scholar-researchers.

These soundscapes provide us with a framework in which to unpack the complexities of being Black (in America); it blends sankofarration with the body as critical sites of learning survival, liberation, and resistance. As such, for many Black women music artists—like Holiday, Elliott, and Monáe—visuality, sonority, and even temporality are entwined with and part of a larger story that needs to be told. In this way, we can see the sonic as a rhetoric that serves to proclaim individual and collective progress.

Now, all of this is not to say that we've "made it" in America or elsewhere or that we are in a great position now because things are "better." Nor am I saying that racism or antiBlack violences are on their way out of fashion. The connections I want to make clear in this chapter are that (1) there is an ongoing practice of a lynching discourse; (2) there is a willful ignorance of intersectional oppressions to maintain some semblance of power by the white supremacists; and (3) it is willful because there is clear documentation of how these acts are carried out. What this means, then, for Black feminist rhetoric—which is concerned with liberation for all—is that a path forward must be built on recognizing the body as a site of knowledge, one that carries with it the generational receipts. These receipts of documentation—be they writing, speaking, making music, and/or creating imagery (and later music videos and films)—suggest a clear intention to name a litany of wrongdoings, which ultimately disrupts the continued willful ignorance of the act as well as provides clear examples of how Black folk resist and survive the changing same—passing the documentation from generation to generation and learning about our struggles. Thus, art and rhetoric have a profound complementary relationship for engaging with the struggle for freedom, particularly when employed by Black folks. I believe there is something personal and important about holding on to a past and acknowledging the generational traumas because, as we have seen here, they continue to inform our daily lives, our political institutions, and our collective consciousness.

3

Queer(ing) Sound, Time, and Grammar
Black Women's Methods for Generative Prosodic Rhetoric

> Reclaiming my time. . . What he failed to mention was: when you're on my time, I can reclaim it.
>
> —Maxine Waters

> #SayHerName
>
> —African American Policy Forum

In her influential TED Talk "The Radical Politics of Time" Brittney Cooper unpacked problems with a long-standing relationship between Black people's temporal reality and Western philosophies. She described the uncritical, racist belief that Black people are "out" of time—a concept passed down generation after generation from one intellectual school of thought to another. She notes that "When white male European philosophers first thought to conceptualize time and history, one [Georg Hegel] famously declared '[Africa] is no historical part of the world.' He was essentially saying that Africans were people outside of history who had had no impact on time or the march of progress" ("The Racial Politics of Time"). In other words, Black folks have historically been seen as having no meaningful subject and therefore no personhood or agency influential enough to matter to the rest of the (imperial) world. Rather than support this commonplace antiBlack theory of personhood, Cooper pushes back on its meanings and implications—like so many other Black thinkers have done for decades. She declares, "that desire to mitigate the impact of race and racism shows up in how we attempt to manage time, in the ways we narrate history, in the ways we attempt to shove the negative truths of the present into the past, in the ways that we attempt to argue that the future that we hope for is the present in which we are currently living" ("The Racial Politics of Time"). Black women—like Cooper, Tamika Carey, Maxine Waters, and even musical icons like Nina Simone—have theorized the many temporal (often generational) adjustments Black folks make for survival. These adjustments of temporality indicate Black folks' cognition and wherewithal to assert our personhood and make space for ourselves even in the most oppressive conditions. With this sentiment in mind, Cooper flips the notion of being "out of time"; she alternatively views subjectivity and agency through a Black feminist lens and positions Black folk (and Black women in particular)—whether they be public intellectuals, pop icons, or political figureheads—as having a profound impact on how we can theorize time as a means for survival.

Similarly, Hortense Spillers wrote a well-received essay countering the same temporal assumptions that Cooper pushed back on forty years later. Spillers's "Mamas Baby, Papa's Maybe: An American Grammar Book" (1987) publicly criticized Daniel Patrick Moynihan's infamous report, "The Negro Family: A Case for National Action" (hereafter referred to the *Moynihan Report*). The controversial *Moynihan Report* relied on binaries of "ethnicity" to un-name and blame raced and gendered bodies for the downfall of American (family) life. More specifically, Moynihan argued that Black women were primarily at fault for the poor and inequitable conditions of (Black) life in America during the 1960s and beyond. However, as Spillers saw it, the "problem" was not located within Black communities; the problem was/is located in the inherited violent thinking of and about Blackness as game pieces rather than as persons. Spillers noted that "Under the Moynihan rule, 'ethnicity' itself identifies a total objectification of human and cultural motives . . . . [Black bodies] are *wholly* generated, with *neither past nor future, as tribal currents moving out of time*. Moynihan's [white] 'Families' are pure present and always tense. [Blackness] freezes in meaning" (Spillers 205, emphasis added). As a rhetorical effect, "Ethnicity," an often-employed written code for Blackness, is "perceived as mythical time [and] enables a writer to perform a variety of conceptual moves of erasure all at once. Under its hegemony, the human body becomes a defenseless target for rape and veneration, and the body, in its material and abstract phase, a resource for metaphor" (Spillers 205). Hence, the rhetorical process to name, categorize, and qualify Black identity through generic, essentialized, often Eurocentric terms for/of the body, including nicknames and broad terms, effectively removed our subject-position—or perhaps more accurately, removed our position as "Subject."

Correspondingly, this removal of personhood signified a social hierarchy, empowered by the white gaze, consigning Blackness as object rather than acknowledging Blackness as Subject, agent, or meaning-maker. This process of un-naming stripped Black bodies of our past and future while also predesigned our present through Eurocentric social expectations, philosophies, and epistemologies. This "traditional" grammar, used by Moynihan, labeled Black bodies not by our proper names—which could give power to our very being and validate alternative social ecologies and epistemologies—but, instead, named us through racist mechanizations of our bodies: labeling us as "she," "boy," "bastard," "vixen," "Sadie," or "absent father," among many others. Spillers points to this kind of problematic grammar in professional documents like the *Moynihan Report* suggesting that the employment of such passive and uncritical language actually aides in cloaking white accountability. Glossing over Black personhood in these ways rationalizes the dismissal of Black temporality and ways of knowing while side-stepping the long history of white folks' participation in creating the very social situations in question.

It is here that Spillers conceives of a theoretical Black grammar to speak back to Moynihan's racist logics—much like Cooper's retheorizing time. To counter his argument, Spillers nuanced language's systematic structure and shifted the meaning of grammar to a theorized application of temporality and agency. Said another way, Spillers suggested a revised "grammar," or what I am calling a Black grammar, to counter the ways white supremacist naming practices influence social life and death. Thus, in her article, she documents this rhetorical unbinding of Black subject position by queering the grammaticality of Black bodies, which was (and has been) fused to an abject culture of displacement. She challenges the temporal implications of Black identity in America by explicitly linking language to the body and rejecting Moynihan's traditional grammar usage. She pushed against applying grammar in a way that uncritically and inappropriately marked the flesh as being indeterminate; she resisted a linguistic structure condoning or promoting essentialized stereotypes and tropes. Her subversion of a normative grammar system calls on readers to reinsert the proper noun, to say her name, to acknowledge a Black Subject-position capable of acting on our own accord and influencing the "march toward progress." Positing a queered grammar, which is a Black grammar, retrieves tense and temporality for Black bodies by centering ourselves as agents. Taking Cooper and Spillers together, we can begin theorizing Black folks' temporality by adjusting our linguistic frameworks. It is in this coupling I believe we can extend the argument of Black folks' rhetorical agency—one that operationalizes a Black grammar.

In this chapter, I take Cooper's and Spillers's arguments in tandem examining the intersections of sound, body, time, and language as a generational roadmap for negotiating resistance, survival, and even self-care. My theorization of Black grammar, then, is the legend to this map. Rather than ceding time, or working from a position of being "out" of time, I suggest Black women music artists, specifically, have indelibly used their platform to convince publics of Black folks' temporality and therefore personhood carving out paths for progress. The Black women music artists addressed in this chapter have developed methods for creating space in time; they have been evolving generational sonic rhetorics of survival, resistance, liberation, care, pleasure, and much more. They vocally levy audiences/listeners as repayment for centuries of silence and patience, audibly giving time back to, or entertaining space for, Black women as stakeholders and agents. Said another way, this chapter investigates and theorizes how Black women music artists make use of their voice, queering grammar and manipulating time on sonic levels, as a means for asserting themselves as agents: proclaiming the right to not only exist but also survive, heal, and indulge. I argue that many Black women music artists operationalize sound, more specifically prosody, for these purposes named above; indeed, they dictate time by weaving tense, tempo, paralexical phenomena, repetition, and duration into their audible, rhetorical messages of autonomy. In publicly asserting their (sonic) bodies and using their social caché to hold attention, they audibly provoke critical reflection and make way for social justice pedagogies. All in all, what this chapter largely suggests is that Black women music artists have perceptibly flipped the script by altering understandings and applications of time with their voice and musicality; they have queer(ed) methods of delay,[1] as Tamika Carey has argued, and recentered grammar through Black modes of meaning-making ("Necessary Adjustments"). In doing this, Black women music artists make visible the many ways we cultivate and reinforce ongoing contributions to change or "progress."

As such, this queer method of sonically manipulating time through Black grammar's prosody can bring into view a (re)claiming of Black bodies' agency in public domains. To demonstrate this relationship between sound, body, language, and time, I first develop my use of queer theory. This reorientation serves as a foundation for reinterpreting time as an embodied, rhetorical, sonic process and a generational part of working through Black grammar. This queered sonic temporality stabilizes ideas of vocality as a Black woman's survival rhetoric that is felt and heard as it travels across space and generations.

Next, I apply my theorization of queer(ing) grammar in time—that is, the manipulation of temporality through voice and sound—by reframing agency through Black grammatical tense, tempo, repetition, paralexical phenomena, and duration. I read Nicki Minaj's "Beez in the Trap," Aretha Franklin's "Respect," Lauryn Hill's "Doo Wop (That Thing)," Megan Thee Stallion's "Body," and Nina Simone's "Mississippi Goddam" as models for understanding a Black sonic rhetoric and grammar that ultimately build on what Cooper and Spillers have argued: that Black folks are doing work; we do have a temporality and therefore are worthy of being seen as agents, as Subjects. Ultimately, this chapter gives attention to the many ways Black women's intellectual ingenuity and agency are present in popular audible soundscapes (and even if some audiences aren't listening). Having said this, I suggest the sonic rhetorics of and listening politics for Black women may be a generative starting place for some as we journey on attempting ways of understanding (rhetorical) sonic agency. The intervention being made here extends frameworks that peer into operationalizing rhetoric and language for social progress and rhetorical agency. I hope this chapter provides some clarity for questions surrounding Black women's ability to survive and create change while enduring some of the bleakest temporal realities.

What We (Don't) Already Know

Theoretically Queering Time

I draw on Bettina Love's explanation of "queer" to inform my methodology, namely for viewing theoretical means of interpreting Black women's sonic rhetoric and grammar. Love unpacks the term "queer" as "a widely used catchall term in the LGBTQ community. It can describe someone's sexuality or nonconforming gender identity, or it can be used to reject labels and binaries (male, female) altogether." However, she adds, "the word also functions as a space to think, act, perform, create, and be outside what is considered 'normal,' particularly what White, straight, middle-class America says is normal. . . . queer is much more than who you love, marry, or have sex with" (141). Moreover, Love quotes Cathy Cohen's mobilization of queerness to point out a gap in operationalizing this theory, suggesting scholars be more critical and open-minded about the affordances of a queer praxis: " 'queer theorizing that calls for the elimination of fixed categories of sexual identity seems to ignore the ways in which some traditional social identities and communal ties can, in fact, be important to one's survival' " (Cohen 450; qtd. in Love 142). Along these same lines, Love additionally includes E. Patrick Johnson's use of "quare"-ness as a survival rhetoric and discourse emphasizing queer theory's utility. "Quare studies" Love writes, "is interested in the ways dark people subvert spaces, identities, and resources to ensure our survival. We all need quare studies as a lens for liberation, freedom, and abolitionism" (143). In broadening understandings of how queer theory can be mobilized as a method for survival, we can continue challenging inherited, oppressive systems our foremothers resisted; we can continue generating layers of understanding oneself in relation to time, place, and culture.

It is in this way that I interpret Black women's sound as a temporal, aural call for selfhood. It is within this vein that I explore Black grammar's relationship with linguistic temporality. For me, a Black grammar operationalizes sound to in/form a particular kind of "non-traditional" rhetoric needed to hear the ways we can survive and mobilize. In other words, I understand some Black women's employment of sound as a method for controlling time in the hopes of communicating agency and personhood now and in the future. My method for unpacking Black women's use of sound and voice as a rhetoric is reliant on this queered logic of meaning-making. My use of queer is not squarely centered in sexualities and genders specifically; rather it is situated in alternative space-making intent on carving out reimagined audible possibilities for Black bodies. My use of queerness is not intended to diminish, trivialize, or usurp the work of queer studies scholars; rather, I use queerness to continue these same calls for/of imagination, care, and survival.

In this chapter, queer(ing) time is seen as a marker of power, like Cooper suggested. Here, time is a praxis capable of countering or disrupting normalized conceptions of progression and ongoing antiBlack notions of being in the world. This alternative temporal view challenges white, heteronormative rationalizations of how events (should) unfold; it suggests that progression from point A to point B is not always a standard straight line. Rather, progressions of events build on each other, sometimes in circular patterns; thus, for many Black folks, progress is nonlinear.

Furthermore, queer(ing) time and language relies on embodied and generational knowledge-making. Queer(ing) time is both a theoretical concept of understanding the self in relation to multiple, simultaneous tenses and an applicable way for transmitting the self across time and place, disrupting bilateral movements. Recentering time within these seemingly abstract constructions of sound and language highlights temporality as subjective and relative to the perceiver; thus, constructing a queer understanding of time through sound and language validates alternative (sometimes subversive) ways for gaining and maintaining power or agency—especially when one views temporality in relation to the body and its methods of communication.

A Black Grammar

Grammar is a structure that allows space for nouns (i.e., subjects) to create a central position from which information originates. Grammar's structure guides expectations of meaning and temporality as it organizes language. As a matter of fact, "Linguistically speaking, the greatest differences between contemporary Black and White English are on the level of grammatical structure. Grammar is the most rigid and fixed aspect of speech, that part of *any* language which is least likely to change over time," noted Black sociolinguist Geneva Smitherman posits (*Talkin and Testifyin* 18). All in all, grammar is the set of rules that helps us explain and understand meanings of provided content in a logical manner by organizing or assigning value to units of information in relation to who is communicating said information; it makes the subject, or (pro)noun, the origin point from which to interpret all other conveyed meaning. It is highly unlikely that this way of organizing information will (ever) change.

While some disciplines, like writing studies, vehemently argue against upholding grammar as a prominent aspect of writing, rhetoric, and communication (particularly in the college classroom and rightfully so), I believe there is still something we can learn from grammar's sociocultural function to better address larger resistive moments like the ones posed in the beginning of this chapter. To be clear, this is not an argument for reinstituting past, prescriptivist models of grammar into classrooms. Rather, this argument is an attempt at theorizing the opportunities for survival when practitioners operate grammar against the grain of "standard" interpretations of language. Smitherman, for example, understands grammar's affordances but advocates for couching such staunch rules within sociocultural contexts so as to not deny the speaker their identity and experiences. Suggesting grammar is attached to its own politics that are embedded within what Charles Mills identified as "the Racial Contract,"[2] Smitherman pushes against a traditional grammar system by mapping its racist practices onto American English's commonly accepted rules. In doing this, she reiterates what some of us already know: a traditional approach to grammar often perpetuates the same continued solipsistic tactics marginalizing nonwhite bodies. Because conditions in America still reveal imperial commitments to oppression, the deployment of Black grammar is still a necessary method for (subversively) resisting persecution, resisting attempted erasure of personhood, as well as determining liberation(s) and educating younger generations about how to care for or protect our agency. As such, I follow Spillers's lead in approaching grammar, recognizing agency in Black voice and Black bodies. Black grammar resists marginalizing Black bodies' Subjectivity/subject-ness. Participating in meaning-making with a Black grammar, then, decommissions some white standards of knowledge-making and instead prioritizes Black consciousness and ways of being our self(s) across time, place, and medium. In making this sonic shift, Black grammar emphasizes the ingenuity of survival needed to press on and continue fighting for liberation(s).

Consequently, Smitherman calls on English teachers and language practitioners to revise and restrict dependency on traditional grammar constructions; in doing this, more generative and equitable learning can take place. She has often suggested that sustaining such a traditional (read: white) perception of our systematic language actually slows down more "progressive" moves aimed at ensuring equitable education. In "Soul 'N Style," Smitherman concludes that "what I been layin on y'all relates to the fact that there are fundamental linguistic-cultural differences between Blacks and whites, and these differences impact on and often adversely affect the communication process" (16). Throughout her installations of "Soul 'N Style," Smitherman repeatedly demonstrates the implications of not understanding meaning across speakers, especially when meaning is made through and grounded in differing perceptions of power-related language principles like grammar (e.g., subject-verb agreement and pro/

noun naming practices). These miscommunications could quite literally result in life or (social) death for Black bodies, as we've seen in Spillers's essay and in the previous chapter with Ida B. Wells's anti-lynching campaign. Smitherman, building on naming practices, illustrates this point with an example:

> the Black executive who had a problem adjusting to the use of first names on various levels of management [is] at his new firm. Now, characteristically, Blacks will cop a 'tude quick when white strangers be callin' them by they first name. . . . See, historically, whites done used this as a sign of disrespect and a verbal mechanism for putting Blacks in they "place." However, in the white business world, being addressed by your first names signals that you in the inner (power) circle. ("Soul 'N Style" 15)

These misunderstandings of language use often manifest in tensions (and fallouts) displayed between communicators, fracturing inter- and intrapersonal relationships needed to (successfully) navigate society. Indeed, under many Black language conditions, the value of grammar lies in its ability to serve as a subversive, multifaceted, collaborative network for interpreting or generating meaning. In this way, more or less, grammar can communicate a pro/noun's positioning as a layered ontological, communal, temporal, and spatial construct essential for understanding and deciphering multiple meanings simultaneously. Thus, there is a need to understand the nuances and implications of using language within and across communities. There should not be an assumption of the same grammar across all communicators, nor should the expectation of a linguistic equivalent to respectability politics (i.e., traditional grammar) be normalized. Both approaches can lead to miscommunication and misunderstanding. Queer(ing) our approach to grammar, that is, asserting the validity of a Black grammar in this instance, is an important intersection, theoretical approach, and applicable component of a Black (feminist) survival rhetoric.

Because language is a complex, systematic, communicative form, it makes sense to examine its relationships with rhetoric, sound, and body through a queered linguistic framework capable of accounting for the speaker's identity.[3] After all, from a speaker's perspective, making sound (or voicing our Subject) *is* part of interpreting the body's communicative needs and methods. Equally important, Smitherman has suggested that

"Black Dialect consists of both language and style. In using the term 'language' we are referring to *sounds and grammatical structure*. 'Style' refers to the way speakers put sounds and grammatical structure together to communicate meaning in a larger context" (*Talkin and Testifyin* 16, emphasis added). Although Smitherman has since changed the way she uses the term "dialect" when referencing Black language, her sentiment of a dynamic, expressive system still holds true.

Being attentive to Black grammar provides a measure for interpreting the interplay of language, style, personhood, sound, and temporality. By characterizing Black grammar through tense, tempo, duration, repetition, and paralexical phenomena as part of a sonic rhetorical process altering aspects of time, we reveal ways Black women have countered demoralizing stereotypes and the (un)naming of Black personhood. By this I mean Black women have used voice's sonority[4] and prosody,[5] as part of our Black grammar, to disrupt racist ideas or problematic understandings of Blackness as a monolithic identity, particularly one bereft of a history and future and one incapable of creating or maintaining the present tense on our own terms. In this way, recognizing Black grammar rationalizes Black women's use of voice as an audible, rhetorical measure of resistance and pedagogy as it temporally reverberates in public soundscapes and imaginations. On the sonic level more succinctly, Black women music artists make explicit the many ways voice challenges the inequitable representations of time used to hold Black bodies hostage, to "freeze" us in place or delay our momentum, and strip us of our Subject, agency, and personhood.

As I mentioned earlier, I specifically employ the linguistic concept of prosody for measuring Black grammar as a functional, sonic rhetoric. Through prosody, then, sound is integrated as part of rhetorical language and grammar; it is helpful in providing us a vocabulary for describing the ways music can make grammatical sense. Linguist James A. Walker defines prosody as a concept that "is used to refer to a number of suprasegmental features of language: the relative prominence of syllables within a word or phrase (*stress*); the height and range of the fundamental frequency of speech (*pitch, tone*, and *intonation*); rate of speech and the relative duration of syllables (*timing*); and the tendency for phonological rules or processes to occur within particular domains, such as the syllable, the word, and the phrase (*prosodic phonology*)" (388).

While this chapter is mostly concerned with prosodic elements relating to timing—that is, repetition, stress, and duration, more or less—it is important to understand the linguistic components of Black women's sonic rhetoric as a means for identifying and interpreting knowledge-making occurring within Black grammar. And, because grammar is the least likely to change over time, exploring the language and performance of influential moments in (Black) popular music can provide us with a sociohistorical genealogy and barometric readings of social atmospheres over time. These Black women music artists' sonic legacies serve as recognizable time capsules for younger generations to explore. As such, I want to take time (no pun intended) to parse out threads of Black temporality that I see as part of this generative, prosodic rhetoric: this Black grammar. I want to dig deeper into how music and sound (specifically the audibility of voice) are used as key instruments for transmitting lessons of survival, resistance, and liberation. What follows is my theorization of how time (in and across generations) can be sonically fractured, reverberated, and repurposed into rhetorical agency that is then taken up as personhood. Sonically mining Black grammar for temporal relationships marks this kind of sonic rhetoric as an embodied philosophical practice and literacy. This embodied knowledge-making process is capable of cultivating agency in relation to past, present, and future. Thus, Black grammar can serve as a method for observing generational exchanges of knowledge and advice.

Applying Methods of Theoretical, Queer Black Time in Grammar

When her 2012 single "Beez in the Trap" received international attention, Onika Tanya Maraj, better known as Nicki Minaj, brought Black grammar to the forefront for listeners worldwide. The song reached number 48 on the Billboard Hot 100 and even gained her a spot on a well-received late-night British talk show, *The Graham Norton Show*. Here she explained the sociocultural context of her title and chorus by decoding one of the most prominent and recognizable aspects of Black grammar, the "habitual be." Minaj states: "No, no, no. It [beez] just means, it's the saying 'I am *always*.' You know, that's our [Black] slang way of saying it. You know, we be like 'I bees doin' such and such and such [crowd chuckles].' So, but, so, it's really like 'I am always in the trap.' Now the trap, ladies and gentlemen, relates to anywhere you get your money. [Norton sighs 'oh,' signaling his newly-formed vernacular understanding] So you in the trap right now, Playboy" (Nicki Minaj Hilariously Explains 'Beez in the Trap,'" 00:24-00:59). She employs Black grammar in her song, which is distributed across radio and TV waves, to connect voice to the body and cultivate a level of independence. Minaj communicates a subversive, generational way for surviving by deploying the habitual *be*. Minaj's emphasis on the auxiliary, or helping, verb is put squarely in relation with her body's ability to maneuver traditional patriarchal and chauvinistic expectations of the Black female body: that is the capitalistic "trap" reinforcing antiBlack assumptions of Black bodies. She is using the broad and demeaning stereotype of the "Jezebel" against the very people who try to keep her in this role: making money to free herself from this literal and rhetorical "trap."

More often than not, linguists focus on the habitual aspect of *be* when contextualizing and investigating Black language and grammar. The habitual *be*[6] poses an interesting method for constructing tense and meaning. Through her song and interview, we can tell that Minaj is acutely aware of and attentive to the habitual *be* form. Employing *be*—rather than "am," as it would be translated in a white, traditional grammar—directly positions Minaj's linguistic identity within a long-standing Black communicative discourse. Looking at this auxiliary verb closely, we can glean a better understanding of how Black grammar can help generate our temporal Subject position.

This specific semantic deployment of the copula (previously referred to as the helping/auxiliary verb or habitual *be*) generally refers to an action or event that is either repeated, reoccurring over time, or (you guessed it) habitual—as its moniker suggests. In this way, the use of *be* is not entirely bound by discrete moments in time; rather, it is describing an event or action (or feeling in some cases) as having the possibility to be represented multiple times across chronologies or spaces. This construction of the helping verb can signal a complex occurrence for the speaker while also communicating a much deeper, personal connection to subversive, temporal relationships between language and the body. The invariant *be* (also known as the habitual *be*) can unpack the subject's positioning in a succinct, concise translation; it allows space for the multiple ways a pro/noun can carry out some action. In other words, the habitual *be* form is not discretely bound by one temporal instance. It can be applied to multiple temporalities of one's past, present, and future tenses/selves. Only the context clues, or the linguistic environment, can decipher in which tense the speaker is referencing—but all tenses are fair play. While the more obvious use of the habitual *be* would insinuate the present tense, as Minaj's definition suggests, the habitual *be* is not solely contained by the present understanding of "doing," or the present perfect comprehension of "having done," something.

The Black grammatical construction of this copula, then, represents a consistent and contextual unfolding over time, an unfolding that can be simultaneously past, present, and (predictive) future. Smitherman surmises that the habitual *be* can be, and often is, translated under multiple conditions. "The Black English speaker," Smitherman notes, "can use *be* to convey a sense of future time, as in *The boy be here soon* and *They family be gone Friday*." At the same time, *be* can represent past actions: "Black English speakers use *been* to express past action that has recently been completed. 'Recently' here depends much more on the particular words in the sentence that express the time, rather than the actual amount of time itself. For example, it is correct Black English to say: *She been tardy twice this semester* (which might have been several weeks or months ago as long as it's what would be called 'this semester')." She goes on to add, "*Be* is also used in combination with *do* to convey habitual conditions expressed in question form and for emphasis: *Do they be playing all day?* (in White English: *Do they play all day?*)" (*Talkin and Testifyin* 20, 21–22). In terms of tense or temporality for Minaj, "beez" communicates both frequency and time of completion. To translate this into a broader Black feminist cultural context, Black folk, particularly Black women, are always, have constantly been, and most likely will be *frequently* struggling to get free (be that economically or socially). For Minaj more specifically, in 2012, she was making money often (and arguably continues to do so) and, makes money in many ways (e.g., dancing, rapping, singing, merchandizing, guest appearances, to name a few), surviving by any means necessary in a capitalist economy. (Un)surprisingly, this seemingly diminutive and ubiquitous helping verb is, in fact, anything but the sort; this word (and its variations) plays a significant role in Black grammar constructions and communicating Black agency and temporality across time.

Because this copula can transpire over time and simultaneously represent multiple points of temporality at once, repetition becomes an exceptionally important aspect to listen to. Indeed, the influence of repetition in this verb's structuring is fundamental to establishing meaning. For instance, Minaj's clarification of "beez in the trap" suggests that Black folk—especially Black women—are repeatedly trying to make money/survive; even more so, Black women are constantly finding ways to survive as they are repeatedly caught in "the trap" of antiBlack ecosystems manifesting in our oppressive realities. In a capitalist society, accruing money means potentially securing one's livelihood, even securing one's family's livelihood. Having money, to some extent, means having some degree of privilege and economic freedom that can translate into a "better" quality of life. However, it is only "better" to some degree, as antiBlackness, sexism, and homophobia among other "-isms" still dictate quality of life around the world, hence the frequency and intensity of *be*ing caught "in the trap."

Constantly being in the trap suggests a much larger ecology of recognizing the many intersectional ways oppression has been and continues to be carried out in the name of white supremacist logics. Black women are often needing to and in the habit of (re)claiming modicums of personhood in the hopes of gaining equitable rights and freedoms. These freedoms can be in the form of fair pay for (equal) labor, reconciliation or reparations, and equal opportunities for cultivating quality lifestyles predominantly afforded to affluent white male citizens—securing "the bags" by any means necessary. This habitual being in the "trap," according to Minaj, linguistically symbolizes the historical imbalance of freedom and Black folks' exhaustive attempts at surviving that result from the generations of antiBlack, temporal misconceptions of "being out of time." Invoking survival shouldn't be a habitual act, but for many Black folks, it is. This way of being in the world also shouldn't have to normalize an inheritance of survival plans that continually need repeating, but for many Black folks, it does. Thus, this Black grammatical function of the habitual *be* does precise work to reverberate and resist the intersectional, generational traumas that people of African descent continue enduring in and through our bodies. Said another way, the habitual *be* can keep track of (nonlinear) time by measuring Black women's (in)frequent gains of "freedoms" and the recurring need to publicly assert our agency and the dependance of our labor. If messages of survival and liberation need repeating, then it is clear to see and hear that "we" have not learned to equally exist in time together.

Minaj's meaning-making through using habitual *be* conveys what she is *doing* at a particular time, what she *has been doing*, and the frequency with which she *does it*; she asserts her agency and aptitude for making money as a means of validating her experiences of being in the world—contextually, historically, temporally, and ecologically. Her use of the habitual *be* communicates her subversive positionality signaling a relationship between tense, modality, and aspect (TMA)[7]—all prosodic methods of Black grammar, which strengthen a connection between various temporal realities, the body, and language. Hence, Minaj's discussion with Norton, the show's host, as well as her performance of the song for public audiences and listeners illuminate this verb's temporal connectivity, offering us a sample of how sound functions in concert with Black grammar and Black bodies. In this way, Minaj lays another generational cornerstone of a potentially robust theory of/for Black women's sonic rhetoric.

"That Big Wheel Keep on Turning," So Let's "Fuck It Up to the Tempo"[8]

Now, I say Minaj has laid *another* generational cornerstone of Black women's sonic rhetoric because she is not the first to employ Black grammar in such audible ways. The prosodic methods of grammar (i.e., stress, tempo, and tense, to name a few) have been employed by the likes of Aretha Franklin, Lauryn Hill, Megan Thee Stallion, and Nina Simone, for example, all of whom have similarly manipulated time and demanded R-E-S-P-E-C-T in one way or another. Thus, this re-sounding process of queer(ing) grammar has long been established, and it continues evolving into a robust theoretical genealogy and pedagogy for Black women's survival and rhetorical resistance. By piecing together, across generations, these kinds of sonic tools employed by Black women, we can delve further into embodied aspects accompanying Black grammar as it appears in our everyday soundscapes. Shifting our focus from how tense is created to the ways in which repetition and tempo mimic our temporalities, for instance, can provide us with other mile-markers on this generational journey.

If we view repetition in its most conventional usage, then we may overlook its influence in Black (feminist) sonic, rhetorical practices. As a result of this overlooking, we may end up sustaining outdating views of repetition as merely a poetic literary device. This "traditional" approach of understanding repetition, like grammar, has an uncanny habit of separating language from the practitioner's body; in effect, this kind of application can reject some of the grounding principles that Black language and rhetoric were built on: the relationship between "soul" and "style." While I do see immense value in poetic literary devices, I do not want us to forget repetition's rhetorical attributes. Repetition can sonically create or manipulate time through its audible *changes of momentum* embedded within the audible speed of aural messages and the affective, internalized clock of "progression." This sonic start-and-stop rhythm allows the performer to, figuratively and literally, push pause and push play for the audience. This intentional stutter of sound dictates the intensity, effectiveness, and motion of the artists' message(s) while giving listeners time to stop, reflect, and act. Queer(ing) repetition, for the sake of Black grammar, can take place in three sonic forms: the repetition of words; the repetition of beats; and the repetition of concepts.

Eunice Waymon (better known by her stage name and alter ego, "Nina Simone") gives us a perfect example of how sound and voice intersect with timing, stress, and repetition (and later duration) to form an intersectional and generational Black feminist sonic rhetoric. Simone performed "Mississippi Goddam" before largely white audiences in 1964, one year prior to Aretha Franklin's release of "Respect." The sonority of "Mississippi Goddam" amplified the kind of intersectional activism Simone, and others since then, encouraged during the early formation of the Black arts movement, and the twentieth-century civil rights movement more broadly. As Ruth Feldstein notes, "What was clear was that in [Simone's] *performance* of ["Go Limp"] and ["Mississippi Goddam"], Simone claimed the power of sexuality from a black woman's point of view and that this power was central to her vision of black political activism" (1368–69). Similar to Minaj's "Beez in the Trap" lyrics and video that highlighted how one can capitalize on the hypersexuality of Black women's bodies to overcome some economic disparities, Simone's song placed Black women's bodies on the front line of these intersectional, generational battlegrounds with her explicit reference to "Sister Sadie" and her unabashed critique of the Birmingham bombing (further explained below). Well after Simone's live performances ended, this song (like Franklin's and even Billie Holiday's songs) still resonates as an activist anthem resolutely calling for Black women's agency, personhood, accountability, and liberation across the globe.

In terms of a Black temporality more specifically, "Mississippi Goddam" audibly fractures listeners' perceptions of time. This is done not just by blending past sonic rhetorics with contemporary lyrics (although this is a significant feature of Simone's and Franklin's prowess) but also by juxtaposing a fast-paced tempo with quick and prolonged lyrics intentionally critiquing temporal impediments of/to Black folks' liberation. Originally written with a tempo of 155[9] beats per minute (bpm), "Mississippi Goddam" is generally considered a "happy" tune. In fact, some music critics, like Liz Fields, have described it as "jaunty" or having a show tune–like melody (2021). In comparison, Franklin's "Respect" is recorded as being 115 bpm:[10] both songs are considered cheerful and uplifting, or inspiring to some degree, largely because of their tempo and key (G major and C major, respectively). According to psychologists Liu et al., the tempo of a song directly correlates with how a listener interprets and connects to a song's emotive appeal, otherwise known as "arousal" and "valence" (2018). More specifically, their findings support earlier research suggesting that fast-tempo[11] music "evoked the most pleasant feelings" and altered listener's threshold of arousal. In other words, "faster tempo could arouse [a] more positive emotion with stronger activation of emotional experience" (Liu et al. 7). This correlates with a listener's valence, a measure of the listener's affective association with feeling positive (i.e., feelings of happiness, euphoria, or cheerfulness when listening to a song), and arousal (i.e., the perceived conscious, active listening altered by affect). What can be interpreted in relation to Simone's and Franklin's Black activist music, then, is that audiences who listen(ed) to this song may develop/have developed more positive feelings toward the kinds of intersectional Black feminist, activist messages sounded out in these songs; thus, audiences were/have been/can be moved more strongly into acting with a (perceived) mentality aimed at allyship.

This tempo range, from a rhetorical aspect, plays an important role in constructing purposeful communication orienting both Franklin and Simone as sonic rhetors and as important contributors to our generational sonic rhetoric methodology. Elizabeth Ellis Miller, author of "Remembering Freedom Songs: Repurposing an Activists Genre," describes the genre of freedom songs coming to power: "Their emergence developed because of the song leaders such as Bernice Johnson Reagon, Fannie Lou Hamer, and Betty Mae Fikes, who taught the songs and offered instruction into their histories" (54). As Reagon, Hamer, and Fikes took on the role of teaching the new generation songs to protest for liberation, a shift or transfer of knowledge took place as they shared, created, and communicated rhetorical acts of and for freedom. These freedom songs are one of many types of generational sonic rhetorics. These songs were easily passed on because they could "easily" be remembered. Using songs, especially with faster tempos that invoke positive feelings, encouraged, connected, and displayed young activists' investment in our freedom struggles.

Their audible playing with time, that is, the speed or tempo of the music in this case, corresponds with understanding Black temporality's unpredictability and precarity. Through Simone's musical composing, for example, she cultivates a sonic method of participative, critical reflection (dis)orienting or displacing (perhaps suspending) anticipated emotions with the juxtaposition of her tempo and repeating lyrics. "Mississippi Goddam" acted as both the catalyst and cohesive structure for audiences moved to act with urgency—connecting their emotional experience of listening to their personal perception of the context in which the sound was produced and digested. The tempo and repetition of contrasting lyrics ushered listeners from a passive listening stance to an active one. If one feels good about listening to the music, then perhaps the listener will be pulled more strongly in the direction of favoring acts of/for Black liberation, as the song suggests. Simone's employment of a fast-paced tempo initially invites audience members to participate in a faux-sonic activism,[12] superficially making listeners feel good about what little change has occurred in recent memory. But, as Feldstein described, "[t]he lyrics were filled with anger and despair and stood in stark contrast to the fast-paced and rollicking rhythm" of "Mississippi Goddam," and her song "expressed on a cultural terrain pain and rage" (1349–50). Rather than rely on tempo to convey the message of progress and leave audiences with a false sense of allyship (i.e., supporting her music and call for liberation just by listening to the song), Simone subversively uses tempo to counter what has been understood as "progress" and to alter listeners' perception of equality's pace with respect to Black bodies. The tempo of "Mississippi Goddam" can create a sense of urgency, rather than euphoria, within the audience. This fast tempo elevates the listeners' heart rates, like one might associate with feelings of fear, anger, and uncertainty. In this way, this song's quickened lyrics are not intended to invoke feelings of happiness or positive emotions, as the bpm would suggest—rhetorically, physically, and neurologically. Instead, Simone's Black grammar and temporal juxtaposition allow her to "weaponize music itself," as Fields writes for PBS. As a result, this contended exchange between sound, feeling, and reality allows audiences to initially digest the tune without much internal resistance, only to then begin reckoning with their own listening perception and reception of time *in* reality.

So, while under the pretense of musical enjoyment—and the theatrics accompanying Black women music artists' live shows (especially Simone's live shows)—audiences are confronted with a lopsided reality of Black temporality in which listeners must negotiate. One side of reality is recognizing that Black subjectivity is steeped in generational violence and oppression and, on the other side, a reimagining of Black subjectivity adorned with hope for change and progress. In other words, the song's musical message confronts what is believed to be true (i.e., the social justice turn that is "progress") and counters the prospects with a much darker reality (i.e., a slow-paced liberation unfolding over generations and hindered by inaction and politics) while asking listeners to engage with the choices at hand.

Alternatively, Franklin's tempo in "Respect" was largely driven by repeating words instead of stroking piano keys. Even though Otis Redding does employ repetition in his original recording of this song, it is Franklin and her sisters who operationalize voice's sonority for cultural progress and mass produce a sonic movement. Because their Black feminist version of *"respect"* became embedded within the song's remix, Franklin's rendition is more inclusive of the greater public sentiment regarding the cultural moment when this version was publicly released, much like Simone's "Mississippi Goddam." Franklin's "Respect" aptly addressed the urgency of the civil rights movement, the momentum of the feminist movement, and the frustration with the Vietnam War. These women's voices transformed the work of the horns and drums that provided the repetition and tempo in Redding's initially recorded track into a vocal Black feminist call of agency and change. By using their voices as the repetition mechanism, they brought audiences' attentions to the sounds and performance of the body and caused listeners to grapple with the often-repeated call for progress through an intersectional frame. The oral manipulation of the lyrics by way of repetition prolonged the audiences' attentiveness, giving these singers more time to espouse their message and assert their agency in public and sonic spaces while also confronting the (ongoing) frequency at which progress is delayed.

Tricia Rose points out, in *Black Noise: Rap Music and Black Culture in Contemporary America*, that "Rhythmic complexity, *repetition with subtle variations*, the significance of the drum, melodic interest in the bass frequencies, and breaks in pitch and time," all aspects of sound, "are not merely stylistic effects, they are aural manifestations of philosophical approaches to social environments"[1] (67, emphasis added). If we think about prosody in this way, then, it's not difficult to understand alternative ways of knowing. We can make meaning that is grounded in our own lived experiences and embodied practices, as our epistemologies mimic our historical context, our pendulum-like march toward progress. As a survival strategy, Black women music artists have audibly queered these sonic devices—like so many other instances of language—for the purpose of reinforcing temporality, addressing precarity, and asserting urgency of Black folks' personhood. These sonic rhetorics of resistance and survival also demonstrate how one can make a way forward by stressing agency in multiple ways. Black women music artists have commissioned repetition, like tempo, within their performances to convey the need for change, to insinuate the changing same, and to "keep that big wheel [of progress] turning," as Tina Turner once sang; they have employed sound to call for reconciliation, acknowledgement, and action in the hopes of moving us toward freedom and liberation on some level. Looking at repetition and tempo through this queered Black lens, then, we can begin unraveling and reconnecting the philosophical underpinnings Rose mentions, tying Black music, Black culture, Black language and literacies, as well as Black rhetorics firmly together.

Aretha Franklin and her sisters do just this in their rendition of "Respect." They sonically give us a glimpse into how that change for progress, equality, and liberation can occur—that is, by giving "just a little bit" of respect to Black women. In Franklin's version of this tune, her sisters, Erma and Carolyn, vocally repeated "just a little bit"; "re-"; and "sock it to me" throughout the song. These three repetitive lines, along with the spelling out of "respect," significantly set Franklin's version of the song apart from the song's earlier rendition—presumably written and originally recorded by Redding. Operationalizing repetition though these various but distinct ways plays a key role in establishing Franklin's wildly popular remix. While these three instances of repetition are important to recognize in their own right, I primarily focus on "re-" in this chapter since it visually and sonically queers grammar for a Black context (i.e., manipulating prefixes/suffixes to communicate a particular temporality).

While some listeners may believe this song only speaks to women's issues, others see and hear this song as a much larger call for Black folks' liberation in general. Whatever the case may be, a general consensus is that "Respect" quickly became Franklin's signature song and, for some, the anthem of the 1970s feminist and cultural movements. Carl Wilson, a writer for *Slate*, invokes a conversation between Jerry Wexler, Franklin's producer; and David Ritz, Franklin's biographer, to spell out how influential Franklin's cover of "Respect" was. Wexler described her number-one hit song as "virtually defin[ing] the national consciousness at that moment in history" (par. 2). Wilson then contextualizes Wexler's sentiment, suggesting that the public reaction to Franklin's version of the song granted her rendition success because [the song] literally spells out a fundamental human need, in a way mainstream pop had not heard before, with both maximum dignity and maximum playfulness. It does it in the names of women, people of color, and anyone else exhausted and exasperated with being treated as less than a full person. All of this somehow packed into 2½ minutes that begin with horns and a string-bending guitar riff and the big bang of "WHAT you want" (question mark, or exclamation point?) (par. 3)

This gravitas was something unattainable, despite relative success, for Redding. Adding to his point, Wilson notes that "Aretha's 'Respect' was an anthem of female empowerment, one that emphasized resistance and self-possession rather than just suffering and forbearance" (par. 18), which was something prioritized in the marketing of blues a generation prior.

Connecting the employment of prosody to rhetorically communicating one's personhood and grammaticality is a significant relationship to acknowledge here. This connection not only signals the importance of Kairos, but also signals a temporal reality attuned to multilayered navigations of being in the world for Black folks. Citing Christopher Small, Rose points out that "[t]he repetitions of African American music have a *function in time* which is the reverse of (Western classical) music—to dissolve the past and the future into one eternal present, in which the passing of time is no longer noticed" (qtd. in Rose 66–67, emphasis added). This is to also say that Black music is an equally important part and complementary way of knowing and expressing our centuries of being in the world; it is not meant to merely sound "good" or "funky," but is used for recognizing our nonlinear temporalities. Black music is an embodied philosophy that records our past, present, and future. Songs like "Respect," and the other songs I discuss in this chapter, continue pushing against such "neat" and "tidy" auditory responses intended to dress up colonized behavior and epistemology as well as continue devaluing Black temporality. These songs resist mindsets that insist past faults are strictly in the past and, as such, have no bearing on present-day ontologies or have no influence on today's political and legal jurisprudence.

Maintaining this functionality, I suggest repetition can communicate our very being in the world, at least in some respects. The repetition of the "re-," for instance, is an intentional sonic disruption meant to blend the past with the present. As Small and Rose suggest, repetition opposes a long-standing white supremacist belief that Black folks have *no* past, present, or future. Similarly, James A. Snead cosigns this connection between philosophy, repetition, and embodied Black grammar by illuminating an origin point of this established antiBlack concept we find ourselves continually resisting. Like Cooper, who opened this chapter, Snead reminds us of Hegel's ignorant proposition, which was an oppressive assertion that Black folk have no culture, and therefore no future and no humanity, ultimately devaluing Black bodies' positioning in the (Western, imperial) world (147–48). But, as Snead points out, Hegel's anti-definition of what we are "not" is much of the same evidence for arguing who we *be* and how we exist. In fact, Black people do have a past, present, and future; it's just that these tenses are often playing out simultaneously at once and in many forms—as we know from the habitual *be*. For many of us, time has the possibility to fold in on itself, conveying our positionality as continuously being in multidirectional motion, and we can prove this with sound.

Snead directs us toward Black grammar complicating repetition as being a more accurate understanding of how Black folk employ prosodic, rhythmic, sonic messages *of* temporality to prove his point. He states that "repetition, first of all, would inevitably have to creep into the dimension of culture just as it would have to creep into that of language and signification because of the finite supply of elementary units and the need for recognition in human understanding" (146). This audible translation has already occurred, as listeners have been conditioned to associate sound with feeling. The prefix "re-" often stands in as a syntactical abbreviation affixed to the user's notions of "return," "go back," and/or "once again. Additionally, Snead suggests that "whenever we encounter repetition in cultural forms [like chart-topping hip-hop and R&B singles], we indeed are not viewing 'the same thing,' but its transformation" (146). We are not recognizing "re-" simply as a prefix now; we are coming to understand Franklin's uses the sound of "re-" repeating as an ongoing (dare I say generational) sonic simulacrum—an audible copy of the start-and-stop process of generating freedom or liberation, healing, and pleasure that accompanies the right to be seen as fully human. Franklin's use of this semantic utterance models an intersectional process of change many Black folk are familiar with: that is, the revving up to do something just for that momentum to be (often violently) truncated, stopped, or hindered in some way to then only be shown and pointed right back to the starting line. Black women especially know how frustrating and aggravating this cycle is, particularly as our voices are refused to be listened to or legitimated.

Snead describes this kind of transformation as being "graft[ed] onto culture of an essentially philosophical insight about the shape of time and history" (146). In other words, the frequency at which this delay occurs has impacted our ability to see ourselves in discrete time, as the past is our present and coalesces to shape our future. He suggests that when we [i.e., people of African descent] recognize and use repetition, it is not just a convenient way to fill a moment in time or create popular, catchy content for the general public's consumption. Instead, it is a method for publicizing how Black folk have acknowledged and continue recognizing just how (little) things have changed over time—that is, how things have transformed and/or been repurposed.

When words or sounds get repeated in popular culture, they provoke the audience to take pause, listen, and think through its sonic message— its characteristics and implications. This threshold for audible exchange can become a moment of solace, peace, and action even within moments of noise, chaos, and rupture. In this way, as Rose suggests, the rhythm created from sound acts as a generative means of equilibrium for both artists and (potentially) listeners (67). From a prosodic approach, then, repetition transforms into a Black sonic rhetoric and extends applications of Black grammar to and through the body.

While our use of repetition may often be a subtle and subversive way to hold the public's attention and demand critical reflection, this method is still a powerful tool of/for resistance. Like tempo, repetition can become a weaponized, rhetorical mechanism for Black folk reiterating how urgent, timely, and deeply engrained our calls for change, survival, health, and liberation are with respect to our livelihood. As such, repetition can be employed as one method for Black music artists' praxis. Indeed, employing repetition to dictate time (that is, the time spent listening to the performer, their message of time, and/or the time spent lingering, remembering, transmitting what was/is being experienced) through the performance of sound is a masterful tool that has been cultivated and passed down through generations. It is a significant symbol for Black folks, as it represents both progress and change in relation to our past, present, and future tense.

The sonic legacy of repurposing sound is not only demonstrated in Franklin's version of her Grammy-winning rendition, but it is also in her methods for developing her sonic identity. As Wilson points out, "Aretha's ways of expanding and exploding the song's rhythms and melodies drew on the techniques of the gospel singers she was close to and admired from both church and the family salon, such as Marion Williams, Mahalia Jackson, and her father's longtime lover, Clara Ward of the Ward Singers" (par. 8). This kind of embodied relationship oscillating between/around sound, language, and identity is a methodological trail that illuminates various pathways for other Black women music artists to follow as we learn new and/or more effective ways for cultivating voice and agency. Furthermore, using repetition as a method and methodology suggests that sound, as a tool, is often generationally cultivated, passing on information about various ways of survival. The sonic aspects of Black grammar are pathways navigating us through these ongoing oppressive conditions; it is an important network for passing on traditions and methods of resistance, especially within a music industry that has for a long time been male-dominated and exploitative.

In fact, we still see these sonic mentorships retain prominence even if there isn't a strong, physical advising presence—although some personal connection is most often the starting point for this audible transfer of knowledge and advice. Wilson writes, "Few of these [contemporary Black women] figures can match Aretha's pipes or her finesse, but a few have been catching up with her political and emotional sophistication. What was Beyoncé's Lemonade, after all, but an album-long elaboration of the themes of 'Respect'—though updated to an era of sexual frankness that makes the once eyebrow-raising 'sock it to me' mantra sound as quaint as a sock hop?" (par. 19). At its core, "Respect" is a call for just that, respect. These generative, audible exchanges of information between Black women reinforces the idea here that there is, indeed, a genealogy of Black women's sonic rhetoric as pedagogy in which to explore. This generational sonic exchange is still being deployed today and with good reason: the need for survival and an urgency to fight for life are still of the utmost importance.

The lessons learned from life, family, and various sonic mentors resonate with contemporary artists like Lauryn Hill and others mentioned here. It is no secret that Hill and Franklin were on similar wavelengths (as were Franklin and Beyoncé for that matter). Hill and Franklin did, after all, collaborate in the late 1990s with their "A Rose Is Still a Rose" (1998) duet. Generational conversations through musical discourses like duets, sampling or remixing, interludes, and iconography, for example, can create a practical progression of argumentation that is "original" enough to grab hold of new audiences while still being familiar enough—to those connected with the penultimate struggle—to continue extending and evolving generational sonic rhetorics.

Generational sonic rhetorics overlap through visual, aural, performative, and linguistic interpretations. Lauryn Hill's entire video for "Doo-Wop (That Thing)" suggests that music can and does connect past, present, and future by sonically passing on lessons worth repeating: lessons like self-love, community support, and (of course) respect. Black women music artists named throughout this chapter, and this book more broadly, have employed sound as a means for calling attention to the many generational traumas imposed on Black bodies. Black women music artists often audibly repeat lessons learned as a means for educating younger generations, hopefully teaching others how to avoid repeating traumas and how to heal and survive in times of oppression/suppression, as I detail in the following chapter. As such, Black folk have sounded the alarm frequently, abstractly, loudly, and concretely; our calls for change, liberation, and freedom still resonate through audible spaces, showing listeners ways for (un)learning.

Hill's song and music video both are indicative of how Black women music artists have traversed time and space connecting and reinforcing generational calls for survival by any means necessary. In this way, Hill's song pays homage to the groundwork laid by her predecessors, including Franklin and Simone, with their manipulation of time through sound, while also extending earlier generations' calls for validation. Thus, repetition's reiterating presence reinforces the prominence and utility of Black women's use of sound as a rhetorical, generational, pedagogical tool.

While there are many instances of repetition in Hill's "Doo-Wop (That Thing)," there is one brief portion of the song that stands out to me as a particularly important example of how prosody has been contemporarily used to embed a Black (sonic) grammar into popular discourses. Between 02:43 and 03:02 of this song, Hill echoes two phrases again and again: "watch out" and "look out" in a "round robin" style complete with acapella, instrumental deviation, and audible breaks. The first time we are introduced to Hill's cautionary phrases, we hear (and see) a pause in the music. This momentary silence is proceeded by Hill and her backup singers (which also includes her own vocals being dubbed and played over her foregrounded lyrics, i.e., doo-wop-ing) initially harmonizing these lines acapella, which is then followed by a change in instrumentation. Operationalizing voice in this way encourages a refocusing on orality as a primary means for communicating information, much like Franklin's rendition did a generation prior. Incorporating doo-wop techniques, then, not only connects past generations' sonic activism with contemporary auditory expectations (driven by "newer" technologies), but this technique of repetition continues the generational threads calling for awareness and reflection of (in)equity. Hill rhetorically centers African-based epistemologies by shifting attention to orality, sound, and performance as part of her embodied, temporal storytelling.

After the first round of acapella advice, Hill introduces a tonal shift caused by repeating, vibrating stringed instruments. Rather than reintroduce the high-pitched staccato of the piano that has been keeping time in the background since the beginning of the song, she introduces the midrange tone of the stringed instruments. The trill of the violin here invokes an affective feeling for the listeners while also amplifying Hill's message—as she repeats these two phrases for a second, a third, and a fourth time. This smooth, sonic transformation of repetition (that is, the initiation of strings instead of the piano and the acapella breaks) bolsters Hill's sonic message of care and concern. Her nuanced prosodic method fuses orality with resonating emotions spurred on by the strings' vibrations.

Juxtaposing the instrumentation with vocality effectively creates an audible chasm in which to pay attention. This use of voice becomes stressed by its simple unadornment, and the body becomes the focal point for meaning-making. The sentiments expressed by these phrases convey the level of vigilance Black folk, and Black women more specifically, have had to negotiate in our daily lives since the days of the Middle Passage (and most likely even before). Hill's temporal sonic echo amplifies generational requirements of vigilance that has become a staple of Black folks' survival methods. As an audience, we are coaxed and directed to sharply tune in to Hill's advisory message of health and safety as the musicality of the song becomes more defined and focused. Rather than having the drums, horns, and beats accompany the voice (as it does before and after this particular break in music), the background noises become stripped away, leaving only the voice, through its various techniques of repetition, creating the sound and tempo that emphasize the message. This is similar to Franklin's remix, which stripped down the bold, brassy notes of Redding's recording as she transformed it into a Black feminist liberation theme song. Additionally, Hill's use of the strings' repetitive tremor parallels the tremor Black folks experience every day as we navigate white, solipsistic societies and structures; the strings are a sonic reminder of the stuttering, the hesitation, the start-and-stop process of progress that is often inundated by fear, sadness, and hope. Blending acapella with this specific tone of the vibrating strings audibly triggers a survival-mode response for many listeners—that is, we should pause and take stock of our surroundings, as we are under surveillance and (most likely) in "trouble." Therefore, the (subversive) use of repetition Hill employs here indicates, for listeners, an urgent moment for attunement to and recognition of her message as an ongoing process for resistance and liberation, one that goes back generations.

The vibration of the strings resonates with our being and warns us not to be lulled into a false sense of "victory" or "progress" as well as to not pacify our agency. Hill's repeating vocalized and stringed tremors oppose white, classical interpretations of orchestral music and listening more broadly. As Dylan Robinson posits:

> [T[he colonial imposition of settling listening seeks to compel sensory engagement through practices of focusing attention that are "settled"—in the sense of coming to rest or becoming calm—and in doing so effect perceptual reform sought through the "civilizing mission" of missionaries. . . . Listening regimes imposed and implemented "fixed listening" strategies [i.e., listening for aesthetic arrangement or intentional harmonizing to calm or assimilate listeners] that are part of a larger reorientation toward Western categorization of single-sense engagement, as well as toward Western ontologies of music located in aesthetic appreciation." (40–41)

Hill's use of Black grammar's prosody reiterates the magnitude of listening for agency outside of "traditional" methods that Robinson called out. In this way, Hill's sonic rhetoric warns us of incoming stressors; her methods of repetition signal caution and awareness for our bodies so we can prepare ourselves for resisting legacies of manipulation. In other words, like indigenous listening practices, Black music—with all its highly functional and specialized techniques—is an aural representation and extension of our personhood, agency, and experience: so much so that Hill's operational sonic rhetoric emphasizes older, decolonial approaches for listening that once served as a means of survival.

As such, Hill uses repetition to dictate time and convey its relationship to the body by creating a multilayered repetitive process of strings and voice. The musical shift defined by the tonal and syntactic phrases are rhetorical, prosodic techniques overtly emphasizing familiar generational messages. She is sonically carving out time through intra-linear repetition and contrasts phrase lengths with quick, frequent, and sustained measures filled with notes and sounds. Ultimately, Hill audibly interrupts our sonic conditioning—both in our anticipation of the meter we have already been accustomed to hearing through the first two verses and choruses as well as in our way of listening *for* information. Throughout this song, and particularly within this specific moment of dynamic repetition, we are undoubtedly being asked to intently listen to her words embedded in the middle of the song while disguising her message as entertainment—an approach so many other Black women music artists have also employed.

Theorizing these effects in this way better solidifies the relationship between body and language. Repetition can harness listeners' attention and focus the audience's awareness on the message from the speaker/performer. As a rhetorical function of Black grammar, repetition can help listeners identify prevailing motifs, themes, and messages. It makes the sonic message easier to digest because the message can become internalized like a habit. This also means that the audible message becomes easier for the audience to recognize, remember, and transmit as time goes on because we've heard it once before.

Prosodic attributes, like repetition, tempo, and tense, allow listeners to impose personal connections or meanings onto the sonic message because it becomes attached to the body in some way. This development, in turn, reinforces rhetorical connections between artist, audience, and message; their ecological and auditory relationships become fortified. Like Norton's superficial understanding of being in the "trap," made possible by Minaj's clarifying the habitual, or in this case the repetitive *be*, the listener latches onto what resonates with their personal understanding of the message, paving a pathway for appropriation and/or transmission. The artist guides listeners to consciousness.

"Look at How I Bodied That"

Even though Hill and Franklin were generations apart, both brought attention to the body through prosody. They recognized Black women (and Blackness in general) as valid sites of agency, personhood, and meaning-making. It is true that Franklin's repeating phrase "sock it to me" was risqué at the time, but, as Wilson noted above, that phrase—in comparison with today's progressive resistance to respectability politics—is mild. And it is true that Hill's song also falls flat in its attempts at addressing multiple kinds of intimate partner violence (the same critique listeners espoused for Redding) and dynamic self-care. The reliance on heteronormative, sexualized social responses can continue inflicting similar, normalized trauma that often lingers behind colonized mindsets. But these repetitions *of* the body *in* sound can still facilitate a smoother pathway for recalling the urgency in validating Black personhood. As we turn to the twenty-first century, the pendulum of more explicit calls for Black women's agency is swinging back toward the brash, queer, and unapologetic tactics of performance and sound, much like Black blueswomen a century earlier, while continuing the development of a sonic Black grammar and rhetoric informed by prosody. In addition to continuing the sonic rhetoric found within repeating words' prefixes and thematic concepts, Megan Pete, better known as Megan Thee Stallion, repeats particular audible and performative gestures to mark time rhythmically, temporally, and linguistically. She modernizes past calls for agency, ramping up the evolutionary trend of prosody as a possible queered mechanism of/for Black grammar.

Similar to Franklin and her sisters' operationalizing "re-" almost forty years earlier, Megan Thee Stallion adds to Black grammar's sonic process by emphasizing sounds made *with* and *about* the body, a method that is especially evident in her third single from *Good News* (2020), "Body" (2020). The certified platinum single that has been emphatically praised by critics as a "twerk-worthy bop" (Lamarre 2020) celebrating and empowering people of all shapes and sizes to be proud of who they are. In this up-tempo song that promotes confidence and encourages listeners to enjoy themselves and their bodies, Megan Thee Stallion models herself as an example as she sings "look at how I bodied that." The hook of the song primarily consists of a partial-word repetition: "Body-ody-ody-ody-ody-ody-ody-ody." Like its sonic predecessor "re-," this repetition of "-ody" narrativizes the push-pull tensions of respectability, objectification, and self-care that have for generations played out over the terrain of Black women's bodies. Thus, the repetition of the "suffix" parallels Franklin's repetition of the prefix "re-" as her audible articulation of the body becomes a response to the (sonic) stuttering of time and reality à la gendered expectations of how to behave in public for the sake (and hope) of proving one's personhood and its effects on moving forward toward "progress."

Vocalizing the repetition of the body creates a focal point for audiences to gaze at and reflect on its positioning in the world. Megan Thee

Stallion's subversion of the gaze (and corresponding expectations of/for Black bodies) rests on auditorily inserting celebrating Black bodies into public imaginations. As such, Megan Thee Stallion sonically operationalizes the "suffix" for resisting generational misconceptions about Black women's bodies (like the ones we saw in the *Moynihan Report*) as being deviant, "naturally" hypersexualized, and/or "oddities," similar to Minaj's argument in "Beez in the Trap." As a result, this message of pleasure and (Black) joy deftly counters long-standing, racist public imaginings of Black (women's) bodies.

By pushing beyond what "-ody" can signify, we can further theorize how Black grammar evolves within such seemingly unapologetic soundbites. As Rose pointed out, "Time suspension via rhythmic breaks . . . are important clues in explaining sources of pleasure in black music" (67). I would also add, sources of pain, regret, frustration, and even disillusionment (as I discussed in the previous chapter) to Rose's point. For Megan Thee Stallion, the body is a respected source of power, memory, and knowledge. The rhythmic breaks created by her repeating "suffix" mark her body as an epicenter of pleasure that gets translated into her music. The body potentially offers listeners a moment of relief from prolific antiBlack expectations. In other words, Megan Thee Stallion's use of her sonic Black grammar can create a suspended moment where our oppressive realities move to the background. She creates a moment where we can release tension, enjoy identities/our bodies, and indulge in playfulness so that we can take care and indulge in moments that carve out space for us: in other words, foster long-term survival. She uses her body repeatedly and emphatically, communicating to and convincing listeners of this mindset: a mindset that is about catering to the self and rejecting the haters. She makes it clear that the body is a site of pleasure, agency, and resistance with her overt and multilayered forms of Black grammatical prosody.

In addition to her identifiable use of repetition, Megan Thee Stallion employs paralexical phenomena as another audible layer of Black grammar's prosodic rhetoric. Definitionally, paralexical refers to things that are adjacent to lexicon and grammar, such as sounds (for example, beatboxing) that are not quite words but are still a part of communicating meaning within a sentence or specific moment of interpersonal communication. Rhetorical tactics like this can be recognized as prosody because "the relative prominence of syllables within a word or phrase," as Walker defined it earlier, is continually stressed over time and is clearly operationalized as the featured linguistic aspect of the song. Said another way, the sound-word formed by Megan Thee Stallion sticking out her tongue and pronouncing "ah" stresses her body's presence by sonically extending the lyric and elongating the time in which the artist is in the spotlight. This paralexical negotiation marks her as a sonic rhetorician as she persuades the audience to give their attention to her for just a little bit longer; they continue listening to her sounds even after her lyrics are complete. These audible iterations of agency radiating from the body, are cultivated as primary focal points in which to give the most time and attention. She signals to listeners that this audible and visual message of and from the body is indeed something to be stressed.

Moreover, Jon Whitmore describes the paralexical as "[a]ural communication includ[ing] spoken words and paralexical sounds (groans, screams, whimpers); sound effects (wind, a car starting up and driving away); and music" (14). These sound-words are not onomatopoeia since paralexical sounds are not so much words that mimic external, audible actions (e.g., "pow" or "bang") but instead are concocted words that create and replicate meaning radiating from bodily experience or emotion. The collective repetition of image, sound, and word works in tandem with an up-tempo and resonating rhythm meant to be physically engaged with (i.e., dance). This "stressed" relationship forcing audiences to recognize Megan Thee Stallion's whole self as a primary agent and her body as a primary site of knowledge. She is audibly taking time from audiences to give to or place on herself, carving out moments of pleasure, joy, and relief, albeit temporarily at the cost of the audience's attention; she does this by mechanizing Black grammar's prosody. These audible iterations of Black grammar emphasize the body and demands we give her our time as we listen to her message. Thus, we begin (or continue—for some of us) recognizing Black bodies (like hers) as cultural knowledge-making sites worthy of attention, appreciation, and validation, not as objects to be gazed upon but as agents.

Having taken a closer look at Megan Thee Stallions' paralexical phenomena, we can also see and hear this rhetorical, linguistic tactic reverberate in another important Black female music artist. Beyoncé's "Daddy Lessons" operationalizes similar paralexical phenomena with her inclusions of "whoops" and "hollers." Although Megan Thee Stallion's deployment is truncated in comparison to Beyoncé's prolonged notes, it does not diminish this kind of sound-making as being any less of an opportunity for sonically marking and communicating meaning for Black women.

In both instances, the paralexical can describe "the interrelatedness of language (in terms of sound and context) and the performance of meaning (in terms of interaction between non/verbal expression) as a method for Black women's delivery and navigation of multiple discourse communities—both public and private" (McGee, "Language of Lemonade" 58). Generationally exchanging information in this manner is an important part of Black women's narrative strategy. As I've written elsewhere, "[t]hese stories and realizations of various ways of knowing developed in connection with the use and delivery of language—the speaking of their (generational Black women's) stories—and the recognition of the hidden performances and meanings of language within nonverbal communication" (McGee, "Language of Lemonade" 59). Pain and joy cannot always be captured by words alone, but the body can remember and communicate both simultaneously.

The influence of paralexical language has been so engrained in Megan Thee Stallion's sonic identity that it is hard to imagine her artistry without such sonic rhetoric. In fact, Megan Thee Stallion has built her career on her paralexical deployment. She so frequently employs this function, described above, that it became a quintessential feature for the singer's sonorous style. I might even go so far as to say that the paralexical sound "ah" accompanied by sticking out the tongue has become a hallmark of a particular contemporary Black women rapper's school of Black grammatical thought: Megan Thee Stallion, Beyoncé, Cardi B, and Nicki Minaj all use this sonic, rhetorical feature, extending their time in public, audible spheres, creating aural and oral space, as well as asserting their grammatical agency (i.e., Subjectivity) with/through the body (see image below). Blake Newby, a writer for *Revelist*, reported that Megan Thee Stallion's paralexical usage (arguably spelled out as "ah," "ahh," "agh," or even "blah") was so iconic that Twitter gave her an official emoji (2019) complementing her trending hashtag #megantheestallion.

Like Franklin's powerful projection and creative arrangements, Megan Thee Stallion's paralexical "trademark" ad lib or, more formally, *ad libitum*, which derives from the Latin phrase "at one's pleasure" or "as you desire," is indeed a hallmark of her sonic identity. Her (em)bodied sound is a prosodic rhetoric informed by a Black grammar; it is a particular audible marker she can use at her discretion until she is pleased with or satisfied by the result. To deploy this paralexical phenomena means she is aware of her timeliness and is aware of how to use sound as a method for creating and holding listeners' attention for as long as or for

Queer(ing) Sound, Time, and Grammar | 129

Figure 3.1. Screenshot from Stallion's "Big Ole Freak" to illustrate sticking out her tongue and taking extra time. *Source*: Stallion, Megan Thee. "Megan Thee StallionBig Ole Freak—[Official Video]." YouTube, uploaded by Megan Thee Stallion, 28 Feb 2019. https://www.youtube.com/watch?v=oBYf6gpVvRA&t=133s

whatever purpose she needs or wants to fulfill. Hence, sounds are audible additions of the body that physically and conceptually extend time and prolong the cultivation of agency for the user. Paralexical phenomena, like this example, ultimately peak the audiences' attention, and, in turn, the audience gives more time and focus to the artist, allowing them to (re)claim agency from and within the public (sonic) sphere. However, as I've argued throughout this chapter, creating and sustaining audiences' attention can take on many forms; the paralexical is one way Black women music artists have evolved their sonic rhetoric and continued asserting agency through Black grammar. As an alternative to deploying paralexical tactics, some Black women (music artists) have showed off their vocal abilities by emphasizing their ability to exhale and sustain sound.

"We All Gonna Get It in Due Time"

Prior generations of Black women music artists have linked their bodies (albeit in subtler ways) to time by explicitly lengthening sounds as they strategically held notes in place. Billie Holiday's elongated, descending cadence when she sang "drop" in "Strange Fruit," for instance, made audiences feel like they were metaphorically falling with her. The time it took to "drop" created a physical uneasiness for listeners as they reflected on the sociocultural implications of the song. Thus, stretching sound is another example of how Black women music artists have prolonged their stay in the spotlight. Instead of using sound-words to create time in audible spaces, some Black women music artists have accentuated or extended time by mechanizing duration as a rhetorical sonic effect. A singer can curate direction, tone or mood, and emotion of the song by using duration to their advantage. This is similar to word choice and spelling, which indicate points of emphasis and develop plots for writers as well as varying sentence lengths to keep a story's flow moving. Mixing forms and styles within these compositions replicates extensions of the author's/performer's voice. In opting for this technique, Black women music artists channel time by explicitly marking it through the elongation of specific moments, sounds, or concepts, getting listeners to pay closer attention. Duration, then, is most effective when artists can juxtapose the lengthening of the voice (and respective breaths) with staccato pronunciations of words or phrases. As a result, artists who employ elongation as a sonic rhetoric can harness listeners' anticipation or focus; prolonging the note's sound as it reaches and lingers within the audience's bodies (e.g., ears, mind, feeling) can signal to audiences that these Black women music artists' control their own voice, illuminating their sonic, rhetorical agency, their message, and (hopefully) their labor. With any luck, this acute sonic sensitivity brings to light the generational toiling of Black women (and Black persons), which is an end goal for many Black women music artists: initiating change and healing.

Additionally—as we have seen, read, and heard from the artists in this work—using and constructing voice through prosody is a means for communicating a Black grammar in form and style. The prosodic and aspectual[13] sonic rhetoric built into Black grammar captures the audience's attention, sparking a new, or uncovering a hidden, connection of empathy or understanding; it fortifies a process of knowledge-making oscillating between composer, message, and receiver as well as adds to the argument of being seen as human. Similar to the effect of Megan Thee Stallion's paralexical "ad lib," employing duration as a sonic rhetoric results in holding the audience's attention and creates a moment in which to recognize personhood in public (audible) spheres by elongating their time. Communicating through these queered concepts can effectively reel in readers and listeners alike while also teaching other generations techniques for generating survival, healing, freedom(s), and agency.

A working definition of duration could be *the amount of time taken* for an event to start, proceed, and then be completed. It is a holistic, all-encompassing interpretation of a series of events within a particular moment. Put more simply, duration is a *specified length of time*. In a musical context, duration is marked by both time signature and by the annotation of notes and rests on a staff. Like grammar, this written musical system of keeping time gives listeners a structure for understanding a musical work's progression, speed or tempo, pitch, and (for singers) intonation, for example. Although writing time in music is a relatively common application in "traditional" composing, it is still a kind of composing with voice. Attitude and personality seep into compositions through these stylistic attributes. Black women musicians have found ways for demarcating these very structures as part of our temporal identity and generational legacy of survival, resistance, and liberation.

Hence, exploring duration as part of our grammar that engages with Black temporality entices us to see/read/hear beyond the words of a text or performance; it provides us with a clearer picture of how Black women use sound in innovative and rhetorical ways for generational praxes including survival and liberation—just as a prior generation of blueswomen did. As Hazel Carby noted, "of course singers were entertainers, but the blues was not an entertainment of escape or fantasy and sometimes directly represented historical events" (475). To this point, the birth of "Mississippi Goddam," for example, came as a response to the 16th Street Baptist Church bombing in Birmingham, Alabama, where four Ku Klux Klan members carried out a violent antiBlack attack for the sake of white supremacy, resulting in the murder of four Black girls. This song was Simone's reflection of her reality and her (lack of) Subject position as a Black woman in America. It has been recorded that upon hearing about the bombing, an irate Simone attempted to make a gun out of household materials for retaliation. However, her husband at the time, Andrew Stroud, intervened and suggested she put her anger into music. In minutes the song was born (Fields 2021, par. 2; Pierpont 2014; Harrington 2003, par. 5). Having been urged by her husband to translate her anger and pain into music and also having been persuaded by her comrade Lorraine Hansberry to take a more active stance in the civil rights movement, Simone unapologetically performed this tune as well as "Four Women," "Young, Gifted, and Black," "Old Jim Crow," and "I Wish I Knew How It Would Feel to Be Free," collating a Black activism soundtrack. For many of us who have come across and/or continue listening to "Mississippi Goddam," this song remains poignant and even cathartic, acting as a release valve for our overdue and overwhelming anger and frustration.

By now you may be asking, "What does Simone's timeliness have to do with duration?" Duration is an overlooked aspect of Black grammar, even though its prosodic measurements are easily quantifiable, and even though our temporality is not inherently linear. Black women (music artists) have queered this concept by layering time on itself. What I mean by this is that Black women (music artists) have complicated the linear approach of measuring time by invoking duration (i.e., the linear representative) as they comment on moments in time (i.e., references of the past, feelings in the present, and hopes for the future). Simone's music, for example, simultaneously operationalized sound's ekphrastic affect and invoked past generational Black (feminist) sonic rhetorics. At once, "Mississippi Goddam" employed themes of liberation and coalition found in "Negro" spirituals and work songs (e.g., "hound dogs on my trail," "lord have mercy on this land of mine," "me and my people") as well as a gendered resistance of body described by and through early blueswomen of the 1920s and even blueswomen of the late nineteenth century (e.g., "stop callin' me Sister Sadie"). As Carby wrote in "It Jus Be's That Way Sometimes: The Sexual Politics of Women's Blues," "[t]he blues singer, [Shirley Anne Williams] says, uses song to create reflection and creates an atmosphere for analysis to take place. The blues were certainly a communal expression of black experience which had developed out of the call and response patterns of work songs from the nineteenth century and have been described as a 'complex interweaving of the general and the specific' and of individual and group experience" (qtd. in Carby 475). In this way we can recognize sound as a particularly important pathway for manifesting generational Black (feminist) sonic rhetorics that incorporate a Black grammar of temporality. This generational creation of voice and sound communicates agency across time and space, purposely centering polylithic Blackness—be that through cultural productions of songs, oral life writings of histories, testimonies', narratives, or progressive political actions that signal a "reclaiming [of] my time," as Maxine Waters[14] has asserted. Sound can be a method for observing, hearing/listening, feeling, and transmitting generational blueprints for how to be seen, how to survive, and how to provoke calls for freedom(s) or liberation into action. Invoking duration in this way, that is, the sonic collapsing of past, present and future, is a prelude to the stretching of notes that Simone (and even Holiday and Etta James) mechanizes for a more precise manipulation, theorization, and subversion of time in Black folks' favor.

Her sonic (and often televised) performances of "Mississippi Goddam" provided generations with a resistance literacy—one grounded by music, voice, and sound—which acted as a rhetorical vehicle for change. The song's lyrics signified a reclaiming of time for Black history, Black humanity, and Black temporalities. The lyrics written by Simone reflected her and other political activists' "fiery denunciations of the well-mannered politics of 'going slow'" (Feldstein 1350). Simone's outlook toward injustice, like Waters's procedural assertion to reclaim time, reject a sense of respectability politics that are often framed by cultural presuppositions of Black womanhood. Just as other Black women music artists (and political figures like Waters) have done, Simone uses sound to address and mimic progress. More specifically, she uses duration to manipulate and mitigate the collective "slow" march to freedom. Ultimately, Simone employed time sonically to give notice that "we" are entering the room, that Black women are (as we have been) determined to move forward, to heal with our pasts, and prophesize a better future. Social justice has, after all, been long overdue.

Moreover, Simone alludes to this "due time" not just by explicitly vocalizing this in her lyrics, but also by tacitly exemplifying duration elongating the breath or the sustained exhale of the voice to make sound. In "Mississippi Goddam," she calls out time's inadequate measurements and foregrounds its historical imbalances imposed on raced and gendered bodies. Simone's "Mississippi Goddam" explains that the amount of time given to/for Black folks (i.e., duration) has been inefficient. The amount of time taken to move from one progressive benchmark to the next is not happening quickly enough; the time Black folks give in exchange for what little freedom(s) are offered over generations is not warranted as equitable.

These "gains" are not ample enough to sustain continuing practices of patience and giving of time—common methodologies of respectability politics and passive, nonviolent movements seen within some Black activist practices in the twentieth century. Something must give. As such, this tension of time is emphatically repeated by Simone's differing pronunciations of "Goddam" throughout the song.

While there are other moments in this song where Simone emphasizes duration by drawing out different phrases via repetition and breath (e.g., "I don't know / I don't know"), the most prominent and spectacular display of duration in this tune is the last audible word to close the song before her narrative commentary: "Goddam." Like Minaj's double employment of *be* in the title and chorus, Simone layers this word's meaning by giving it a prominent role in which to be repeated, that is, in the title, in the chorus, and in its exponential buildup to the penultimate lengthening of the note. As the song progresses, the amount of time given to the word "goddam" increases. Although this measurement varies from recording to recording, many of the words in the song are generally held for a half- or full second; meaning, the majority of the lyrics are primarily designated as either an eighth or a quarter note; they are the staccato moments of the musical sentences. The frequency and speed at which these words are sung translates to the fast-paced tempo of this song noted earlier in this chapter, which is also a rhetorical factor in persuading audiences to give their attention to the artist.

Throughout the song, Simone holds "Goddam" for approximately two seconds (or two beats)—twice as long as many of the other lyrics. In doing this, she marks this word as a half note. This sonorous lengthening implies that this word is significant. These brief vocalizations of "Goddam" in the body of the song sonically signify the frustrations of being on the receiving end of generational oppression, violence, and ignorance from hegemonic social structures, audiences, and communities. However, this is not the case for the ending note/word: "Goddam." This last iteration of this word, regardless of the version, is held twice as long as the previous vocalizations—changing the half note to a full note. She sustains her breath for four seconds, or beats (as it is in the official live recording posted on YouTube); this ending note has been doubled once again. Stretching the time needed to carve out audible space in this song amplifies the rhetorical effect of Black grammar within this tune; elongating this term signals a final exasperated attempt at calling for change from her listeners, a call that is both urgent and overdue.

Even in this brief aural encounter, Simone's sonic application of duration notably marks a method for amplifying Black folk's temporality, urgency, and emotions—emotions that have been (and continue to be) carried from generation to generation as we attempt to shirk off Hegel's lasting antiBlack philosophy regarding Black personhood and temporality. Furthermore, exponentially expanding the time taken to sing "Goddam" in the end audibly emphasizes Simone's message of being tired and fed up with the changing same. Just as Tamika Carey (2020) and Brittney Cooper (2020) remind us of Fannie Lou Hamer's call, "freedom now," so too does "Mississippi Goddam." Even though this song's lyrics changed over the years, depending on where Simone was performing it and what city made the news for its egregious antiBlack acts, she still managed to mechanize sound as a rhetorical tool. Using duration in this way continually and audibly recounts the lasting effects of racist actions in the United States (particularly the South). Thus, the duration of the final vocal call is, indeed, a reflection of anger, conviction, and/or resolution, feelings all culminating in a final, desperate climax directed at an attempt to gain progress, survival, and liberation for Black folks.

Thus, the urgent need for change, which is at the heart of Simone's sonic argument, is given a new life as she reiterates the continuous and daily mistreatment devaluing Black life. With lines like "too slow" and "yes you lied to me all these years," for example, Simone emphasizes how patience is wearing thin. She describes how normative, white supremacist logics invoke patience as a stall-tactic for attempted appeasement for Black folk and for maintaining the dominant power structure. Unlike the previous examples in this chapter, "Mississippi Goddam" unapologetically addresses how patience, or as Robison describes it, as listening's "calming" effect (37–73), is not the solution for countering continued practices of (un)naming often associated with negative or demeaning stereotypes ("washin' the windows"; "pickin' the cotton"; "too damn lazy"; "Sister Sadie"). As Feldstein suggests, "[i]n 'Mississippi Goddam,' when Simone rejected the impulse to 'talk like a lady,' she effectively claimed that doing so would not halt such discriminatory practices as calling black women 'Sister Sadie'" (1365). To this end, an engagement with patience may not always provide pathways to personhood; it won't get us there in a timely manner either. The conviction to employ patience, then, was/is losing steam since it has only moved the needle of social justice so far over one hundred plus years ("They keep on saying 'Go slow!'/But that's just the trouble"). Using patience (often synonymous with "quietness" and/or passivity) as a main resistive method for survival and liberation may even, sometimes, support a white savior mentality—a mindset that Ida B. Wells poignantly noted as a pervasive part of the Southern lynching legacy, a cloaked rationale for violence hidden behind chivalry and decorum that can propagate forms of racism from altruistic misconceptions.

As such, the duration of this progress, signified by Simone's prosody, prioritizes Black folks' subject position through a collective reckoning with our past, present, and future tenses/selves. Simone ultimately espouses a liberatory rhetoric of/for urgency by sonically employing duration–countering patience with tempo and sound. Moreover, "Mississippi Goddam" explicitly and critically asks listeners to not waste any more time because we simply don't have time to waste (or we have wasted enough time). This song, then, calls on its audiences to shift their civil rights methodology and favor acts of urgency—rather than maintain a slow and steady walk toward progress—by any means necessary. Thus, Simone queers time to interpret our temporality for large, public audiences, making her music an entry point for understanding the importance of Black grammar—one that calls for the recognition of Black Subject positions throughout time. In other words, Simone rejects the notion that Black folk are merely space-takers.

"Mississippi Goddam" marks time not by syntactical morphemes[15] like Minaj's *be* but by verbally (re)counting or describing what time has been and continues to be for us Black folk. This sonic rhetoric of duration, then, reinscribes this sense of urgency as one that has been developing over time for her audience. "Mississippi Goddam" is an audible, vocal response to generational tension and violence circling a presumptive and intentional void that is an absence of Black subjectivity, just like Hortense Spillers's cultivation of (Black) grammar as a response to and rejection of the *Moynihan Report*'s logics and argument. The urgency, the anger, the unheeded generational call for personhood, liberation, survival, and other emotions culminate in this song's foreshadowing of what will happen when our patience runs out ("I can't stand the pressure much longer"; "You're all gonna die and die like flies"). "Mississippi Goddam" documents the present feelings of uncertainty ("I think every day's gonna be my last"), of being stuck, of feeling static ("Where am I going? / What am I doing?"), and the quickness of losing hope while still grasping for a future ("Just try to do your very best"). How long are we gonna have to wait for freedom and for the recognition of our temporal agency as

Subject? Alternatively, how does this kind of temporal immobility factor into a cultivation of agency or Subject position?

Why So Tense?: Reading Time through a Queer, Sonic, Black Grammar

Black women music artists' Black grammar is frequently grounded by rhetorics of survival, pedagogy, and liberation; it is intent on asserting our agency. Generations of Black women music artists navigate and survive these harsh realities by reverberating Black grammar: testifying, witnessing, and invoking call and response to gather critical masses as we push for change. Prosody is one of many ways we survive, teach, and liberate ourselves by whatever means necessary. All in all, time continues functioning as a significant aspect of cultivating personhood. By altering specific amounts of time (initially designated for or given to the artists to perform), these Black women music artists have sculpted time to assert themselves as agents, showcase their personhood, and—however briefly—demonstrate their ability to own time. So we are not out of time; we are time masters. These methods of controlling time through various manipulations of sound highlight the importance of a Black grammar in communicating our temporal legacies. Black grammar can assert power and agency in social contexts even as publics often view our Black bodies as commodifiable objects. Thus, controlling time is, in effect, a particularly useful power move to counter superficial notions of Black bodies being "out of time."

In fact, this push-pull of who controls time and by what means has been qualified by Tamika Carey as "temporal hegemony." Carey defines temporal hegemony as "where ideological and material structures converge into a culture of hostility that pushes equity for a group further out of reach. These [are] legal practices of delay and social forms of displacement" (Carey, "Necessary Adjustments" 270). In my argument here, the prosodic aspects of Black grammar (like tense, tempo, repetition, paralexical phenomena, and duration) are speaking back to these inherited solipsistic practices that center white control of time and dictate when and how liberation can occur.

I hope this point came across clearly even though you may have found my musical organization/argumentation a bit disorienting or scattered. That was mostly by design; part of what I argue here is a messy yet systematic view of time. My aim in organizing this chapter was not to present you with another linear logic that fits nicely into discursive expectations, but rather to center Black rhetoric and epistemologies. You have been engaging with time from an Afrocentric purview.

What I present here is an application of "Sankofa." Sankofa is a West Africa concept, proverb, and pedagogy that, expressed in the Akan language, is communicated as "se wo were fi na wosan kofa a yenki." An approximate English translation of the meaning is "it is not taboo to go back and fetch what you forgot." In other words, it is not unheard-of or irrational for many Black folks to formulate understandings of reality and self through practices of "looking back to move forward." Thus, this chapter presents my argument in the form of sankofarration[16] (Brooks et al. 240). This chapter (even in the subheaders) presents Black women music artists as looking back and talking to each other on various sonic frequencies and across time periods to make meaning and theorize our temporality. While the artists presented here are a small and homogenous sample, they do provide a glimpse into how robust and dynamic this genealogy of Black grammar and Black (feminist) sonic rhetorics are and how useful their audible theorizations of personhood, survival, and even healing can be for younger generations.

My construction/narrativization of the self through this particular lens is intentionally grounded by an understanding that time can be cyclical, not just linear. I use these artists to reach back and reconnect our social contexts that inform our being in the world and to push against antiBlack arguments and actions like the long-standing and problematic notion that Black folks are "out of time." I use this framework as a pedagogical form to show others how to go back and reflect on informative teachings even if these lessons are outside "traditional" four-walled classrooms because even those structures (like grammar) can be oppressive. Juxtaposing tense, tempo, duration, repetition, and paralexical phenomena—all audible associations of time—showcases Black women music artists' (and many others not named here) ability to collapse imaginary boundaries between past (i.e., enslavement), present (i.e., civil rights), and future (i.e. post-racial America) as a method for calling listeners in/to action.

4

Audible Advice, or Mentorship in Sound

A Black (Feminist) Practice of Care through Sonic Rhetorics

The term "mother tongue" can be understood on several levels. Most obviously, mothers transmit their language into their children who develop facility with it. In this sense we all inherit the condition/ing of our mothers if she has a word in our socialization. But more basically, our language, our mother tongue, is at least partly how we know what we know.

—Richardson, *African American Literacies* 75

Scene 1

My mother used to preach to me that my body was a precious gift. When I was just twelve years old, she sat me down for "the talk." I was just developing a woman's body. My breasts were getting large, and boys were starting to notice me. My mother sat across from me on my twin bed in our room of our Littleton Avenue apartment, and we discussed her version of the birds and bees . . . . "Guys will try to have sex with you, Dana," she told me. "Your body is precious—the most precious thing you can give to someone. Make sure they deserve it. Don't give it to just anyone." That was rule number one. "That first time should be special, and it should be with someone you love. You should be married, but knowing how people are today, let me be realistic with you. If you have sex, make sure you're protected. Use, use, use protection! You have dreams, and you don't want to mess your life up" .... My mother was on point on all fronts with that advice. I wished I had listened a little more closely to the things she said then. But, as always, I had a mind of my own. (129)

Reflecting on her own maturity, Queen Latifah gives her wise mother credit for passing on such important information—even though she might not have understood the value of such advice as a preteen.

Scene 2

Latifah describes another older Black woman who lived in the neighborhood who publicly voiced her concerns for how the preteen's body would be perceived in public. "'Dana, are you wearing a bra?' Miss Tamara asked me. I said 'No,' but I was thinking something like 'Hell, no.' A bra? I didn't even own a bra." Miss Tamara's response was "'Well, you need one,' ... Miss Tamara ... must have noticed me bouncing around. That's when she pulled me aside to tell me I needed a training bra. ... Miss Tamara was this fly lady who had a lot of style, much like my mother. And she was big on the neighborhood girls carrying themselves like ladies" (137–38).

Scene 3

Working in conjunction with her mother's "talk," Latifah described how poetry helped her see the beauty in herself. She writes, "I am not the prototypical 36-24-36. Never have been, never will be. And although society tells me I'm too big, what I try to keep in my head are words from Maya Angelou. As she says in her poem 'Phenomenal Woman,' 'It's the arch of my back, / The sun of my smile, / The ride of my breasts, / The grace of my style. / I'm a woman ...'" (qtd. in Owens 140). Latifah's advice network did not only consist of mothers and mother-figures; she also drew mentorship from musical influences and poets like Maya Angelou.

In addition to the epigraphs above, I begin this chapter with a few scenes from Dana Owens's autobiography, *Ladies First: Revelations of a Strong Woman*. Both the epigraphs and opening scenes document the very real, vibrational intersections of materialized, embodied sound[1] and generational advice. Within these excerpts, Owens, better known by her rapping personae, Queen Latifah, describes the impact "motherly" advice has had on her development as a Black woman (music artist). Pointing toward her mother's, her neighborhood-mothers', and other artists' words, Latifah directs readers' attentions to the advice she was given, advice she subsequently used, to develop her sense of self(worth) over the years. Their care and concern informed how Latifah matured as she developed her career across media and genre—from rapper to jazz vocalist, to writer and actress. These shared moments of advice across vocal registers[2] acted not only as guiding principles for her own life journey, but also for the ways she mentors thousands of readers who engage with her life story.

These auto/biographical scenes tell us that material sounds are rhetorical and can lead younger generations to a "better" life by encouraging us to use, think of, or act out more efficient negotiating methods for our everyday situations and lived experiences. It is these sonic applications of advice, or mentorship in sound, that speak to and soothe our souls when we are up against improbable odds; they demonstrate the urgency and necessity of knowing ourselves and finding community. This informative exchange represents something we can hold onto as we hope and work for a "better" future.

In sharing these lessons and experiences across generations, we are warned of possible incoming stressors. These "warnings," or pieces of wisdom meant to ensure safety and survival, offered to an audience are what I am thinking through as the *audibility* of advice. Audibility, here, refers to the degrees in which things are heard or understood; it signifies the *acts of sharing*, conveying, or communicating various understandings of realities when one's vocal register(s) are used for transmission. The audibility of advice perceived in this chapter broadens what Amanda Nell Edgar discusses in "Speaking Identities" (2019) and focuses more on the intra- and interpersonal relationships with meaning-making and agency than the sonorous aspects of voice that can be quantifiably measured. This partnership between mode, content, and persons, then, often results in some kind of mentorship—being seen as a mentor when one listens to the exchanged gossip, for example, or even when one listens to the experiences of others and responds with acknowledging, validating, or vindicating one's own "gut feelings."

Said in another way, transmitting collective information, as discussed here, can be interpreted through a more recognizable framework of "literacy" that researchers like Jacqueline Jones Royster and Deborah Brandt identify. In *Freedom Writing: African American Civil Rights Literacy Activism, 1965–1967*, Lathan draws on Royster[3] and Brandt to contextualize the intersectional and social applications characterizing literacy. For Royster, literacy is "'the ability to gain access to information and to use this information variously to articulate lives and experiences and also to identify, think through, refine and solve problems, sometimes complex problems, over time'" (Royster, *Traces* 45; qtd. in Lathan xxii). This view of literacy not only (1) identifies Black women's ways of knowing—across genres of "texts"—as being centered in our lived and embodied experiences, and (2) explicitly acknowledges the temporality of Black women's intellectual traditions as an ongoing generational endeavor, but also (3) centers Black women's ways of knowing as a quintessential praxis for its practitioners—especially in the face of naysayers and their methods, which often erase Black women/Black bodies/Black thought from ongoing conversations. After all, as Barbara Christian wrote, "those who have effected the takeover have the power (although they deny it) . . . to determine the ideas which are deemed valuable. . . . For people of color have always theorized—but in forms quite different from the Western form of abstract logic. . . . How else have we managed to survive with such spiritedness the assault on our bodies, social institutions, countries, our very humanity?" (41). And, in terms of Black feminist (rhetorical) theory, Lathan describes Patricia Hill Collins's proclamation that "'The dilemma'" of current intellectual frameworks which maintains the power that Christian wrote about "'is that Black women intellectuals,'" out of necessity, "'must place our own experiences and consciousness at the center of any serious efforts to develop Black feminist thought'" (qtd. in Lathan xxv).

This chapter responds to these calls by embracing Lathan's appeal "for varied methodologies originating in an African-derived cultural epistemology, where self is understood as a process of continual interaction" (xxvi). More specifically, deriving from a culmination of Afrodiasporic theorizing, Lathan puts forth a "gospel literacy"[4]—which includes components of "acknowledging the burden," "bearing witness," "call-and-response," and "finding redemption" (xviii)—to investigate the ongoing contributions of African epistemologies within Black sacred and secular modes of communication. Blending Royster's and Brandt's contributions to literacy with Lathan's intentional blurring of sound and song in Black rhetorical activism, in this way, illuminates the innovative methods Black women (music artists) use to share their lessons learned. Thus, drawing on these social constructions of literacy, with special attention to Black women's embodiment of sound, helps us better understand the intersecting politics of knowledge-making that Black women (music artists) have long been employing to theorize and change our day-to-day realities for the better—written, verbal, or otherwise. Therefore, my methodological reorientation attempts to clearly tie together Black women (music artists') liberatory, embodied, sonic rhetorics with Afrodiasporic epistemological sites of resistance and survival. These inter-and intra-communal relationships are especially evident when viewed from Black sociohistorical and cultural understandings that recognize knowledge-making processes as being found in and between any type of "text" including the body/bodies.

Moreover, Lathan reiterates this long-standing multimodal and multivocal literacy practice and theoretical methodology as part of a foundational exigency for Black feminist theory. The audibility of advice, then, works as documentation, validating our existence beyond tokenism or the derogatory assumptions and demeaning stereotypes about Black life and language (and by extension voice and body) by centering our ways of knowing and being in the world—historically, socially, and politically. The audibility of advice, or mentorship in sound, further displays components of the gospel literacy as this intergenerational, diasporic praxis developed and evolved between mentors and mentees. For this chapter's purpose, I find it useful to think through Lathan's unpacking of "acknowledging the burden," and "call-and-response," in particular, to identify and link the teleological benefits of audible advice that Black women (music artists) employ across time, space, and vocal register(s) with long-established practices of intellectualism, leadership, and mentorship. As such, looking into Lathan's construction of a "gospel literacy" aids in understanding the extent of, and reciprocal nature between, the sacred traditions of African epistemologies and the secular rhetorics found in Black women's discourses of sound and music. The audibility of advice resonates with us on deep levels and provides us with tangible means for cultivating (social) health and well-being by mechanizing subversive, written, aural, and oral "hush harbors."[5] Ultimately, these sonic relationships transform us into leaders, mentors, and intellectuals who guide our visions forward.

Interrogating methods of how this intersectional practice of audible advice, or mentorship in sound, "honor[s] the traditions and thus the people who are still too often not present in our classrooms, on our faculties, in our scholarship," as Adam Banks has written, offers us additional critical approaches for expanding conversations beyond the mere acceptance or validation of Black language and rhetoric (*Digital Griots* 14–15). My hope in doing this is to provide another sketch of Black women's rhetorical pathways of being and doing. Because their prowess, activism, and intelligence often go unrecognized in the dominant, hegemonic and gatekept structures of knowledge-making, my contribution to similar interventions (Bradley 2017, 2021; Daphne Brooks 2021; Lordi 2013, 2020) continues the necessary work of amplifying these scholars' care of Black women and sound identifying and networking the prior lineages (that are often operating outside of but well within view of public gazes). Moving beyond such initial and superficial engagements requires Lathan's call and necessitates a response to Brittney Cooper's invitation, suggested in *Beyond Respectability: The Intellectual Thought of Race Women*, to "care more" and (en)trust more Black women's intellectual legacies (2). As such, the experiences translated in, around, and through voice's various manifestations noted in this chapter—acutely recognized in interludes and gossip—are helpful vernacular roadmaps that can aid in identifying and cultivating additional interpretations of generational rhetorical agency, survival, and progress mentioned throughout this book.

This chapter primarily focuses on (1) how advice and/or mentorship is translated through Afrocentric interpretations of oral and audible vocal register(s) and (2) what the implications of such generational transmissions are for Black women and girls. The answers to these questions and the others posed in this book lie at the heart of voice, embodiment, and Black rhetorical praxis more broadly. In addressing these questions, I first excavate Black feminist public intellectual[6] legacies through a "gospel literacy" with the goal of identifying who can communicate embodied advice and mentorship across generations and why. Explicitly reframing Black women (music artists) *as* public intellectuals (à la leaders and mentors) encourages the recognition of Black women's vernacular vocal register(s) as another valid, organic form of knowledge, text, and sonic rhetoric. Next, I describe where we can find audible advice, or mentorship in sound, applying these shared communal values in a contemporary, technological setting. This section focuses on the implications of conversational talk across different media, specifically theorizing how audible information can be operationalized and interpreted as a generational Black feminist sonic rhetoric. Transforming voice in these ways reiterates the leadership necessary for Black feminist theory and reflects Black feminists' emphasis on accessibility to reach the critical masses needed to change something/ someone. These methods of audible advice, or mentorship in sound, are meant to be passed on as instruction, which often helps others navigate the less than perfect conditions of Black (social) life. More specifically, building on Vorris Nunnley's "hush harbors," I reimagine these methods of interludes and gossip as metaphorical and subversive, sonic third spaces where Black folks can plot liberation and further validate our existence. Finally, I propose that these applications of audible advice, or mentorship in sound, can guide our generational practices of care by advocating for representation, social health, and rhetorical healing: practices that ultimately work to resist antiBlack traditions of dehumanization. With that in mind, this chapter aims to present Black women's voice, written and otherwise, as a multidimensional, multigenerational, and Afrocentric composing process of social justice pedagogy capable of traversing media and time.

Caring for Black Feminist Public Intellectual Histories

It is true that some publics have a hard time separating some Black women (music artists') personal life from their on-stage personas (Richardson, *Hiphop Literacies* 2006). But Black women (music artists), like Latifah and others named throughout this work, also take on many other, more positive, roles. Many of us, as audiences, view these larger-than-life public figures not just as performers, but also as intellectuals, leaders, mentors, and even mother-figures as they pass on information gained from their own lived experiences, sometimes in coded or explicit messages. The audibility of advice found in their messages firmly connects Black folks' traditions of literacy as social action to our methods for gaining personal freedoms, including the expression(s) of hope, joy, peace, pride, honor, and safety. The content of these messages (i.e., rhetorical survival and care strategies) are so fundamental to developing a sense of self and community that the meanings behind the messages are continuously transmitted and recognized among various audience members across generations.

Using Alice Walker to support the idea that literacy is a social activist methodology mobilized by Black women in their use of vocal register(s), Royster writes that alternative forms of knowing take shape across various media, including, as Walker points out, "folklore [which may include storytelling, wise sayings, community rituals] [and] is at the heart of self-expression and therefore at the heart of self-acceptance" (qtd. in Royster, *Traces* 29). The mobilization of these literacy narratives infiltrates many aspects and genres of composition (oral, written, or otherwise), and these strategies continue drawing on effective uses of sonic rhetoric to build community and facilitate spaces of self-love. We can see this mobilization of generational literacy narratives play out in Black women (music artists') vocal register(s) as they mimic[7] their predecessors and continue Black composing genres (e.g., the essay, gossiping, or autobiography) extending Black women's voice and agency. As Royster notes in *Traces of a Stream*, "in the case of African American women's essay writing, rhetorical analysis is one mechanism for paying attention to both generic form and the 'performance' of" the relationships between "voice, vision, agency, audience, form, and so on" (*Traces* 23–24). As the spectator engaging with the audibility of advice found within these artists' media, we are offered a hyper-focused account of celebrities' personal growth and hardships. Interpreting their lived experiences is part of Afrocentric traditions meant to help us find ways of bettering ourselves and conditions. We would be foolish if we believed that Black women (music artists') lives were independent of each other and/or if we believed that the lives, and the words they share with us, were purely meant to be digested simply as entertainment. There is, indeed, a much larger, historical legacy of rhetoric and intellectualism being performed behind and between these Black women (music artists') words on the page and stage.

Black (feminist) theory and rhetoric are especially important frames for unpacking these vernacular roadmaps used by (younger) generations in their navigation of various, complex landscapes. An equally important consideration is our recognition of Black women's public intellectual legacies. These legacies model the effects of intercommunal kinship- and knowledge-making by asserting representation and social well-being as overarching themes for action, collaboration, and resistance to "historical erasure" (Pritchard 2016). Lathan reminds us, for instance, that "Angela Davis and Deborah Gray White's Afrafeminist work on enslaved African women confirms that the roles within African communities were clearly defined, with women fulfilling essential functions as keepers of the ancestral heritage" (4). Black feminist theory provides a contemporary thread and outlook on this much older legacy. Thus, the role that Black women (music artists') vocal register(s) play in transmitting essential information generationally continues the already established Afrafeminist view of communal knowledge-making processes and productions while further supporting Black feminist traditions and praxis.

Central to this approach of recognizing the audibility of advice is, then, understanding the role that Black (feminist) rhetorics and Black (feminist) theory play in shaping and transmitting shared knowledge. Both perspectives of Black women's intellectual thought (that is, the Black feminist theoretical underpinnings and Black rhetorical approaches to communication) offer crucial insights for unraveling coded messages lying in plain sight. Said another way, Black women sharing what we've learned from our life experiences (including the messages handed down to us) is just as important as how we share information through our vocal register(s)—tone, indirection, word choice, media, form, and so forth. These sonic rhetorical choices inform how we interpret and recognize essential pedagogical transmissions of information within the established Afrodiasporic epistemological frameworks and cultural practices.

(Re)defining Common Archetypes of (Black Women) Public Intellectuals

It is not a stretch to envision Black women (music artists) as public intellectuals/leaders/mentors because of this griotic[8] role that Black women have historically and culturally inhabited. However, Black women's contributions to this role often get overlooked when defining this archetype. Indeed, Antonio Gramsci is often credited with outlining the pragmatic shift for intellectualism with his Marxist classification of intellectual labors.[9] For Gramsci, intellectual labors can be categorized by their social function—that is, how the production of knowledge is operationalized—either as an expectation of one's (class) status or as a way of moving others toward change and enlightenment via a blurring of social status (Gramsci 3–13). Extending the public intellectual into Afrocentric constructs, Banks ties the digital griot, the DJ, to the Gramscian organic intellectual model, noting that this person is "the intellectual who is nurtured and sustained by local communities rather than professionalized in universities or think tanks or foundations" (3). However, what is often overlooked by Gramsci's Marxist examinations on thought (and to some extent Banks's work on DJs) are the implications of race, sex, and gender in tandem with class. Gramsci's postulations are contextualized within a

European philosophical discourse and seldom account for a more diverse identity politic and worldview. Thus, this section of the chapter builds on Banks's Black rhetorical use of the griot and the Afrocentric ontology found within (organic) public intellectualism. I do this by centering Black women (music artists') contributions to the development of this archetype and emphasizing activism that centers liberation, resistance, and survival for all—quintessential collective themes found throughout the Black diaspora because of the overt and ongoing legacies of colonization, genocide, extraction, and so forth.

The responsibilities and intentions of a public intellectual, especially Black public intellectuals (e.g., engaging with communal dialogue, rationalizing lived experience of one's self and of others as a theory in the flesh,[10] and mobilizing agency of one's self and of others to change a situation), often becomes synonymous with leadership in many Black communities. According to Lathan's postulations, drawn from Bernice Reagon's accounts, a leader is "expected to both motivate and stimulate the group toward active participation. A good leader must manifest strength, energy, and enthusiasm to make a group want to participate" (10). This motivation can be heard in the arrangement of sound, like Simone and Franklin did with tempo, seen in the pronouncement of words. Additionally, Lathan cites Craig Werner's description of a leader's modus operandi by examining the relationship between the gospel and call-and-response:

> Call and response begins with the call of a leader who expresses his/her own voice through the vehicle of a traditional song, story, or image. This call, which provides a communal context for exploration of the "individual" emotion, itself responds to a shared history that suffuses later stages of the process . . . . Whether it affirms or critiques the initial call, however, the response enables the leader to go on exploring the implications of the material. . . . When working most effectively, this process requires individuals not to seek a synthesis, to deny the extreme aspects of their own experiences, but to assert their subjectivity in response to other, equally personal and equally extreme, assertions of experience. (qtd. in Lathan 9)

To motivate the public, the public intellectual or leader *must* understand the sociocultural histories of their communities. Black women (music artists) are exceptionally positioned at the forefront of directing popular culture; they are trailblazers and curators who initiate rememory and translate ancestral knowledge and heritage for the masses in ways that are easily consumed (for better or worse). These intersectional ecologies of identity and action greatly influence knowledge-making processes and contribute to the many rhetorical practices found within the pragmatic public intellectual model, methods, and methodologies that Black women (music artists) operate.

Richardson's opening epigraph suggests our mothers' advice and mentorship often guide us in developing our own ontologies. Denying *all* her voices (Royster 2000; 1996) and vocal register(s) limits our understandings in how we navigate our ongoing social conditions. Taking this into account, we need to look closer at the possible applications of public intellectual archetypes, especially in ways that solidify and reorient us toward Black epistemologies and Black feminist (rhetorical) legacies as equal forms of knowing. In doing so, we not only reiterate the timeliness of Christian's and Collins's remarks posed earlier in this chapter, but also further support our efforts to validate the contributions of Black women's thought and rhetoric in discourses of knowledge-making. Focusing on the sonic rhetorics enabled within these public intellectual forms acknowledges intersectionality beyond class and disrupts and resists static, white constructions of thought and being. Viewing public intellectualism in this way illuminates possibilities of hope while offering avenues of change through dynamic and multivocal intersectional (con)texts.

Centering Black women (music artists') agency, when viewed as public intellectual/leader/mentor, can alter our comprehension of sociohistorical moments; this is especially evident when we retrace historical narratives and various sites of resistance (e.g., the evolution of "feminism") informing our understandings of what and whom public intellectualism can refer to. As an example of this point, Sojourner Truth's "A'n't I A Woman" speech delivered in 1851 at the first women's rights convention in Akron, Ohio, is often recognized as a starting point for Black women's public intellectual histories. Truth's speech forcefully earmarked intersectionality as an essential praxis for Black women who generate and interpret meaning from the inside-out. As bell hooks suggested in *Ain't I A Woman: Black Women and Feminism*, "Sojourner Truth was not the only black woman to advocate social equality for women. Her eagerness to speak publicly in favor of women's rights despite public disapproval and resistance paved the way for other politically-minded black women to express their views" (160). To further explain, hooks asserts that "Black women were placed in a double bind; to support women's suffrage would imply that they were allying themselves with white women activists who had publicly revealed their racism, but to support only black male suffrage was to endorse a patriarchal social order that would grant them no political voice" (3). In describing the importance of Truth's speech, which explicitly calls out the problematic history and approach to suffrage from a US context, by addressing intersectionality, hooks notes that "[n]o one bothered to discuss the way in which sexism operates both independently of and simultaneously with racism to oppress us" (7). Truth's advocacy for all women's liberation highlighted the oppressive paradoxical constraints of being Black, woman, poor, and a non-citizen. It is from this interstitial reality that Black feminism manifests. This site also illuminates what is overlooked when we do not critically engage with the kinds of intellectual labor that philosophers, leaders, *and* everyday folk take on to initiate necessary transformations.

However, the historical account of Truth's oratory is not the oldest example of Black feminism that we know of, and she surely wouldn't be the last. In fact, in a less overt manner, Katherine McKittrick describes how New France (also known as Montreal, Canada) (in)advertently acknowledges Black women's agency in the (un)making of the city's geographical, historical, and economic situatedness. Describing Marie-Joseph Angélique's presence in Montreal and her allegedly setting a fire to cover up her attempted escape from slavery (which resulted in burning down much of the city), McKittrick writes that

> The question of her alleged arson spatializes . . . the terms through which blackness can become a convincing historical and contemporary Canadian geography. Those orderly places and spaces of captivity, gender, and race . . . were radically challenged by Angélique, not only because she was a geographic subject, but also because she was and is so familiarly implicated in (and deemed responsible for) the fire of 1734. . . . She endured a two-month trial, which included her *making "confessions" that documented the story of her life*. (115–16; emphasis added)

Even though Angélique's proclamation of existence and historical situatedness during the public trial (and before her execution) may not offer the same rhetorical situation that recognizes Truth as a public intellectual and protofeminist, Angélique's intention to document her narrative and the unfair social conditions placed on her body provides evidence of Black women's ability to publicly theorize our existence—just as Truth did in her speech.

While the example of Truth's speech shifts focus onto Black women's strategies for countering the roadblocks laid before them (i.e., protecting themselves against dangerous coalition-making), the example of Angélique highlights how the roadblocks were/are simultaneously and generationally constructed (i.e., nonBlack "citizens" in Montreal needing to erase Blackness so as to not have to name it, and their need to reinscribe why Blackness is "less than" so as to continue justifying horrendous antiBlack behavior). Both cases in point provide important glimpses into the kinds of ongoing, performative, and embodied rhetorical maneuvering Black women (music artists) as public intellectuals and leaders have continually negotiated.

Their theorizing of one's self aligns with "the African concept of *Ubuntu*, which means 'I am because we are.' This philosophy rests on the belief that individual existence (and knowledge) is contingent on relationships with others. Sacred and secular ways of knowing cannot—within an African worldview—exist separately" (Lathan 5). Both Angélique's and Truth's use of lived experiences are not independent of one another; they are intimately tied together as markers for (younger) generations to continue thinking through and pressuring for change that allows our whole selves to be recognized as equals. Taken together as part of our critical reflection, they illuminate how rhetorical strategies can change over time, even though the call and response may stay the same. Both Truth's and Angélique's narratives highlight one of many ways Black women have altered public perceptions of who is or can be "free"—which lies at the heart of Black feminist theory and remains a driving force for cultivating public intellectual models, methods, and methodologies—that is, by communicating our theorizing of our sociocultural and historical situatedness through the body and experiences.

Therefore, tethering the rhetorical effects of these personal narratives to the responsibilities of public intellectualism amplifies what Black feminism is largely and historically concerned with: that is, universal freedom, or, as, one of my mentors, Joycelyn Moody has said, "liberation for all." In *Black Feminist Thought: Knowledge, Consciousness, and the Politics of Empowerment*, Collins describes Black feminist thought as

> Consist[ing] of theories or specialized thought produced by African-American women intellectuals designed to express a

> Black woman's standpoint. The dimensions of this standpoint include the presence of characteristic core themes, the diversity of Black women's experiences in encountering these core themes, the varying expressions of Black women's Afrocentric feminist consciousness regarding the core themes and their experiences with them, and the interdependence of Black women's experiences, consciousness, and actions. This specialized thought should aim to infuse Black women's experiences and everyday thought with new meaning by rearticulating the interdependence of Black women's experiences and consciousness. (32)

I think it important to quote Collins at length here because this definition encapsulates the boundless approaches of/to Black feminism permitting us to envision who a public intellectual can be beyond Gramsci's initial description. This broad definition also reflects commitments to (mass) freedoms that motivate Black women's public intellectual topics and methods—exemplified by Truth and Angélique. Reframing the public intellectual archetypes through raced *and* gendered lenses allows us to further investigate processes of rhetorical reclamation[11] while explicitly tying Black women (music artists') sonic, rhetorical legacies to important factors grounded in various African epistemologies. In doing this, we help (re)define our sense of self in and beyond our communities.

In this same vein, the common archetypes for Black women as public intellectuals/leaders/mentors can also be identified across various disciplines. Some oral traditions may recognize Black women activists as public intellectuals, but some literary traditions may recognize them as (Black) literary foremothers—a parallel, rhetorical figure rooted in written word discourses. These synonymous figures divulge information to the community with the understanding that transmitting "ancestral knowledge" or shared lived experiences not only builds communities but also provides blueprints for developing the kinds of literacy needed to survive, resist, and heal. Jacquline K. Bryant (2004) and Alice Walker (1983) discuss the literary foremother as a figure that is prominent in Black women's writings. This figure is often an older Black woman who freely dishes out words of wisdom "despite the constraints of physical and mental abuse, space, and time." This figure "pass[es] on creative genius in the forms of storytelling, language style, and creative arts [e.g., quilting, dairy writing, testimonies, speeches, etc.]. This gifted, older Black woman, this foremother, is unaware that her voice is laden with cultural wisdom, spiritual insight, and generative power. As the unassuming visionary that possesses a hope so intense that it directs circumstances" (Bryant 74). I believe these Black women are indeed aware of, and strategically use, the power within their voice and vocal register(s); they recognize their agency as part of a sonic rhetoric and as part of compositional traditions whose purpose has, for so long, been the "keeper of ancestral knowledge." Both (Black) literary foremothers and Black women public intellectuals embody the leadership qualities outlined above. Regardless of genre, we can identify aspects of Black women's voice, whether it be in written or oral form, as being grounded within and derived from prior, lived knowledge and intersectional experiences passed on from older generations.

From a more contemporary view, Cooper redefines this cerebral-activist legacy for Black women's rhetorical lineages. In doing so, Cooper expands and complicates prior traditional notions of Gramscian public intellectual models. Drawing from Lucindy Willis to broadly define Black women's intellectual traditions, Cooper writes that "the term *public intellectual* is fairly contemporary [. . . and] 'connotes a distinct shift in perspective, making the concept less theoretical and more pragmatic.'" She continues, it is "[r]elated to, but distinct from, thinker/philosophers like Socrates or Virgil, [intellectual], in the nineteenth century, referred to individuals who 'generated, applied and dispensed culture. Like great thinkers, [public intellectuals] were philosophers of sorts, but they seemed to possess a more developed sense of audience. . . . they viewed life in its broadest contexts—socially, politically, and economically'"; however, they "'often took active roles in challenging contemporary social conditions'" (qtd. in Cooper 15–16). Along these same classificatory lines, Cooper also drew on Ponchitta Pierce's essay, originally published in *Ebony,* which (re)defined common archetypes of Black women public intellectuals into three shifting classification types: the purist, the public, and/or the pragmatic intellectual. Like our review of Gramsci's definition above, we are most concerned with Pierce's outlining of the public intellectual that describes the Black woman thinker as "a second type of intellectual, 'whom circumstances have thrust into the limelight.'" She goes on, adding certain characteristics to this identity such as "'morality, creative vision, objectivity-integrity and a disciplined mind.'" Also, according to Pierce, "'[a]s secondary characteristics, she should have 'wit, urbanity, *sound* education, grasp of the humanities, appreciation of the arts, travel background. She is also expected to be action-oriented, to translate the ideas she creates into practical, socially useful programs.' This type of intellectual constituted the quintessential definition of a public intellectual" (qtd. in Cooper 123–34, emphasis added). Triangulating the "who," "what," and "how" of Black women's public intellectual histories, Cooper also mentions Gwendolyn Brooks's influence in Pierce's description, recognizing that "'an intellectual is one who observes and/or claws out facts and ideas, worries them, turns them inside out, assembles them, relates them, and—on the *highest* level—enhances or nourishes them'" (qtd. in Cooper 124).

Taken together, we can appreciate Cooper's efforts to realign and extend notions of Black women's intellectual traditions, which can now bridge together Truth's proto-feminism and Angélique's unwarranted notoriety, for example, with contemporary redefinitions while still emphasizing our much older Black rhetorical and cultural roots grounded by Afrocentric ontologies. This expanded view of public intellectual traditions validates the ways Black women theorize knowledge as being more than just thinking through issues of class in political speeches or essays. Black women's public intellectual legacies often manifest outside "traditional" academic genres in forms such as song, storytelling, and life writing; it operationalizes sonic rhetorics through its vocal registers as part of the quest for accessible distribution or transmission. This is because, as Richardson writes, "African cultural forms that are constantly adapted to meet the needs of navigating life in a racist society influence these practices and ways of knowing and coping." She continues:

> African American females communicate these literacies through storytelling, conscious manipulation of silence and speech, code/style shifting, and signifying, among other verbal and non-verbal practices. Performance arts such as singing, dancing, acting, steppin', and stylin', as well as crafts such as quilting and use of other technologies are also exploited to these purposes (e.g., pots, pans, rags, brooms, and mops); African American females' language and literacy practices reflect their socialization in a racialized, genderized, sexualized, and classed world in which they employ their language and literacy practices to protect and advance themselves. Working from this rhetorical situation, the Black female developed creative strategies to overcome her situation, to "make a way outa no way." (*African American Literacies* 77)

With this in mind, "Black women thinkers have always been public intellectuals, both because they cared about producing accessible forms of knowledge for and with communities involved in the Black freedom struggle, and because the confluence of racism and patriarchy exempted them from access to academic institutions and from the protections of the private sphere. Black women have never had the luxury of being private thinkers" (Cooper 15). Reliance on "traditional," academic genres is often used as a gatekeeping mechanism and weaponized for continued enforcement of antiBlack logics. Notably, Angela Y. Davis supports this thought, writing that "what are constituted as black feminist traditions tend to exclude ideas produced by and within poor and working-class communities, where women historically have not had the means or access to publish written texts. But some black women did have access to publishers of *oral* texts," namely blues (and later R&B and hip-hop) records (*Blues Legacies* xii-xiii). Both racism and sexism systematically stymied Black women's collective liberation. Continued enforcement of such discursive and social limitations provided an urgency for developing such alternative forms of knowledge-making literacies. But, in true Black feminist fashion, we flipped that traditional script: Black feminist intellectual traditions and literacies continued flourishing as they were translated through aural and embodied spheres.

These alternative frames in which to view, recognize, and understand Black women (music artists) as public intellectuals lays the foundation for thinking through the methodological examination of audible advice and mentorship suggested in this chapter. Black women public intellectuals can negotiate various publics simultaneously; they can provide meaningful communication through vernacular literacies and multimodal composing practices as they shift and take on different roles and identities at one or multiple times: Black women (music artists) are experts at negotiating this multidimensional identity and responsibility.

As such, Black women public intellectuals and music artists reflect on knowledge gained from our ancestors and our present experiences, informing our collective and individual futures in a variety of ways. The agency resulting from the shared advice mitigating feelings of isolation or "craziness"[12] positions these Black women public intellectuals and music artists as mentors and leaders within and across sonic media. As a rhetorical model similar to the griot, audible advice frames the potential mentor role that Black women take on reflecting our long-standing responsibility of and ability to hold onto previous generations' teachings while simultaneously translating these teachings in context with present experiences; this relationship forms innumerable types of kinships and connections, all of which inform our daily decision-making process. Black women enable embodied knowledges and pedagogies to support the cultivation of rhetorical agency as we operationalize our sound, voice, and/or music to "git free." Cultivating vernacular literacies in antiBlack spaces, as public intellectuals and Black women (music artists) do, always proves meaningful when it can be translated into effective moments of resistance and (en)acted agency. Black women (music artists) are exemplary practitioners who embody and extend Black women's public intellectual traditions as they repackage the "theory in the flesh" in their materialized sound, continuing transmissions of advice and mentorship because of their innovation, commitment, and persistence regarding liberation for all.

Hush Harbor Sound E/Scape Discourses

Spaces like the stage, page, or podium are essential, subversive moments carrying weighty meanings and cloaked directions for some listeners to follow, especially if you are privy to various vocal registers circulating in Black culture. Over time, Black folks have responded to and resisted antiBlackness by cultivating our own sonic support networks by operationalizing advice or mentorship in sound. We use our voices as subversive, mechanized "hush harbors" communicating kinship and continuing legacies that validate the self and our shared ontological, epistemological beliefs. There are many (un)documented instances of Black folks forming and carrying on interpersonal communication strategies in shared spaces, often as part of a public intellectual methodology. Those spaces, those audible moments of advice like the one described in the opening scenes, are integral to cultivating and sustaining mentorships; they are embedded with kairotic exchanges that provide advice to younger Black generations that help us navigate a (hopefully) less strenuous way forward. It is in these spaces that audible advice transmits meaning and knowledge across generations. Recognizing audible advice, or mentorship in sound, as a Black feminist process building on robust legacies of Black women's public intellectualism addressed earlier means that we can imagine more clearly what and how we operationalize third spaces and how we recognize voice as an extension of it.

In "The Commitment to Theory," Homi Bhabha theorizes the third space as an intersectional exchange of information between communicators in which the message is given life not only by enunciation but also by generating shared meaning or understanding of what was communicated. Bhabha writes that

> The linguistic difference that informs any cultural performance is dramatized in the common semiotic account of the disjuncture between the subject of a proposition (enonce) and the subject of enunciation, which is not represented in the statement but which is the acknowledgement of its discursive embeddedness and address, its cultural positionality, its reference to a present time and a specific space. The pact of interpretation is never simply an act of communication between the I and the You designated in the statement. The production of meaning requires that these two places be mobilized in the passage through a Third Space, which represents both the general conditions of language and the specific implication of the utterance in a performative and institutional strategy of which it cannot "in itself be conscious." (20)

In Black (rhetorical) studies, we may recognize this transactional concept as Nommos. For Keith Gilyard, "*Nommo* 'is the belief in the pervasive, mystical, transformative, even life giving power of the Word'" (qtd. in Lathan 20). In later works, Gilyard and Banks provide another definition (based on other Black author's conversations, such as Smitherman and Asante, as well as Asante and Robb) as being "the traditional African belief in the visionary, creative and community-building capacity of the performed word"; this is "the intense African belief in the potency of the word" (11–12). As such, Nommo not only encompasses oral and aural spheres, it also represents "a more elaborate idea . . . denot[ing] the practice of eloquent public speaking . . . . [t]he goal is to fascinate as much as it is to instruct" (50). Likewise, in *Talkin and Testifyin*, Geneva Smitherman interprets Nommo as part of African teleological legacies, noting that "African Americans reinterpret this linguistic orientation as a way to actualize the 'fundamental unity between the spiritual and material aspects of existence.' She adds that "the oral tradition, then, is part of the cultural baggage the African brought to America. The preslavery background was one in which the concept of *Nommo*, the magic power of the Word, was believed necessary to actualize life and give man mastery over things" (77–78). Therefore, "[t]he African belief in the power and necessity of *Nommo* was so strong that" the enunciation or communication of words and the resulting meaning were to be followed, understood as a social contract or agreement existing between not only people and communities but also between people and the supernatural forces guiding our everyday existence (Lathan 20).

Broadly speaking, these sonic third spaces are a postcolonial (for Bhabha), theoretical intervention challenging the sociocultural presumptions of binaries informed by language and culture. For Bhabha, the third space ruptures notions of "East vs. West" that is pervasive in the sociocultural languages and literacies informing homogentisic perceptions of identity. He states that "[s]uch an intervention quite properly challenges our sense of the historical identity of culture as a homogenizing, unifying force, authenticated by the originary Past, kept alive in the national tradition of the People" (21). The moment in which interpersonal communication takes place is also the moment where resistance to normative exceptions and temporal logics can and do occur.

To clarify, these third spaces are not just shared moments that bring together two seemingly distinct epistemologies; they are also shared moments of meaning-making that bridge past, present, and future. Each communicator uses these moments in cultivating their own intrapersonal growth. "It is that Third Space, though unrepresentable in itself," Bhabha suggests, "which constitutes the discursive conditions of enunciation that ensure that the meaning and symbols of culture have no primordial unity or fixity; that even the same signs can be appropriated, translated, rehistoricized, and read anew" (21). In allowing and acknowledging the flexibility (or "hybridity" that Bhabha suggests) of the third space, these moments of communication and shared knowledge-making sustain immense (potential) power for remaking or redirecting the self in flashes of uncertainty.

Vorris L. Nunnley theorizes these third spaces as part of a Black rhetorical tradition. More specifically, he conceptualizes them as "hush harbors" in *Keepin' It Hushed: The Barbershop and African American Hush Harbor Rhetoric*. Hush harbors are extensions of these third spaces in that they are similar communicative and subversive knowledge-making webs helping to construct or validate one's identity. The "hush harbor," for Nunnley, represents shared moments of meaning-making that result in immeasurable possibilities for reimagining Black life beyond binary thinking and demeaning stereotypes. Nunnley asserts that "hush harbors are rhetorical free zones of emancipatory possibility precisely because they are internally directed, working from the terministic screens of African American life and culture rather than being anchored in a concern of countering White or mainstream surveillance" (34). Used in this way, audible advice, or mentorship in sound, supports Black radical imaginations of liberation and Black feminist public intellectual methodological legacies by starting from a point of Black subjectivity. Because African (American) public discourses are largely developed against the grain of hegemonic "traditions," Nunnley suggests that these spatialized rhetorical spheres where Black folk communicate and make meaning are often "relegated to hidden African American spaces, thereby bracketing these knowledges out of democratic deliberation" (2), and, as a result, they flourish "on the lower frequencies" (3). In fact, Nunnley surmises that hush harbors are essential for creating legacies of Black rhetorical traditions because these subversive third spaces validate Black rhetoric and logics that are "frequently alluded to but *rarely named*, theorized, or taken into account in the public sphere or in the public spaces because of the danger of its hidden transcripts containing Black perspectives" (2). In other words, for audible advice, or mentorship in sound, these shared moments of interpersonal communication may happen in plain sight, but the exchange of information is bound and protected by exclusive "Black cultural codes."[13] As a result, the inherent relationship between the Black rhetoric produced by audible advice and the establishment of the public intellectual/leader/mentor simultaneously safeguards and promotes Black (social) life while also continuing legacies of Afrocentric epistemologies, ontologies, and teleologies. These sonic, spatial constructs once again reiterate the concept of Ubuntu, which prioritized the framing of meaning-making process by the exchange of information through inter- and intrapersonal communication—prevalent in Black women public intellectuals' and music artists' messages.

As an origin point for Black survival rhetorics, which Teresa Zackodnick (2010) and Nikole Hannah-Jones (2019) date back to the early seventeenth century, hush harbors are "spaces where such talk has occurred during and since the Middle Passage and the enslavement of the minds so often kept to themselves; and it is about the spatiality where, since the early twentieth century, Black [wo]men could be philosophers and fools, thoughtful and ignorant, progressive and sexist, but mostly where they could be everything that being human allows" (Nunnley 2). Moreover, hush harbors are informed by, and reciprocally inform, hegemonic publics about "an awareness of not only how Blackness and Black knowledges are tethered, not sutured, to such African American spatialities and rhetorics, but also of how rhetorical *kairos* (opportune moment)—which always involves material-rhetorical spatiality—influences the donning or the removing of the hush harbor mask" (Nunnley 4). Thus, in addition to being a space of information exchange, hush harbors provide an underlying performative structure for surviving and healing through talk. Rather than propagating Black dis-assemblages for capital gain, as I've addressed in earlier chapters, these sonic third spaces serve as resting stops to gather, reflect, in/form, and organize information, which is then used to manufacture a way forward while we navigate oppressive terrains. These hush harbors, these moments of advice and resulting mentorship, are performative and theoretical spaces aiding us in making sense of our experiences and ultimately (re)orienting us in directions that will help further develop our communal and self-identity. These spaces are, as Nunnley argues, places and traditions of "knowledge generation" for many Black folk (6). It is in these spaces that Black women (music artists) invoke the long-standing Black feminist theories undergirding public intellectualism as they exchange information in, about, and through voice and vocal registers to those in our shared communities.

Vocal Applications of Hush Harbors

I emphasize the audibility and vocal registers within these sonic third spaces because, as Smitherman points out, Black language is a shared experience and a "tie that binds" (*Word from the Mother* 3). These relationships fasten together generations, concretizing the importance of drawing from our ancestral knowledge and recognizing the rich spectrum of Black thought and being in the world. After all, "The Africanization of U.S. English has been passed on from one generation to the next . . . provid[ing] a common thread across the span of time, even as each new group stamps its own linguistic imprint on the Game . . . . the language has not only survived, adding to and enriching the English language," but it also continues informing our way of life (*Word from the Mother* 3). As such, audible advice, or mentorship in sound, is an important aspect of Black (feminist) sonic rhetorical traditions; it extends the temporal and spatial directions of orality while validating our languages' and literacies' multidimensionality.

To further illustrate how and who operates audible advice to inform a mentorship in sound, I shift to examining two iterations of this sonic spatiality, proposing that sonic third spaces like interludes and gossip play important roles in transmitting knowledge and mobilizing subjectivity for Black women and girls. Focusing on these aspects of Black women's sonic rhetoric demonstrates how voice operates in our public intellectual traditions. It also highlights how oral and aural texts perform as generational, subversive, sonic hush harbors communicating generative moments of exchange and continuity informing Black (social) life.

INTERLUDES

Thinking about the evolution of audible iterations within Black women's public intellectualism, contemporary Black women music artists like Solange Knowles and Solána Imani Rowe (better known by her stage name, SZA) have used interludes as an extension of third spaces facilitating the transmission of advice or mentorship in a twenty-first-century fashion. Both Solange and SZA critically engaged with this intellectual rhetorical legacy when they formatted their albums *A Seat at the Table* (2016) and *Ctrl* (2017), respectively, by including interludes between songs. These interludes bridge musicality with their mothers' and grandmothers' advice, connecting performance, rhetoric, and sonority of voice and vocal register(s) with who they are as Black women—as daughters, mothers, aunts, friends, and sisters. The interludes used in these two albums carry on the pedagogical public intellectual blueprint for Black feminist rhetorics and being—one that is grounded in past, present, and future imaginations as well as experiences of self. These interludes theorize their intersectional situatedness and historically contextualized identities; they alter conceptions of humanity by countering the assemblage of Blackness for mere capital gain and/or public spectacle that is often foundational in the music industry. Their interludes illuminate our humanity, which is central to many of our generational calls for freedom.

Solange Knowles's *A Seat at the Table* includes twenty-one songs; of those twenty-one songs, eight of them are designated interludes where she dedicates time to transmit advice from family members and mentors. Two interludes, tracks eight and fifteen specifically, are exclusively composed with Black women's voices: "Tina Taught Me" and "I Got So Much Magic, You Can Have It." The interlude highlighting Tina Knowles's reflection is a particularly powerful example of motherly words of wisdom, and I find it necessary to quote it at length:

> I think part of it is accepting that it's so much beauty in being Black. And that's the thing that, I guess, I get emotional about because I've always known that. I've always been proud to be Black. Never wanted to be nothing else. Loved everything about it, just it's such beauty in Black people. And, it really saddens me when we're not allowed to express that pride in being Black. And that if you do, then it's considered anti-white. No! You just pro-black, and that's okay. The two don't go together: because you celebrate Black culture does not mean that you don't like white culture, or that you puttin' it down. It's just taking pride in it, but what's irritating is when somebody says, you know, "They're racist!," "That's reverse racism!" or "They have a Black History Month, but we don't have a White History Month!" Well, all we've ever been taught is white history, so why are you mad at that? Why does that make you angry? That is to suppress me and to make me not be proud. ("Tina Taught Me")

Tina Knowles's interlude operationalizes the theory in the flesh as a praxis to serve as a teaching opportunity for both her daughter, Solange Knowles, and Knowles's audiences listening to her album. On the surface, this interlude unapologetically embraces Black identities and teaches her daughter to not only feel comfortable in her skin but also take pride in the sociocultural, historical, and political legacies centering Blackness (e.g., the Black Power movement).

Further excavation of this message reveals another prominent Black feminist theoretical teaching, that is, part of "what Patricia Hill Collins describes as a 'politics of containment' (*Fighting Words* 33) wherein black women are controlled, monitored, and scrutinized through surveillance and highly achieving and visible figures are rendered silent" (qtd. in Carey, "Necessary Adjustments" 142). Tina Knowles recognizes the impact white, dominant, public gazes can have on social movements that (and by extension icons, celebrities, or leaders who) center Blackness. She alludes to a public gazes' rhetorical effect that freezes Blackness in place (i.e., ensuring Blackness remain "out of time") and reinforces the containment of Black mobility inhibiting the march of progress. The interlude ends with Tina Knowles questioning this antiBlack rhetorical method, signaling to Solange Knowles that it is okay to challenge these problematic and often racist tactics stalling liberation and freedom. By connecting these teachings and personal experiences, the mother encourages, supports, and motivates her daughter to continue prior generations' efforts to secure a more equitable existence by emphasizing the beauty in/of Blackness.

The literacy act embedded within this interlude necessitates an understanding of reading between the lines and applying generational information to various types of microaggressions that show up in our daily lives. This sonic, rhetorical tool reflects what Lathan has described as "adhering to the West African philosophy of *mate masie* (wisdom, knowledge, and prudence). The philosophy weaves together both wisdom and knowledge while having the good sense to consider other perspectives." Lathan continues, "[w]ithout critical knowledge of how social customs and power dynamics within African American culture vary from one situation to the next, it is difficult to negotiate rhetorical situations and to participate in a way that is meaningful and even comprehensible to the collective" (Lathan xxi). The imagined dialogue between mother and daughter calls for critical reflexivity when thinking through how best to respond and move forward at this time; the advice necessitates an intentional accounting of one's personal situation and for other possibilities that may involve people other than one's self. In conjunction with the other interludes, Solange Knowles's interlude highlights audible advice as a kind of multivocal and multimedia Black feminist creative process for mobilizing knowledge, making it public and accessible; her interludes creatively make way for the visible, inherited praxis of our generational lived experiences and our sonic rhetorics.

In a similar manner, SZA's *Crtl* includes fourteen songs; of the fourteen, five songs include advice solely from her matriarchal lineage: her mother and grandmother. All the interludes include either her mother's or grandmother's voice, unlike Knowles's interludes, which also sample interviews from family and friends like Master P. While Knowles's interludes are produced as separate entries between the songs, lasting anywhere from seventeen seconds to one minute and fourteen seconds, SZA's interludes are attached to the song, taking on either the "intro" or "outro" position—fading in or out of the composition—seamlessly transitioning between the sonic collection of lessons learned and her own personal, critical reflections embedded within the lyrics.

Listed on the credits simply as "Mommy" or "Granny," SZA's inclusion of matriarchal figures are reminiscent of many of our own blood or fictive kinships who dish out advice about overcoming hardships and taking care of ourselves, just as we saw in the scenes from Owen's autobiography. For instance, in the last seconds of "Love Galore," we hear "Granny" say, "Princess Solána, if you don't say something. Speak up for yourself. They think you STUPID! You know what I'm sayin'?" (4:24–4:35). Similarly, in "Garden (Say It Like That)," "Granny" advises, "You ain't got shit to say to me, I ain't got shit to say to you." Both she and SZA chuckle, and SZA interjects, "and that's the truth!" Granny continues, "And step on. I said you Black heffa, you. You stand yo ground. Cause, I, like, I feel the same way. If you don't like me, you don't have to fool with me. But, you don't have to talk about me or treat me mean. I don't have to treat you mean. I jus gonna stay outta ya way. That's [how] you work that one" (3:00–3:28). Both of "Granny's" snippets describe how to navigate moments of distress where you feel out of control and/or unlike yourself.

While her grandmother advises SZA on how to navigate moments of external pressure and frustration, her mother's interludes mentor SZA about the effects of holding onto these painful moments of (self) sabotage and theorize about navigating internal distress like anxiety. This is apparent from both the opening and closing of the album, signaling to SZA (and her audiences) that Black feminist (rhetorical) theory is always intimately tied to "acknowledging the burden"—that is, simultaneous external *and* internal stressors dictating our Black sociohistorical and cultural existences. Her mother's theorizing of the flesh initiates the first track, "Supermodel," where she notes that "my greatest fear; that if I lost control, or if I did not have control, things would just, ya know, I, would be, fatal" (0:00-0:12). In a world, or society, that does not often view Black women as being fully human, the urge to control our surroundings is tantamount to our many methods of trying to survive. This want of control can filter into aspects of how we take care of ourselves and our communities—from beauty standards, body image and eating disorders, depression and anxiety, and other performance-related labors like working beyond retirement or without sleep and proper nutrition, and being without access to adequate housing and/or equitable financial means, as noted in the first chapter—all to make the statement that we belong. Charisse Jones and Kumea Shorter-Gooden, authors of *Shifting: The Double Lives of Black Women in America*, assert that there is a sustained belief in the antiBlack myths, particularly in the "strong Black woman" myth that superficially constructs all Black women as

> invulnerable and indefatigable, that they always persevere and endure against great odds without being negatively affected. This is one myth that many Black women themselves embrace,

and so they take on multiple roles and myriad tasks, ignoring the physical and emotional strain, fulfilling the stereotype. There is peer pressure among Black women to keep the myth alive, to keep juggling, to keep accommodating. Some women who desperately need balance in their lives, who greatly need assistance, never seek or receive it. Instead, their blood pressure soars. They overeat. They sink into depression. Some kill themselves or try. Other simply fantasize about making an escape. (3)

Likewise, as Carey noted earlier, Collins asserts that "the seamless web of economy, polity, and ideology function as a highly effective system of social control designed to keep African-American women in an assigned, subordinate place" (*Black Feminist Thought* 7), and these antiBlack mythic stereotypes are effective forms of imposing psychological terror onto Black bodies. Wanting to control the world around you may be a result of these lasting and damaging remnants of white solipsism. "Indeed," Jones and Gooden-Shorter write, "society's stubborn myths continue to do tremendous damage to Black women. They often seep into their inner psyches and become permanently internalized, battering them from within even if they're able, for a time, to wriggle free and live the truth" (4)—which makes the interlude by Tina Knowles so perceptive. Working through issues affecting our social health, SZA's mother's last interlude on the track "20 Something" shares her own process for how she manages these feelings, serving as instruction to/for SZA: "And if it's an illusion, I don't wanna wake up. I'm gonna hang onto it because the, the, the alternative is an, an abyss, it's just a hole, a darkness, a nothingness and who wants that!? Ya know. So that's what I think about control. And that's my story, and I'm sticking to it!" (2:49–3:18). This interlude featuring SZA's mother reflects how a relationship between two or more people from a shared community who recognize the value in social (activist) literacies and pedagogies can mitigate the effects of oppressive social expectations and respectability politics that often disproportionately affect Black people—especially Black women and girls.

The sonic, rhetorical practices outlined here invoke Nommos through a theorizing of the body in particular. SZA's mother names the visceral reaction to understanding "control" in context through embracing Black radical imaginations of what could be possible; she recognizes and names the vibrational patterns, resonating internally, as a means for understanding how to facilitate some agency through an intimately tenuous hold on "control." This juxtaposition and power of naming help "illuminate the actual definitions and break down the stigma attached to terms, . . . gaining power and control over dominant oppressive language" that is the antiBlack expectation of not having control; "this is an act of *Nommo*—actualizing the unity between spiritual and material aspects of existence" (Lathan 103). This is "gaining control."

Instead of being a placeholder or a form of entertainment giving respite between main acts, these generational Black feminist sonic, rhetorical interludes hold as much importance as the songs that come before and the songs that follow. These two Black women (music artists) choose not to use the interlude as a means for granting temporary relief but as a way to take great care of the knowledges passed onto them by evolving more traditional sonic hush harbors and embedding them into widely circulated (and appropriated) pop culture. As Cooper states, "Black women's knowledge production has always been motivated by a sense of care for Black communities" (*Beyond Respectability* 2), and this extends to the creative uses of media and materialized sound, continuing this long-last legacy of "keepers of ancestral knowledge."

McKittrick describes this Black, embodied geographical relationship in connection with sociocultural, historical, racialized and gendered spatiality, noting that the Black body is often an " 'imperceptible' social, political, and geographic subject who is rendered invisible due to his highly visible bodily context" (18). Since Black (women's) bodies are often hypervisiblized to the point of being deemed invisible and fungible (Browne 2015), Black women (music artists) mobilize sonic, rhetorical methods to "hide in plain sight" and continue various praxis for survival, liberation, and healing. As Cooper suggests, these alternative but parallel strategies flourished "in part because they were acutely aware of the limitations of making themselves invisible in a world predicated in the surveillance of Black bodies" (*Beyond Respectability* 3) but still committed to transmitting information. Thus, sound, music, and/or voice and vocal register(s) afford us with other ways of understanding complementary possibilities and (re)imagining alternate modes of communicating meaning for and between Black folks in public spheres, especially when filtered through the public intellectual/leader/mentor model.

Emphasizing the audibility of advice, or mentorship in sound, by operationalizing interludes, for example, reinforces the importance of Black women's generational sonic rhetoric as a means for transmitting messages of survival, liberation, and healing; these interludes solidify the importance of orality and vocal register(s), which communicate Black epistemologies by any means necessary. Taken together, we can see the various ways interludes can inform generations. The ways in which these two Black women (music artists) innovatively use interludes are a testament to how Black women public intellectuals and music artists pedagogically communicate across time and space, solidifying and catalyzing central forces in Black women's (rhetorical) theory supporting advice and mentoring frameworks.

Gossip

While interludes are an important part of evolving oral traditions grounding audible advice, or mentorship in sound, the vernacular analog predecessor, gossip, also demonstrates this dynamic Black feminist rhetorical and sonic praxis. When we investigate life writing, like auto/biographies, for instance, we catch glimpses of orality transposed onto written (often vernacular and informal) forms of communication. These textual moments help pinpoint the exchange of generational advice, or mentorship in sound, that was originally transmitted through word of mouth. This sonic rhetoric demonstrates a commitment to at least one pillar of Black feminist thought: politicizing the personal. The written transcriptions of these vernacular exchanges for Black women are a testament to Black feminist (rhetorical) theory used by Black women public intellectuals who "'challeng[ed] contemporary social conditions'" (qtd. in Cooper, *Beyond Respectability* 16) and even challenged disciplinary expectations staking a claim of rhetorical agency. However, the oral hush harbor that originally facilitated these written transcriptions still needs to be taken seriously; the sonic rhetoric found in these embodied and vocal transmissions of meaning-making needs the same kind of scholarly care exemplified in this book's prior sections.

Many scholars have identified gossip's long history and placement in various public discourses as an influential rhetorical endeavor. From salons and parlors to news columns and vlogs, scholars like Patricia Bizzell and Bruce Herzberg[14] have described gossip as a kind of rhetorical public space where shared, subversive secrets inform and guide the actions of larger audiences—but they, too, fall short in addressing gossip as an intersectional, sonic, rhetorical practice. These oral/aural teachings, learned from family, friends, church members, music artists, and community workers, for example, reflect the same applications of literacy that Royster and Brandt described. Broadly speaking, "Black women's discourses," Olga Idriss Davis notes, "is a story of rhetorical strategies of women who transformed the 'ordinaries of daily life' into rhetoric of survival not only for themselves but for generations beyond" ("Theorizing African American Women's Discourse" 36; "A Black Woman as Rhetorical Critic" 81). "Unlike the traditional rhetorical model," states Davis, "a discourse of *experience* celebrates a racial and gendered consciousness of self that comes from knowing and locating multiple strategies or resistance in order to create a progressive means for change in the context of the community" (38, emphasis added). These aural/oral cultural teachings/ literacies/Black woman discourses can be used by anyone, but particularly by the younger generations of Black women and girls to guide and navigate life choices—hopefully ensuring a "better" quality of life, which is the ultimate goal and profound measurement of "liberation for all." Gossip, in these ways, facilitates the audible exchanges of counsel and care for any Black woman or girl across the diaspora; it is an accessible way for mentors to ensure that we all have the opportunity to see and hear ourselves in the narrative. Black women (music artists) continue these practices as they create and share their versions of audible advice, especially in genres like the blues and R&B.[15] Gossip, then, is another effective mode of communication for Black women and girls to learn different methods of survival, liberation, and healing. Under those circumstances, we can understand gossip as another metaphysical sonic hush harbor extending the audibility of advice across time and space, much like interludes, as it weaponizes the opportune moments to manufacture shared knowledge between Black folks and promote ways surviving and healing as we talk.

Rhetorically, gossip "connects with shared local timespace and moderates the perception of conflicting or incongruent desires within social contexts. Thinking of it as a resource for identifying and transmitting the common logic of the community offers a productive point of entry for examining the social norms grounding shared identity," as Heather Lee Branstetter notes (384). Branstetter illuminates the ways gossip pushed fields like rhetoric and composition forward by recognizing the embodied, intangible, but wholly present kinds of rhetorical exchanges or communication: "Layers of narrative built from collective memory construct worlds in which the 'validity of truth or personal veracity' is secondary to 'the feeling and the experience they create between the storytellers'" (qtd. in Branstetter 386). However, like Gramcsi's public intellectual models, common traditional contexts normalizing gossip often maintain gendered and classed critiques—not always racialized—further demonizing this practice as messy and destructive. This viewpoint often diminishes the productive sonic rhetoric gossip affords women of color, especially Black women and girls.

Moreover, the negative and incomplete view of gossip can result from the potentially deleterious aftermath of mobilizing such private information against said individuals and communities. Eric K. Foster writes that "Most societies have explicit sanctions against gossip, and numerous cautionary narratives demonstrate its unwanted outcomes" (78). In the United States and Canada, for example, legal action can be taken against instances of liable and slander, often referred to as defamation laws. These legal proceedings aim to protect the rights of citizens who have been targeted by unfair or untrue statements because "[t]argets [of gossip]," Foster adds, "may be hurt by seeing how others perceive their affairs, by distortion or manipulation of information, or by the violation of private matters. Many ethical condemnations of gossip revolve around presumed rules of privacy" (78). However, for Black and other marginalized folk, privacy, citizenship, and time are luxuries not often afforded to our personhood—let alone our rhetorics and literacies. Maintaining gossip's traditional, deleterious framework does little to address or acknowledge the effective sonic, rhetorical strategies employed by Black women and girls within these hush harbors.

As such, gossip, particularly as it is confined to "feminine" and "conversational" discourses, has long been held as a motive for contempt or erasure directed toward women and "women's talk" (Mary Ellen Brown 1990; Eric K. Foster 2004), especially when factoring in race and sexuality.[16] These unilateral misrepresentations of gossip are also evidence of antiBlack rhetorical strategies meant to thwart, stall, or delay opportunities for progress by maintaining silos and weaponizing social pressure. As a result, traditional understandings of gossip may dictate the kinds of pathways Black folks can operate in public spheres and dimmish the effective rhetorical nature of gossip. More specifically, engaging in traditional gossip practices may be seen as an access point to be exploited by others, increasing opportunities for the hegemony to gain power or ammunition needed in their efforts to continue controlling Black and marginalized bodies. Upholding the stigmatized, cultural belief of uncritically rejecting gossip can also unintentionally support continued antiBlack legacies and surveillance. Perhaps, however, people fear gossip simply because it has the power to alter marginalized people's direction in life, often for the better, making it especially useful for Black women navigating things like racism, ableism, and sexism in their careers.

While gossip's stigma may hold true for most social communities, the effects of gossip can impact different social groups in different ways. It is true that there is a particular stigma surrounding gossip even in Black communities: a frequent vernacular gesture of chastisement to not "air dirty laundry" in public or a warning reminding us that "snitches get stitches." This hesitation surrounding not telling our secrets from within our inner circles may stem from a belief that this "open" discussion can result in harm and/or trauma. It may stem from the belief that gossip can tip off the hegemony, making them privy to our hardships, plots, and/or our moments of vulnerability—and there is some truth to this. Additionally, this "airing of dirty laundry" may also be seen as "weakness" (an action opposing the Strong Black Woman myth) by some in our communities. However, contrary to the harmful connotations and normative applications of gossip, there are positive ways gossip can also function for Black women and girls. Geneva Smitherman writes in *Talkin and Testifyin'* that "black talk is never simple cocktail chit-chat, but a functional dynamic that is simultaneously a mechanism for learning about life and the world and a vehicle for achieving group approval and recognition" (80). There is, indeed, a high level of risk associated with gossip for Black folks in that if "caught" we run the risk of losing our ability to hide in plain sight, or our strategies for freedom become delayed or thwarted (not to mention the very real possibility of social death). It may be riskier, however, to withhold information from close friends, family, and colleagues. Therefore, when Black women enact gossip, it is often for specific life-giving reasons—especially in our professional environments.[17]

For many of us, gossip is a Black feminist sonic rhetoric and literacy that can provide some protection against external forces because of its ability to weaponize advice. Gossip can manufacture a network of support by sharing stories and narratives detailing past experiences from prior generations—validating and expanding the testimonies of other Black women and girls. In other words, we can talk about other people and events to warn those close to us, those we care about, of potential hurdles as well as similar mistakes and resulting downfalls that we retroactively learned from. Daryl Cumber Dance, editor of *Honey, Hush! An Anthology of African American Women's Humor*, expands on this same notion, writing that "These warnings often become more ominous, however, for the black female, who (especially in the South) has historically been the victim of legalized, random, and often ritualistic sexual exploitation." She continues, "[F]or black girls, the necessary behavior," of gossip, for instance, "is not just a matter of etiquette and amenities, but also often practical ways of defending themselves against commonplace disappointments, intimidations, and dangers from every possible source (the white community/the black community/white men/black men/white women/other black women, not to mention natural disasters, illness, and spells)" (40). Black women's sonic rhetorical practices, like gossip, remain a functional and necessary practice of survival and care, especially because the condition of Black life in America (and beyond) remains strongly connected to systematic oppressions of marginalized people.

Additionally, like the literary foremother and public intellectual archetypes described earlier, Mary Ellen Brown personifies those sociocultural, gendered definitions of gossip: "The woman friend or relative who, in the first definition, comes to *give comfort and spiritual support* at times of crisis or transition, establishing an ongoing network of mutual support and obligation between women is seen in the latter definition from outside the women's network as a threat, as the agent of a subversive and malicious information service" (184, emphasis added). Similar to Richardson's listing of African American women's literacy methods, Brown describes informative gossip within these engendered and raced discourses as being found in "[t]he performance of songs, the telling of tales, the arrangement of marriages, discussion of health problems, kinship gossip and work-related hints" (185). This dynamic and multivocal iteration of gossip, as a Black feminist rhetorical practice, firmly roots the sonic in African-derived embodied knowledge-making legacies.

Ruth Brown's auto/biography describes one moment where her life changed because of her intentional vulnerability when she divulged personal information to an inquisitive bystander, pushing expectations of privacy aside for her own survival and mental health. "One day I was out buying groceries when a lady approached me," writes Brown. " 'You're Ruth Brown, aren't you?' She asked. 'I sure am,' I replied, 'but please don't hold that against me.' She turned out to be a friend of Valerie Carr, a buddy of mine from the fifties who'd enjoyed a big record," Brown carries on, "What was I doing these days, she wanted to know. 'To be truthful,' I replied, 'not a whole lot. Things aren't too good right now.' I explained my situation and told her I was searching for an apartment of my own." The mutual friend replied, " 'I got a friend in Atlantic City, and she has a one-room apartment up on 165th street,' . . . 'I keep the keys while she's away and she hasn't stayed there for almost a year. You could ask her if she's prepared to sublet. Let me give you her number'" (Brown 169). Both Brown and the newly acquainted mutual friend exchanged personal, insider information, establishing and expanding this network of friendship and care. With the help of each other, they found ways to survive mentally, emotionally, and physically.

In a more public setting, Brown describes a social scene where gossip is integral to an artist's promotion and career advancement:

> I met Brook Benton that afternoon in Beefsteak Charlie's, a bar between Broadway and Eighth Avenue where musicians and actors congregated. Its walls were lined with sheet music and if you waited long enough you met everyone who happened to be in town, Dizzy sitting at the bar, Mr. B at a table, LaVern table-hoppin' with her husband, Slappy White. It was *the* meeting place, with every mother's child, you can believe it, dressed to the nines. Shooting the bull was the name of the game, for in those days we had no PR teams, we did it ourselves." (Brown 131)

Taking these scenes into account, gossip can reinforce characteristics of "gospel literacy," that is, "acknowledging the burden" and "call-and-response" more specifically, when transmitting important information. "'[A]cknowledging the burden,'" Lathan posits, "relies on one primary conviction: that history and power are synonymous" (16–17). Moreover, "acknowledging the burden . . . link[s] individual and community experiences [,] . . . practices, meanings, and values . . . . it is an empowering practice motivating participants to choose a liberating response . . . [and] relies on spiritual principles such as freedom, hope, and perseverance, which people use to consciously and aggressively resist systems of oppression" (Lathan 17). Brown uses the lessons learned from gossiping to connect nodes of information along her vast network. This sonic rhetoric and literacy position her as having an important role as an advocate, friend, and leader; this act also reinforced her connections to Black communities who could not only help promote her career but also provide a network of rootedness she'd need to survive antiBlack recording industry practices. Particularly impactful for Brown's narrative, gossiping transformed the vulnerability behind "acknowledging the burden" and changed the interpersonal response into action, a request for/of help from someone who understood the intersectional constraints stemming from the sonic sharecropping she'd experienced. Thus, the resultant "call-and-response becomes [the] analytical practice that requires the admission of diverse voices and diverse experiences. It's an ideology that supports an inclusive critique greater than any individual analysis" (Lathan 62). The gossiper, in this intersectional context, draws on "[t]he core of call-and-response [that] is a West African ethos of valuing an interrelationship between individuals and community . . . . Practitioners must engage in an individual process of decoding and making meaning for use in a larger context, all of which is bound by time and space" (Lathan 10). Leaning on these literacy components that accept and reinforce the public intellectual model represented by Black women (music artists) as "keepers of ancestral knowledge" in these ways develops a framework for audible advice and mentorship in sound that is based in reciprocity (or balance) between theory and experience.

It is no wonder that audible advice, or mentorship in sound, cannot only be found across media, but can also be operationalized by various (Black) women. As Dance notes, "most African American children grow up surrounded by those working mothers as well as grandmothers, great-grandmothers, aunts, great-aunts, cousins, friends, roomers, and sundry other mother-substitutes," extending gossip's role as both a theoretical and practical application of Black women's generational sonic rhetorics. "[T]he African American female is likely to receive an even larger and more varied dose of motherly advice than others," Dance writes. "The goal of these mothers, of course, is to keep their daughters safe and to provide them a little common sense and mother wit . . . whatever resources will allow them to avoid the mistakes they made, and to enable their daughters to grow up to be healthier, happier, more secure financially, and better educated than they were" (41). Gossip—in this sonic, intersectional, and rhetorical viewpoint—is a valuable, culturally responsive vehicle for transmitting social knowledge and instruction about expectations as well as necessary methods for day-to-day survival. As Branstetter writes, gossip is "[r]epeated sayings [that] offer community members clues to resources that have been persuasive in the past, while improvisational adaptations create new possibilities" (386). When Black women gossip, we can interpret and translate these "repeated sayings" to make the most effective choices for our career pathways as well as our (social) life and health in real time. These repeated sayings are tweaked and redistributed through different pathways, ensuring maximum survival. "Gossip oriented cultural values and social life by reverberating at a frequency that harmonized the traditions of the past with the unpredictable developments of the future" (Bransetter 391). This speculative reinscription of gossip can change how we communicate over time and within hush harbors; this includes nuances in why we gossip in spaces (and out of sight) of systematic oppression.

Many audiences view these Black women (music artists) as taking on the public, organic, intellectual role by asserting their accessible, familiar, intercommunal, and rhetorical practice of mentorship, counsel, and/or verbal support of individual members who share in our generational struggles for freedom. "These thousands of rules, guides, admonitions, and threats that older women rain down on female children" greatly influence the way we mature and come of age. Dance writes, "Later in life, they are inclined to thank God that their mothers protected them from some of the pitfalls that befall so many women; or to bewail the fact that they did not listen to their mother and therefore had to pay the price. Even later in life, they are very likely to quote their mothers to their daughters . . . and thus the cycle begins anew" (39–40), just as Latifah does in the opening scenes of this chapter.

Personal reactions to gossip or intercommunal (informal) conversations are seen in Black women music artist's materialized sound. Artists like Ruth Brown, for example, theorized the advice gathered from life experiences or the advice told to her by her (other) mother(s), translating their mentorship in sound to reverberating advice on the page. Reading between the lines of these exchanges of gossip allows us to peer deeper into the affordances of audible advice, or mentorship in sound. Reading advice as part of a gossip tradition demystifies and simultaneously theorizes what people talk about in our public hush harbors as we sonically position ourselves out of reach of white hegemonic spotlights.

"Look at My Big Dream!": Drawing the Curtain Back on Generational Struggles

As we have read, audible advice, or mentorship in sound, is a vehicle for transmitting knowledge across time and space. In the life writings of auto/biographies and albums above, we recognize this process of fleshing out and applying advice in our daily lives as a means of countering the many ways Black (women's) bodies are systematically devalued. These mentoring processes foster supportive networks uplifting and encouraging each other to do our best in the moment. Genres of life writing, be that on the page or in the album, offer us a code for interpreting Black women's public intellectual legacies through our collaborative, audible narratives (Cooper, *Beyond Respectability* 68; A. Davis, *Blues Legacies* 1998). This exchange is so frequent and so common that it is seamlessly embedded within our own literacy practices. In fact, Richardson writes that "African American females repeatedly use their stories as vehicles for the transmission of their special knowledge and truth" (85). The sonic rhetoric within these narratives and literacies provides us a relatively stable glimpse into how these oral and audible processes of vocal registers transmit knowledge across and between generations.

These strategic communicative inventions speak directly to what Tamika Carey defines as rhetorical healing. She postulates that rhetorics of healing "transcribe problems into lessons by invoking messages of personal affirmation, notions of familial belonging, institutional responsibility, or broader racial uplift. More often than not, the effects of these discourses are potent." As a result, "Readers [and listeners, I'd argue] feel that they have taken away valuable coping strategies, while the most popular proponents of these projects feel that writing texts that pursue a goal of healing is something of an activist endeavor. Teaching individuals the ways of knowing, being and acting that enable them to reread their pasts, revise a way to help ensure individual and community survival" (*Rhetorical Healing* 6). As a methodology, "rhetorical healing is both an analytical and conceptual framework for identifying the innovation and implications in how writers construct and instruct Black female audiences" (7). Both the audibility of advice and the resulting mentorship in sound found in interludes and gossip can lead (younger) generations of Black women and girls to the kinds of rhetorical healing that Carey defines. The conclusion of Billie Holiday's biography, for instance, exemplifies this exigent connection between African epistemologies, African American female literacy practices, and rhetorical healing and/or social health that Carey identifies as a goal of Black women's sonic rhetorics. Holiday reflects on her own experiences and the many ways she had to "make a way outta no way" as she struggled to own her voice and body. This urgent and generational call for care *as* survival and liberation is translated from her past lessons learned and fuels her vision for future generations:

> "Look at my big dream!" . . . a big place of my own out in the country someplace where I could take care of stray dogs and orphan kids, kids that didn't ask to be born; kids that didn't ask to be black, blue, or green or something in between. . . . I'd have room for twenty-five or thirty, with three or four big buxom loving women just like my mom to take care of them, feed them, see to it the little bastards go to school; knock them in the head when they're wrong, but love them whether they're good or bad. . . . But I'd always be around to teach them my kind of teaching—not the kind that tells them how to spell Mississippi, but how to be glad to be who you are and what you are." (195–96)

Holiday's dream is remarkably like the feelings Tina Knowles espoused on her interlude. Holiday (and the other artists named in this chapter were) was aware not only of the legacies entrusted to her, but also of her own ability to pass on information garnered by her own experiences, her materialized sound, and her status as a public intellectual figure, singer, activist, and author. She writes, "I don't want to preach to nobody. I never have and I don't want to begin now. But I do hope some kids will read this book and not miss the point of it. Maybe because I have no kids of my own—not yet—I still think you can help kids by talking straight to them. . . . It's worth [talking about my past] if just one youngster can learn one thing from it" (Holiday 213). Here, she translates her own sonic realities into written dreams as she sketches out a blueprint for tangible applications for/of mentorship grounded by her own advice she wished to pass on. Her dream is better social health and opportunities for rhetorical healing, especially for younger (Black) generations.

As this chapter closes, as the curtain is drawn together again, it is important to re/emphasize the value of Black women's voice and vocal register(s) across media as the energy (em)powering these vehicles—that is, Black women's sonic rhetorics and intellectual traditions. Sonja Lanehart reiterates this importance of Black women's language, writing that Black women's "stories are too often untold and unreflected upon . . . . They appear independently of one another, but, as you know, all of our stories are interdependent. The interdependence resonates with a clear voice because we are not alone" (*Sista Speak!* 1–2). Within these examples of audible advice, or mentorship in sound, we can see the formation of what

Lanehart identifies as "Ideology of Emancipation."[18] We operationalize our voices, our generational sonic rhetorics, to "git free."

As such, this chapter's discussion of audible advice, or mentorship in sound, highlights the legacy of Black women's generational sonic rhetoric by connecting forms of voice and vocal registers across sonic soundscapes. This work continues Cooper's (re)reading of Black women's public intellectual traditions not by continuing to redefine the term but by emphasizing those "accessible forms of knowledge." More specifically, audible advice, or the mentorship in and through sound, can mobilize a particular form of accessibility maximizing dispersion of knowledge—one that is subversive, liberatory, resistive, and embodied, all of which are needed to survive and communicate meaning on deep, personal levels. Said another way, what this chapter does is prove that Black women (music artists) were/are also public intellectuals who, through telling our stories, generated a variety of ways to operationalize sonic third spaces. This reorientation and collapsing of public intellectual archetypes allows us to better recognize the important rhetorical contributions of Black women who often found ways to continue the Afrocentric traditions of communication and knowledge-making while further ensuring that (younger) generations know their self (worth).

Even though Black women (music artists) have not always been recognized as public intellectuals, activists, or communal leaders, these examples show us that we/they indeed are. Black women (music artists) not only remake what it means to be a public intellectual through our vernacular communicative methods, but they also *bin* remaking this role for centuries as Black women pass on methods of survival, resistance, liberation, validation, representation, and social health to each generation. Carey writes that "Vernacular spaces and practices that affirm and reinforce one's sense of self-purpose foster the rhetorical acts of resistance necessary for an individual's survival in a hostile environment" (*Rhetorical Healing* 34). Additionally, "Vernacular customs and discourse practices such as call and response originated because African Americans have needed ways of 'self-identification' and communication that are apart from the dominant cultures that embrace their labor and reject their humanity. Counterlinguistic practices . . . are the means African Americans have used to make their lives better" (34). Therefore, ultimately, what these moments of audible advice, or mentorship in sound, represent are the various ways knowledge transmission can take place across generations of

Black women and girls in vernacular and sonic ways. In cultivating these practices of transmission, Black women (music artists) provide methods for navigating and resisting antiBlack measures like surveillance and temporal hegemony. The mechanization of reciprocal relationships between orality, audibility, and Black women's language resists the inaudibility of Black death, fungibility, and Black pain by supporting representation, social health reform, and methods of healing.

5

Reverb

A Coda for a Quiet, Undisputed Dignity in Sound

> Indeed, to channel the late Barbara Christian who cited Black women's use of "pithy language to unmask power relations" as evidence that they were always "a race for theory," these ongoing conversations and independent efforts suggest Black women are also a race for healing. This race hasn't stopped and it cannot stop because if it does, Black women lose the right to define for themselves what wellness and healing can and should be.
>
> —Tamika Carey, *Rhetorical Healing* (167)

Reverb (n): /rə'vərb/

A quick Google search tells us that *Oxford Languages* defines "reverb" as a noun: "an effect whereby the sound produced by an amplifier or an amplified musical instrument is made to reverberate slightly" or "a device for producing reverb on an amplified musical instrument." That is what this book is to me (and I hope for you as well): a mechanism for continued acts of amplification.

Unraveling within these chapters are themes of care, embodied theory, resistance, and hope. These threads, time and time again, reorient public (re)views of the ways Black women frame social health/care, acknowledge the burdens and joys of being Black, encourage continued validation of Black creativity and innovation, and intentionally celebrate who we are together. As such, the politics and ecologies of sound, music, image, and voice offer us a means for exploring the nuances within, behind, and between the methods of Black folks' communication. As the opening quote from Carey suggests, Black women's rhetorical language is influential in all our forms of healing and care; it's also essential for our methods of survival and liberation. Regardless of what discipline these themes are centered in, it's clear that Black women's sonic rhetorics have historically, socially, and culturally worked together to amplify our ongoing call for liberation, freedom, and equality—in any and in as many ways as possible.

At times, these sonorous exchanges may have seemed inconsequential, overlooked, ignored, passed over, diminished, or mocked. But, to me, the work that Black women (music artists) do is overwhelmingly important. Their work is amplified when we put them in conversation with each other; when we excavate their rhetorics; when we care to engage with them on their terms; when we follow our imaginations to new possibilities, as they have shown us; when we allow ourselves to be motivated by their presence—even on quiet, lower frequencies. Moreover, Black women (music artists') generational sonic rhetorics embody the quiet and undisputed dignity that Anna J. Cooper (1891) and Brittney Cooper (2017) name and identify across generations, events, and media. Throughout these chapters, we've seen and read about many ways Black women (music artists) use sound to demarcate the body as a rhetorical agent—particularly through the recognizable pop culture lenses of image, music, written and spoken dialogues. It is hard to deny the work and the "wreck" that Black women (music artists), addressed here and elsewhere. They are innovators, intellectuals, mentors, visionaries, activists, and change-makers. After all, as I alluded in my last chapter and elsewhere in the book, the mechanization of Black women's generational sonic rhetorics reverberates in the works/advice of Tamika Carey, Gwendolyn Pough, Brittney Cooper, Simone Browne, Hortense Spillers, Frantz Fanon, Deborah King, and many other Black feminists as it intentionally resists the "inaudibility of Black death," "Black fungibility," and "Black pain" they discuss by supporting representation, social health reform, and rhetorical healing.

I cannot unsee the relationships between sound, music, and language any more than I cannot disregard my own feelings of vulnerability, anger, and joy as a Black/mixed woman. The music I was brought up on and the music I enjoy listening to help facilitate my own way forward, as they have for many audiences and generations alike. The lyrics, images, concepts, and narratives explored within these pages are words I turn(ed) to for comfort, for solace, for understanding, for catharsis, for healing. I tune into their rationales to aid in my progression and movement through the world. These Black women (music artists') performances and lessons reverberate within me as they continue demonstrating the same strands of care, resistance, survival, and liberation threaded throughout this work.

While the goal of this book has been amplification, to magnify the generational work Black women have been putting in for centuries, I am still trying to formulate more inclusive and perhaps more concrete responses to my lingering questions and questions that I am continuously tasked with answering: Why should academia continue to pay attention to (early) Black feminist rhetoricians and how can we better incorporate their contributions? What is the payoff for investing in approaches that "care more" about Black women and their public intellectual frameworks? What can be gained by resituating these frames at the precipice of other rhetorical venues or within multiliteracy and multimedia contexts like sound? How are we to understand the materialized sound being transmitted as knowledge across media, space, and time when Black women inhabit (harsh) public and sonic spheres? In what ways can (and do) gender-nonconforming sonic rhetorics amplify similar social justice pedagogies filtered through these pages? I have also, undoubtedly, begun posing new questions as I come to this book's close. I moved to Canada amid writing this book and have witnessed small differences in Black Canadian languages, literacies, and politics, so I am also wondering how this process of knowledge-making in sound and through the sonic mutates across various geopolitical iterations. In what ways does land and nation (un)making shape the sonic soundscapes that Black women inhabit, cultivate, and in/form? Indeed, more collaborative work must be done on a transnational level to keep caring for Black women/Black bodies across borders.

To answer questions found within this book, I intentionally listened with my body to what these Black women (music artists)—as well as the women in my family—have taught me, but I know more investigation needs to be taken up. Pritchard argues that literacy practices often parallel the consistent manipulation and upholding of the fantastical master narrative. This dominant and discursive practice also incurs harm and violence to voices, literacies, and knowledges deemed marginal like Black LGBTQ communities and respective histories. Pritchard asserts that "Literacy is also implicated in historical erasure in that it can also occur through oral and other nonprint texts. Historical erasure of Black LGBTQ history is literacy normativity because such erasures suppress the life, history, culture, contributions of those positioned outside normativity on the basis of racialized gender and sexuality" (104). I position this work as an attempt to decode those intersectional rhetorics of language, discourse, and identity that are fused between the oral and written knowledges, literacies, and rhetorics hopefully working against what Pritchard has so eloquently identified. But, even in my attempts to not contribute or extend the same harms noted above, I dare say I could've done more to prevent it. I do focus primarily on cisgendered Black women in America, and I don't engage enough with sexuality as a factor in my analysis even when I do address queer Black women like Latifah or Sister Rosetta Tharpe or the homophobic language of Billie Holiday. Undoubtedly more research beyond the scope of my chapters is needed to carry on these fruitful methods for queering subjectivities.

Nevertheless, this initial work does hold significance for future research. I tried to recognize how capitalism influences and supports antiBlack practices in recording companies in chapter 1. In chapter 2, I argued ways sound and visual images combat evolutions of the "changing same" with hope and innovation. And, while chapter 3 demonstrated that Black grammatical temporality can communicate rhetorical agency in sound, chapter 4 relieved us (to some degree) of a sense of everlasting frustration by highlighting the intentional care behind audibly transmitted words or conversational talk. Taken together, I wanted to focus on the temporality of Black women's sonic rhetorics because I see the value in this work; I believe investigating Black women's sound more broadly is important enough to take up space and stand on its own.

While this work may be too "safe" in its analysis for some, it may even be too unconventional, too blurred in its disciplinary, "commonplace" dialogues for others. Maybe we can reorient some of those discussions—I hope we do. Black women's generational sonic rhetorics can be conceptualized through sonic applications, as I have mapped out here, and we can continue complicating Black women (music artists') generational sonic rhetorics to get more nuanced understandings of the expansive networks we can mobilize for individual and collective change and care. I hope this work spurs some of the conversations that are coming and trying to change how we are represented in our fields and elsewhere.

Since I began this journey with *Lemonade*, it seems only fitting that I end with a line from Beyoncé's husband's grandmother, who inspired the album and so many Black women and girls around the world: "I was served lemons, so I made lemonade." This saying signifies my own investment in caring for Black women's sonic rhetorics by writing this book. This pithy advice encompasses our long-standing traditions of "making a way outa no way" and our everlasting attempts of manufacturing agency in even the most quotidian acts. I hope this reverberating saying, along with the messages found within these chapters, continues inspiring the next generations of scholars and readers and offers a space to take more care of Black women's sonic rhetorics.

Notes

Introduction

1. My use of the term "Black" in relation to (but not limited by) the American context and histories in the introduction, and throughout this book, is not meant to erase the local and global differences among people of African descent and heritage. I position Blackness as a central and dynamic phenomenon—one that mirrors the ubiquitous transmission of sound, image, and music—as an ongoing, resonating reference point for individual and collective understandings of identity. Additionally, I opt for the term "Black" to align my work with the ongoing work of my predecessors and other scholars who fight for the ability to be seen, heard, and be in any context that attempts to erase our intersectional humanity. This legacy of/for freedom is not solely restricted to an American (or even North American) context. Many of these Black women (music artists) named throughout this book traveled to other countries, partnered with Pan-African movements, and have roots all across the diaspora. Their experiences, histories, and vulnerabilities frame the ways in which they operate and invoke agency; it is from their contributions that I find myself following their lead. I have thought a lot about the use of the term "Black" and, in this attempt, tried to correlate the breadth of this term with its central positioning in the book rather than isolate Black women's experiences as "exceptional" occurrences that don't speak to one another. I am very cognizant of how "Black" can universalize individuals' experiences, but, at the same time, I hoped to highlight common threads of anti-Blackness around the world that many communities may face by opting for the broader, connective moniker. To not use the term "Black" because I am largely positioning myself within a US (and somewhat Canadian) context would devalue the overarching point of my (and other's) arguments—that Black women and girls have a long, shared history of how to call for freedom, liberation, survival, and health: rhetorically and otherwise. To pigeonhole Blackness in this work simply as being Black in America would also downplay how I see and understand my

own positioning in the world. Hopefully, this use of the term orients readers to the broad applications and uses of rhetorical methodologies and allows readers to feel more comfortable about accepting the elasticity and dynamic feature of ties that bind communities of Black folks while also leaving space to find themselves (potentially) in the taught threads of socially constructed identity markers.

2. Putting this into a contemporary perspective, Sister Rosetta Tharpe (a queer Black woman who was the mother of rock and roll) had a net worth of roughly $1 to $2 million by today's standards; Dylan sold all his recording rights to Sony for $300 million.

Chapter 1

1. See Bettina Love's *We Want to Do More Than Survive: Abolitionist Teaching and the Pursuit of Educational Freedom* pp. 34–39.

2. Sharecropping was an extra-legal practice of abuse in the United States from 1877 to 1955.

3. Lexicon "is a mental dictionary, the vocabulary that one has stored in the brain" (Rowe and Levine 4).

4. Coined by Moya Bailey, misogynoir refers to "the uniquely co-constitutive racialized and sexist violence that befalls Black women" (2021).

5. Prosody, as it is used in this context, is a linguistic measurement of sound. For further discussions, see chapter 3.

6. Black grammar, broadly, refers to an alternative method for meaning-making that centers Blackness. For further discussions, see chapter 3.

7. Within political philosophies, "liberal" or "liberalism" generally refers to the support of individual rights.

8. See Greenfield 19.

9. Munir Ertegun was the ambassador of the Republic of Turkey to the United States in the late 1930s and 1940s and lived in Washington, DC. This family's social status afforded Ahmet Ertegun with access to influential policy makers, business entrepreneurs, and wealthy family friends. As a boy, Ahmet Ertegun attended Landon School in Bethesda, Maryland—an affluent, all-male private school. He enjoyed a relatively stable life until his father died of a heart attack in November 1944. After his father passed, Ahmet Ertegun's mother and sister decided to return to Turkey while he and his brother, Neshui, stayed in the United States. His brother eventually moved to Los Angeles, and Ahmet decided to stay in the Northeast and attend school. He studied at Howard University for his undergraduate degree and then enrolled in Georgetown University for a graduate degree in medieval philosophy, which he did not acquire. While in college, he found himself drawn to Black music and culture. He and his brother collected

records and enjoyed listening, watching, and interacting with Black musical life for years, ultimately providing a foundation for his business venture.

10. American Federation of Musicians changed their name in 1900 to American Federation of Musicians of the United States and Canada.

11. Atlantic was able to re-record and produce this song because the original label, Harlem Records, went out of business in addition to having a signed contract by McGhee, reportedly.

12. In terms of the 2021 US economy, this profit of $10 would equate to $116.21 under current conditions.

13. "The US Copyright Act of 1909 created the first compulsory mechanical license stipulating royalty payments be paid by the user of a composer's work. Unfortunately, the law left out the professional musicians who bring a composer's ideas to life" ("125 Years"). The US Copyright Act of 1909 states that if an applicant receives a copyright, then they also receive five exclusive provisions to "print, reprint, publish, copy, and vend the copyrighted work" of their own volition; "[t]o translate the copyrighted work into other languages or dialects, or make any version thereof" even if it is in another genre of text than the original; "[t]o deliver or authorize the delivery of the copyrighted work in public for profit," particularly in the form of copied material; and "[t]o perform the copyrighted work publicly for profit if it be a musical composition and for the purpose of public performance for profit." Section € of this law is especially relevant to this chapter, as it states that "shall include only compositions published and copyrighted after this Act goes into effect, and shall not include the works of foreign author or composer unless the foreign state or nation of which such author or composer is a citizen or subject grants, either by treaty, convention, agreement, or law, to citizens of the United States similar rights" Additionally, "And provided further, and as a condition of extending the copyright control to such mechanical reproductions, That whenever the owner of a musical copyright has used or permitted or knowingly acquiesced in the use of the copyrighted work upon the parts of the instrument serving to reproduce mechanically the musical work, any other person may make similar use of the copyrighted work upon the payment to the copyright proprietor of a royalty of two cents on each part manufactured . . . the manufacturer shall furnish, a report under oath on the twentieth day of each month on the number of parts of instruments manufactured during the previous month." To make clear, "The payment of the royalty provided for by this section shall free the articles or devices for which such royalty has been paid from further contribution to the copyright except in case of public performance for profit" (par. 5–35). In sum, a royalty is a fee paid to the creator of the work in question any time the work is duplicated and dispersed publicly.

14. Sonic labor is the work of sound. In other words, it is the energy and mechanisms needed to produce sound, including the voice.

15. Brown theorizes what comes to be known as "Jane Crow"—a term coined by Pauli Murry. Brittney Cooper expounds on Murry's influential activism and legal career, which served as the foundation for this term, in *Beyond Respectability: The Intellectual Thought of Race Women*. Cooper wrote that "Jane Crow also named a sociospatial race and gender formation that shaped Black women as knowledge producers and intellectual leaders. Whereas intersectional approaches have always sought to make Black women socially and juridically legible, Jane Crow exposed the ways in which the culture of legal institutions in the Civil Rights era" (102) blatantly ignored the multiple factors compounding upon raced and gendered bodies as a way of upholding legally practices governing citizens' rights and freedoms.

Chapter 2

1. As I noted in the previous chapter, the "sound" is a quantifiable aspect of some audible moment, calculating attributes like pitch, tone, or dialect for voice; the "sonic" is how such attributes are used to meet an end goal. Therefore, the phrase "Strange Fruit" sonic rhetorics is intended to focus on how the song "Strange Fruit" became a moment and method for resisting antiBlack violence.

2. In America, lynching was only recently made illegal in 2020.

3. To encompass the various renderings of lynching over the centuries that Ore outlines, I use lynching(s) as a descriptive shorthand. This is not to truncate the social and/or judicial manipulations of Black life (in America), but to emphasize the multiple ways in which Black life is systematically eradicated.

4. According to Erick Borg, "John Swales, an influential analyst of written communication, described discourse communities as groups that have goals or purposes, and use communication to achieve these goals" (398).

5. In *A Red Record*, Wells describes the change in the white South's reasoning for lynching over time as white defensiveness grew: (1) protecting themselves and communities from "race riots" to (2) protecting their (read: white) way of life within the country to (3) protecting white female respectability (76–78).

6. I refer to R. Murray Schafer's notion of the "soundscape" here. However, rather than use his definition of a soundscape that is "our sonic environment, the ever-present array of noises with which we all live" (1994), I imagine a soundscape as "our sonic environment" that not only embraces the frequencies that create life but also creates a social ecology that is felt or embodied.

7. "Convict photos are a genre of identification photography that Susanne Regener describes as 'compelled photos'—images taken without the permission of their subjects" (Campt 75).

8. Meeropol was a white Jewish man from New York who felt passionately about civil rights even during the height of McCarthyism. Meeropol's involvement

in/with the development of "Strange Fruit" sonic rhetorics made New York lawmakers and others uncomfortable. Blair reports, "In 1940, Meeropol was called to testify before a committee investigating communism in public schools. They wanted to know whether the American Communist Party had paid him to write the song. They had not" ("The Strange Story of the Man Behind 'Strange Fruit' "). It was in this sociocultural and political climate, and shortly after Meeropol's questioning, that Meeropol and his wife, Anne, adopted the two sons of Ethel and Julius Rosenberg, who had been executed by the US government in 1953 for espionage, after having meet the young boys at W. E. B. Du Bois' Christmas party.

9. Petchauer defines this as "As an amalgamation of the words *entertainment* and *education*, it refers to a process during which people learn or have their consciousness raised as a secondary or simultaneous result of listening to music for entertainment or enjoyment. More broadly, it refers to education that happens indirectly or as an implication of an activity" (72).

10. In *We Want to Do More Than Survive: Abolitionist Teaching and the Pursuit of Educational Freedom*, Bettina Love contextualizes "grit" by pointing out that "[t]he Character Lab defines grit as 'perseverance and passion for long-term goals' " but challenges the (for profit) educational system's over-reliance on assessment, arguing that "I take issue with this line of research focused on dark children's behavior by way of examining their character 'strengths' and 'weaknesses' because we live in a racist, sexist, Islamophobic, patriarchal, homophobic, transphobic, and xenophobic world where grit is not enough to fight these systems. Yes, it is needed, but to insist that dark children need, do not have, and can function on these characteristics alone is misleading, naïve, and dangerous" (72–73).

11. The "bootstraps" motif was originally made popular in American literature, as mentioned in *Critical Survey of American Literature*, by Horatio Alger Jr. (McGee, "Horatio Alger, Jr.," 53–58).

12. This "making something of one's self" does not always necessarily adhere to carefully crafted notions of respectability, which could make itself into cannon fodder for circumlocutions of harmful stereotypes and classist divisions. Particularly in terms of sound, what is expected as a norm for Black sound/Black music often becomes translated into a quantifying process that prepackages Blackness respective to a genre of sound; this siloing also makes it easier to promote a "respectable" type of sound for public consumption and, ultimately, appropriation by largely white, middle-class consumers.

13. "Emotion picture" has been described by Rap Genius as a narrative film that includes an embedded accompanying musical album.

14. Brooks, McGee, and Schoellman position sankofarration within a speculative discourse: "John Jennings coined the term sankofarration and defines it as a conflation of Sankofa and narration, a cosmological episteme that centers the act of claiming the future as well as the past. Jennings is specifically expanding upon a central notion of Afrofuturism—that the Western construct of time as

linear is a fallacy. In sankofarration, time is cyclical" and it "rejects the idea of enslavement as the primogenitor of Black horror" (238–39).

15. A byte is traditionally understood as a unit of digital information. Like the proteins in our DNA, the byte is a referent for coding specific characteristics.

16. Lillian Smith, a white feminist from Georgia, wrote *Strange Fruit, A Novel* in 1944.

Chapter 3

1. Building on Brittney Cooper's lecture, Carey points our methods of delay in reference to "the lived realities of racism or the slow speed of racial equity, and practices such as gentrification and restrictive voting laws that displace and disadvantage future generations," which "converge into a culture of hostility that pushes equity for a group further out of reach. These legal practices of delay and social forms of displacement" ("Necessary Adjustments" 270).

2. For Mills, "The Racial Contract is that set of formal or informal agreements or meta-agreements . . . between the members of one subset of [white] humans . . . to categorize the remaining subset of humans as 'nonwhite' and of different and inferior moral status, subpersons, so that they have subordinate civil standing in white or white-ruled polities the whites either already inhabit or establish or in transactions as aliens with these polities, and the moral and juridical rules normally regulating the behavior of whites in their dealings with nonwhites or apply only in qualified form . . . but in any case the general purpose of the Contract is always the differential privileging of the whites as a group with respect to the nonwhites as a group, the exploitation of their bodies, land, and resources, and the denial of equal socioeconomic opportunities to them" (11). In other words, the racial contract is both the said and unsaid regulatory policies that aim to establish and keep (and extend if possible) a system of hierarchy where whites are positioned as exemplar.

3. To account for such an interdisciplinary process, I bridge work from rhetorical theory, Black feminist theory, queer theory, and linguistics as a means for investigating Black language on an aspectual and sonic level. Actually, I find linguistic approaches to prosody as essential to my analysis here because it offers me a method for interpreting sound as part of (rhetorical) language; I find that linguistics offers a particularly helpful vocabulary for describing why these songs make rhetorical sense. Unpacking the linguistic components, or vocabulary, can, indeed, lead us to new interpretations of whole songs and retune our frequencies to sound. My hope in connecting and then applying these theoretical paradigms across time and genre is to provide a better understanding of Black women's rhetorical use of sound as means for asserting agency at different kinds of times and to open doors a little bit more for further comprehensive exploration into

Black women's contributions to sonic rhetoric. Moreover, I organize my analysis of these sonic performances not by chronological order, but by rhetorical grouping to emphasize the generational means for cultivating agency through sound. In doing this, I reconsider the implications of applying an embodied sonic framework to a more nuanced grammar, one that communicates the various ways Black women can employ rhetoric through sound. My hope in laying out this framework is to demonstrate possibilities for reimagining ways we can understand Black women's rhetoric as ingenious and creative measures geared toward agency and liberation—even in the smallest of places where sound is the primary escape.

4. Sonority is generally understood as the volume or amplitude of speech sounds in relation to pitch, stress, and duration or length of soundwave for the respective "note."

5. Prosody, from a linguistic standpoint, is concerned with patterns of larger speech elements or units such as intonation, tone, stress, and rhythm.

6. "In addition to being identified as an "auxiliary" or a "helping" verb, this linguistic phenomenon can also be annotated or referred to as "invariant" *be,* "unconjugated" *be,* or more generally, the "copula" and written as "bees," "be's," or "beez"—as in Minaj's linguistic remix.

7. Charles E. DeBose relates *tense* "to the part of the meaning of a sentence that expresses the time of a predicated event with reference to the time at which the sentence is spoken. . . . *Modality* . . . may be thought of as the part of the meaning of a sentence that expresses a degree of doubt or uncertainty about the truth of a predicated event, or makes its truth contingent upon circumstances. . . . *Aspect* refers to how a predicated event is viewed as ongoing or completed at a particular point in time, or recurring in a manner expressed by adverbial forms like usually and on occasion" (371–72).

8. "Fuck It Up to the Tempo" is a reference to Lizzo's song "Tempo."

9. Recorded at 115 bpm (https://songbpm.com/@aretha-franklin/respect-393ee2c9-501b-4e42-beb1-859658c9a1c1).

10. "Respect. Aretha Franklin" has suggested that listeners play this tune at 120 bpm.

11. Defined as any tempo of 120 bpm or more.

12. Pritha Prasad recently defined this superficial engagement as "idealized coalitions [that] are characterized by uneven, non-reciprocal, and usually idealized/imaginary collective relationships between groups with differential positions of power and vulnerability, and crop up exclusively in response to acute anti-Black racialized violence" ("Coalition Is Not Done in Your Home'" par. 4).

13. Here I am referring to aspect in both layman's terms—which is a characteristic or feature of something—and as a linguistic feature—which is the denotation of the verb used to communicate how an event, action, or state is expressed over time. This is to say, then, the feature of sonic rhetoric and the tense of sonic rhetoric do much to capture an audience's attention.

14. In July 2017, US Representative for California's 43rd congressional district, Maxine Waters, sonically interrupted yet another display of oppressive white supremacist rhetoric by repeating the phrase "reclaiming my time." In this televised House Financial Services Committee hearing meeting, Waters asked Steve Mnuchin, then treasury secretary, about his office's absent response to Waters's inquiry of then-President Donald Trump's connections to/with Russian banks. When the time came to answer Waters, Mnuchin responded by saying, "So, uh, ranking member Waters, first of all, let me thank you for your service to California. Being a resident of California, I appreciate everything that you. . ." Waters quickly shut down Mnuchin's niceties, which cloaked his attempt to co-opt time, by interrupting his loquacious, empty answer. Waters interjected, "thank you for your compliments on how great I am, but I don't want to waste my time on me," ultimately asking him to "go straight to the answer," which, of course, he did not. Perturbed by not being in control of both the time designated for speaking and the public narrative, Mnuchin turned his attention to the chairman [Hensarling] of the committee, ignoring Waters's procedural calls of action, and quietly requested the chairman's help to get back some control of the situation. Addressing the chairman, Mnuchin pleaded, "Mr. Chairman, I thought when you read the rules you acknowledged that I shouldn't be interrupted and that I would have the opportunity . . . ." Without missing a beat, Waters again repeatedly announced "reclaiming my time" and informed Mnuchin that "what [the chairman] failed to tell you was when you're on my time, I can reclaim it. He left that out, so I am reclaiming my time. Will you please respond to the question?" ("Ranking Member Waters Q&A with Secretary Mnuchin—07/27/2017" 1:06–2:11).

15. Syntactical morphemes are word formation arrangements directing sentence constructions.

16. "John Jennings coined the term 'sankofarration' and defines it as a conflation of Sankofa and narration, a cosmological episteme that centers the act of claiming the future as well as the past. Jennings specifically expands upon a central notion of Afrofuturism—that the Western construct of time as linear is a fallacy. In sankofarration, time is cyclical" (Brooks, McGee, Scholleman 240).

Chapter 4

1. Materialized sound is the tangible ways information manifests in our daily lives. From songs to scripts, from posters to performances, materialized sounds are the documented messages we interpret once we receive information from the oral, the audible, and the embodied spheres; it is the transcripted sensation that recognizes the (un)said truth behind the message. Materialized sound is the resonating vibrations of information passed on, and it serves as the foundation for audible advice.

2. Vocal registers are typically understood as an arrangement of tones produced by the body (specifically in the larynx) as the vocal cords vibrate according to manipulative patterns often resulting in different voice registers (i.e., normal voice, creaky voice, high-pitched voice, or whistling). Here, I use vocal registers to amplify the kinds of manipulation the voice can undergo, emphasizing not only things like pitch but also medium (e.g., written text, spoken word, hushed speech, etc.).

3. More broadly, Lathan points out that "Royster identifies literacy as a sociocognitive acquisition" and says that "literacy 'is the ability to gain access to information and to use this information variously to articulate lives and experiences and also to identify, think through, refine and solve problems, sometimes complex problems, over time' (Traces 45). Brandt illuminates how individual acts of writing are connected to larger cultural, historical, social, and political systems (Literacy)" (qtd. in Lathan xxii). Similarly, Royster's and Brandt's definitions initiate a paradigm shift in composition studies through a methodology of recovering, while accounting for, the intersections of a material and cultural form of literacy activity. These theories' components of literacy as a social process, including multiple stages of participation, intertextual relations, and cultural knowledge, are ways to understand not only the social process of literacy but also its multi rhythmic nature as it functions in African American literacy activism" (Lathan xxii). For Lathan, "literacy [i]s a way of knowing, a process by which decoding and making meaning take place in social contexts: in other words, individual acts of composition . . . are attached to larger social systems" (Lathan 23).

4. "As a religious concept," Lathan writes, "gospel music is a synthesis of West African and African American culture, gospel expressions most often call to mind joy, hope, and expectation, including narratives that provide a sense of security" (xix).

5. "Hush harbors" are metaphysical, rhetorical third spaces—an interstitial moment—employed within African American rhetoric.

6. A rich and rigorous discussion of Black women's traditions of intellectual thought has been published by Brittney Cooper and addresses this legacy as one of "race women." For Cooper, "The term race woman has no uniform meaning. But it does name and help to make visible multiple generations of Black women who dedicated their lives to the Black freedom struggle, not only by theorizing and implementing programs of racial uplift but also by contesting limiting notions of Blackness and womanhood. In doing so, these women created a robust and enduring tradition of Black public intellectual work" (139).

7. Holiday listened, studied, and theorized her predecessors like Bessie Smith by reflecting on how music could move her. When Holiday was a teenager, she ran errands for nothing "less than a nickel or dime" while employed by Alice Dean and other girls who worked in Alice's "whorehouse" (9). Holiday recalls, "When it came time to pay me, I used to tell [Alice] she could keep the

money if she'd let me come up in her front parlor and listen to Louis Armstrong and Bessie Smith on her victrola" (9). It was in moments like these that Holiday learned how music, more or less, could be a rhetoric. She remembers listening to Pop's [Bessie Smith's longtime partner] "West End Blues" and critically engaging with his "scatting": "It was the first time I ever heard anybody sing without using any words . . . . it had plenty of meaning for me—just as much meaning as some of the other words that I didn't always understand. But the meaning used to change, depending on how I felt. Sometimes the record would make me so sad I'd cry up a storm. Other times the same damn record would make me so happy I'd forget about how much hard-earned money the session in the parlor was costing me" (9–10). While some of Holiday's recordings do include scatting, some of her other songs also incorporate Bessie Smith's penchant for big volume, which she learned by mimicking and listening to her predecessors. Within her own voice she developed a sonic, generational bridge between her predecessors and herself—and ultimately to other newcomers after her like Sara Vaughn and Lena Horne through her mentorship of the new generation.

8. Adam Banks describes the griot as "standing between tradition and future, holding the power to shape how both are seen/heard/felt/known[;] exhibiting mastery of techniques, but always knowing that techniques carry stories, arguments, ways of viewing the world, that the techniques arrange the texts, that every text carries even more stories, arguments, epistemologies" (3). For Banks, a griot is also "an archivist, a canon maker, time bender; someone with an encyclopedic knowledge of traditions, a searing and searching awareness of contemporary realities, and the beat-matching, text-bending abilities to synchronize traditions, present realities, and future visions in the future texts" (16).

9. Quintin Hoare and Geoffrey Nowell Smith, editors and translators of *Selections from the Prison Notebooks of Antonio Gramsci*, summarized Gramsci's perspective: "[t]he notion of 'the intellectuals' as a distinct social category independent of class is a myth. All men are potentially intellectuals in the sense of having an intellect and using it, but not all are intellectuals by social function . . . . In the first place there are the 'traditional' professional intellectuals, literary, scientific, and so-on, whose position in the interstices of society has a certain inter-class aura about it but derives ultimately from past and present class relations and conceals an attachment to various historical class formations. Secondly, there are the 'organic' intellectuals, the thinking and organising element of a particular fundamental social class. These organic intellectuals are distinguished less by their profession, which may be any job characteristic of their class, than by their function in directing the ideas and aspirations of the class which they organically belong." They also underlie [Gramsci's] study of history and particularly of the *Risorgimento,* in that the intellectuals, in the widest sense of the word, are seen by Gramsci as performing an essential meditating function in the struggle of class forces (Hoare and Smith 1; Gramsci 8–14). They also mention that "[t]he working class, like the bourgeoisie

before it, is capable of developing from within its ranks its own organic intellectuals, and the function of the political party, whether mass or vanguard, is that of channeling the activity of these organic intellectuals and providing a link between the class certain sections of the traditional intelligentsia. The organic intellectuals of the working class are defined on the one hand by their role in production and the organisation of work and on the other by their 'directive' political role, focused on the Party. It is through this assumption of conscious responsibility, aided by absorption of ideas and personnel from the more advanced bourgeois intellectual strata, that the proletariat can escape from defensive corporation and economism and advance toward hegemony" (Hoare and Smith 4).

10. Facilitating a coming to consciousness by sharing lived experiences has been called, by Cherríe Moraga and Gloria Anzaldúa, as "theory in the flesh" ("Entering the Lives of Others" 19).

11. Drawing on Christina Sharpe's work, Louis. M. Maraj defines *rhetorical reclamation* as "rhetorical acts (gestures, performances, language use, embodiment) do[ing] 'wake work' (Sharpe 2016); they draw on cultural histories, contexts, and traditions to suggest agency through re/asserting racialized identity in instances of fracture when white institutions stigmatize Blackness. Such reclamations respond to *white institutional defensiveness*, policies, and practices that posture tentatively (often in racially colorblind ways) so as to avoid causing racial stress for white individuals in institutional spaces" (16). Additionally, I've defined rhetorical reclamation as part of a Black feminist means for constructing agency, as it encourages a "radical feminist rhetorical practice which supports more marginalized voices that resist normalized constructions of identity by: (1) deconstructing foundational vocabulary; (2) instituting creative re/spelling of terms as a means for reclamation of terminology [or naming practices]; (3) emphasizing critical self-awareness or critical self-reflexivity to navigate contexts; (4) complicating shifting identities; and (5) transmitting intergenerational knowledge and literacies" (McGee, *Legacies of Black Womenhood in Blues, and Hip Hop: A Critique of Feminism, Sonic Rhetoric, and Language* 4).

12. As a theoretical model, audible advice translates Black feminist theoretical content and affirms our existence, minimizing what the Combahee River Collective refers to as the "feelings of craziness before coming conscious" (233).

13. Banfield defines "cultural codes" as "sets of principles, representations, practices, and conventions understood to be embraced by artistic community. These are cultural, ideological inscriptions of meaning conceived, created, and constructed, and then projected by performances which suggest that certain ways of being, thinking, looking, and styling are normative, preferable, and validated. They are reflective of ideas, and they project powerful images and imaginings that are sustaining and impressionable" (9).

14. See Bizzell and Herzberg's introductions to Christine de Pizan (540) and Madeline de Scudéry (761).

15. With this in mind, we often recognize cultural icons like Bessie Smith, Billie Holiday, Beyoncé and others as popularized counterparts to our (Black) literary foremothers/public intellectuals/activist/leaders/mentors who usher in paradigm shifts for/of agency and autonomy; these women are profoundly influential in our collective push toward social health and the betterment of Black (social) life. It is not uncommon for authors and artists to share the same rhetorical lineages that we saw when Latifah pointed out Maya Angelou's useful poem. These life lessons are archived and revolutionized as part of Black feminist communal, shared knowledge-making and disciplinary tactics.

16. See Pamela VanHaitsma's work "Gossip as Rhetorical Methodology for Queer and Feminist Historiography."

17. In a professional context, contemporary Woman of color feminist scholar Pirtha Prasad describes "backchannel pedagogies" as akin to gossip. She constructs "backchannel pedagogies" as divulging advice; she contextualizes this feminist methodology by unpacking messages she received as an emerging scholar that unfolded beyond the prying surveillance of white eyes and ears, which helped her "safely" navigate the oppressive terrain and deadly personal and professional attacks within academia ("Backchannel Pedagogies" par. 10). Additionally, Prasad mentions, "*backchannel pedagogies* with the potential to both deflect the racial forgetting that underpins ongoing calls for white teaching/learning moments and make possible alternative temporal logics to white institutionality. In refusing a futurity that recruits us into the teaching moments that repackage racial injury as abstract pedagogical inspiration for whiteness to "do better," backchannel pedagogies highlight the transformative power of the spaces that exist "in but not of" white institutions (Harney and Moten 26): hushed advice during office hours, stealthy text messages at conferences, shady memes shared on Twitter, sarcastic notes I write to my future self in the margins of books. These moments of joyful, silent rage are often ephemeral in the face of a white racial forgetting that continues to force us into unpaid, unrecognized pedagogical labor in the form of diversity service, university committees, and infinitely generous emails to white colleagues" ("Backchannel Pedagogies" par. 12).

18. Lanehart defines "Ideology of Emancipation" as part of Black women's generational rhetorical and literacy prowess, stating that "The Ideology of Emancipation purports: (1) autonomy; (2) empowerment due to the development of critical thinking; and (3) emancipation (real or symbolic) because of the control one will be able to achieve as a shareholder in what can constitute or lead to real power. In this view, literacy is empowering, transformative, emancipatory, and self-enlightening. It inspires confidence. It is emancipatory through revolution" (7).

Works Cited

"125 Years: Musicians Staying Stronger Together." *American Federation of Musicians*, https://www.afm.org/125-years-afm-history/. Accessed 11 Nov. 2021.

Franklin, Aretha, with Lauryn Hill. "A Rose Is Still a Rose." *A Rose Is Still a Rose*, Arista, 1998.

Abdul, Paula. *Forever Your Girl*, Virgin Records, 1988.

Adams, Toney E., et al. *Autoethnography: Understanding Qualitative Research*. Oxford UP, 2014.

Akom, A. A. "Critical Hip Hop Pedagogy as a Form of Liberatory Praxis." *Issue 1: Hip Hop and Social Justice Education*, special issue of *Equity & Excellence in Education*, vol. 42, 2009, pp. 52–66.

Alexander, Michelle. *The New Jim Crow: Mass Incarceration in the Age of Colorblindness*. Rev. ed., The New Press, 2012.

Alim, H. Samy. *Roc the Mic Right: The Language of Hip Hop Culture*. Routledge 2006.

Alim, H. Samy, and Geneva Smitherman. *Articulate While Black: Barack Obama, Language, and Race in the U.S.* Oxford UP, 2012.

African American Policy Forum. "#SAYHERNAME," https://www.aapf.org/sayhername. Accessed Jan. 2022.

Anderson, Tim. "'Buried under the Fecundity of His Own Creations': Reconsidering the Recording Bans of the American Federation of Musicians, 1942–1944 and 1948." *American Music*, vol. 22, no. 2, Summer 2004, pp. 231–69, https://www.jstor.org/stable/3593004. Accessed 11 Nov. 2021.

Anzaldúa, Gloria. "Now Let Us Shift . . . Conocimiento . . . Inner Work, Public Acts." *This Bridge We Call Home: Radical Visions for Transformation*, edited by AnaLouise Keating, Routledge, 2002, pp. 540–76.

Bailey, Moya. *Misogynoir Transformed: Black Women's Digital Resistance*. New York UP, 2021.

Baker, Houston A. *Blues, Ideology, and Afro-American Literature: A Vernacular Theory*. U of Chicago P, 1987.

Baker, Nancy Kovaleff. "Abel Meeropol (a.k.a. Lewis Allan): Political Commentator and Social Conscience." *American Music*, vol. 20, no. 1, 2002, pp. 25–79.

Banfield, William C. *Cultural Codes, Makings of A Black Music Philosophy: An Interpretative History from Spirituals to Hip Hop*. The Scarecrow P, 2010.

Banks, Adam J. *Digital Griots: African American Rhetoric in a Multimedia Age*. Southern Illinois UP, 2011.

Baraka, Amiri [LeRoi Jones]. "The Changing Same: R&B and New Black Music." *Black Music*, De Capo P, 1998, pp. 180–211.

Bhabha, Homi. "The Commitment to Theory." *New Formations*, no. 5, 1988, pp. 5–23.

Bizzell, Patricia, and Bruce Herzberg. "Introduction" [Renaissance Rhetoric]." *The Rhetorical Tradition: Readings from Classical Times to the Present*. 2nd ed., Bedford/St. Martin, 2001, pp. 555–80.

Beitler, Lawrence. Photograph [of Lynching Scene in Marion, Indiana]. 1930. Series 7-9. H.P. Dexheimer/Lawrence H. Beitler collection ca. 1897-ca. 1930. Indiana Historical Society Library Visual Collection P 0379, Indiana Historical Society, https://indianahistorylibrary.on.worldcat.org/search?queryString=au%3D%22Beitler%2C%20Lawrence%20H%22&clusterResults=true&groupVariantRecords=false. Accessed 22 Mar. 2023.

Blair, Elizabeth. "The Strange Story of the Man Behind 'Strange Fruit.'" *Morning Edition* from NPR, 5 Sept. 2012, https://www.npr.org/2012/09/05/158933012/the-strange-story-of-the-man-behind-strange-fruit. Accessed 20 July 2020.

Blow, Kurtis. "The Breaks." *Kurtis Blow*, Mercury, 1980.

Borg, Erik. "Discourse Community." *ELT Journal*, vol. 54, no. 7, 2003, pp. 398–400.

Borloryn, Robin M., and Mark P. Orbe, editors. *Critical Autoethnography: Intersecting Cultural Identities in Everyday Life*. Routledge, 2014.

Bradley, Regina. *Boondock Kollage: Stories from the Hip Hop South*. Peter Lang Publishing, 2017.

———. *Chronicling Stankonia: The Rise of the Hip-Hop South*. U of North Carolina P, 2021.

Branstetter, Heather Lee. "A Mining Town Needs Brothels": Gossip and the Rhetoric of Sex Work in a Wild West Mining Community." *Rhetoric Society Quarterly*, vol. 46, no. 5, pp. 381–409.

Braverman Vishay, and Stiglitz, Joseph E. "Sharecropping and the Interlinking of Agrarian Markets." *American Economic Review*, vol. 72, no. 4, Sept. 1982, pp. 695–715.

Brooks, Daphne A. *Liner Notes for the Revolution: The Intellectual Life of Black Feminist Sound*. Belknap P of Harvard UP, 2021.

Brooks, Kinitra D., et al. "Speculative Sankofarration: Haunting Black Women in Contemporary Horror Fiction." *Obsidian: Literatures & Arts in the African Diaspora*, vol. 42, no. 1, 2016, pp. 237–48.

Brown, Mary Ellen. "Motley Moments: Soap Opera, Carnival, Gossip and the Power of the Utterance." *Television and Women's Culture: The Politics of the Popular*, edited by Mary Ellen Brown, Sage Publications, 1990, pp. 183–200.

Brown, Ruth, with Andrew Yule. *Miss Rhythm: The Autobiography of Ruth Brown, Rhythm and Blues Legend.* Donald I. Fine Books, 1996.

Brown, Ruth Nicole, and Chamara Jewel Kwakye, editors. *Wish to Live: The Hip-hop Feminism Pedagogy Reader.* Peter Lang, 2012.

Browne, Simone. *Dark Matters: On the Surveillance of Blackness.* Duke UP, 2015.

Bryant, Jacqueline K. "The Literary Foremother: An Embodiment of the Rhetoric of Freedom." *African American Rhetoric(s): Interdisciplinary Perspectives*, edited by Elaine Richardson and Ronald L. Jackson II, Southern Illinois UP, 2004, pp. 73–85.

Burke, Kenneth. "The Four Master Tropes." *The Kenyon Review*, vol. 3, no. 4, 1941, pp. 421–38.

Campt, Tina. *Listening to Images.* Duke UP, 2017.

Carby, Hazel. "It Jus Be's That Way Sometimes: The Sexual Politics of Women's Blues*." *The Jazz Cadence of American Culture*, edited by Robert G. O'Meally, Columbia UP, 1993, pp. 470–83.

"Cardi B Defends Trademarking 'Okurrr.'" ET Canada. *YouTube*, 22 Mar. 2019, https://www.youtube.com/watch?v=mZrmwXqmRek. Accessed 7 Mar. 2021.

Carey, Tamika L. *Rhetorical Healing: The Reeducation of Contemporary Black Womanhood.* State U of New York P, 2016.

———. "Necessary Adjustments: Black Women's Rhetorical Impatience." *Rhetoric Review*, vol. 39, no. 3, 2020, pp. 269–86.

Chang, Heewon. *Autoethnography As Method.* Left Coast Press, 2008.

Chang, Jeff. *Can't Stop Won't Stop: A History of the Hip-Hop Generation.* Picador, 2005.

Chávez, Karma. "The Body: An Abstract and Actual Rhetorical Concept." *Issue 3: Keywords: A Glossary of the Pasts and Futures of the Rhetoric Society of America*, special issue of *Rhetoric Society Quarterly*, vol. 48, 2018, pp. 242–50.

Cheng, William. *Just Vibrations: The Purpose of Sounding Good.* U of Michigan P, 2016.

Christian, Barbara. "A Race for Theory." *New Black Feminist Criticism, 1985–2000, Barbara Christian*, edited by Gloria Bowles, et al., U of Illinois P, 2007, pp. 40–50.

Cohen, Cathy. "Punks, Bulldaggers, and Welfare Queens: The Radical Potential of Queer Politics." *GLQ: A Journal of Lesbian & Gay Studies*, vol. 3, 1997, pp. 437–65.

Collins, Patricia Hill. *Black Feminist Thought: Knowledge, Consciousness, and the Politics of Empowerment.* Unwin Hyman, 1990.

———. *Fighting Words: Black Women and the Fight for Justice.* U of Minnesota P, 1998.

Cooper, Anna Julia. *Anna J. Cooper (Anna Julia), 1858–1964. A Voice from the South.* U of North Carolina at Chapel Hill, 2000, docsouth.unc.edu/church/cooper/cooper.html.

Cooper, Brittney. "The Racial Politics of Time." TED: Ideas Worth Spreading. *YouTube*, 14 Mar. 2017, https://www.youtube.com/watch?v=kTz52RW_bD0. Accessed 22 Sept. 2021

———. *Beyond Respectability: The Intellectual Thought of Race Women*. U of Illinois P, 2017.

D'Angelo, Frank. J. "The Rhetoric of Ekphrasis." *JAC*, vol. 18, no. 3, 1998, pp. 439–47.

Dance, Daryl Cumber. *Honey Hush!: An Anthology of African American Women's Humor*. W. W. Norton, 1998.

Davis, Angela Y. *Blues Legacies and Black Feminism: Gertrude "MA" Rainey, Bessie Smith, and Billie Holiday*. Vintage Books, 1998.

———. "Angela Davis Introduces Billie Holiday's "Strange Fruit," performed by Kim Nalley and Tammy Hall." *YouTube*, uploaded by SFJazz, 12 June 2020, https://www.youtube.com/watch?v=SvqHpJDS19E. Accessed 23 Feb. 2021.

Davis, Olga Idriss. "Theorizing African American Women's Discourse: The Public and Private Spheres of Experience." *Centering Ourselves: African American Feminist and Womanist Studies of Discourse*, edited by Marsha Houston and Olga Idriss Davis, Hamilton Press, 2002, pp. 35–52.

———. "A Black Woman as Rhetorical Critic: Validating Self and Violating the Space of Otherness." *Women's Studies in Communication*, vol. 21, no. 1, 1998, pp. 77–89.

DeBose, Charles E. "The Systematic Marking of Tense, Modality, and Aspect in African American Language." *The Oxford Handbook of African American Language*, edited by Sonja Lanehart, Oxford UP, 2015, pp. 371–86.

de Veaux, Alexis. *Don't Explain: A Song of Billie Holiday*. Harper & Rowe, 1980.

DeGruy, Joy. *Post Traumatic Slave Syndrome: America's Legacy of Enduring Injury and Healing*. Joy DeGruy Publications, 2005.

Edgar, Amanda Nell. "Speaking Identities." *Culturally Speaking: The Rhetoric of Voice and Identity in A Mediated Culture*, by Amanda Nell Edgar, Ohio State UP, 2019, pp. 1–23.

Eidsheim, Nina Sun. *The Race of Sound: Listening, Timbre & Vocality in African American Music*. Duke UP, 2019.

Elliot, Melissa. *Iconography*, Atlantic, 2018.

———. "I'm Better (feat. Lamb)." *YouTube*, uploaded by Missy Elliot. 26 Jan. 2017, https://www.youtube.com/watch?v=TwyPsUd9LAk. Accessed 23 Feb. 2021.

Emdin, Christopher. *Urban Science Education for the Hip-Hop Generation*. Brill-Sense. 2010.

Feldstein, Ruth. " 'I Don't Trust You Anymore': Nina Simone, Culture and Black Activism in the 1960s." *The Journal of American History*, Mar. 2005, pp. 1349–79.

Fields, Liz. "The Story Behind Nina Simone's Protest Song, 'Mississippi Goddam.'" How It Feels to Be Free Series, 14 Jan. 2021, PBS.org, https://www.pbs.org/wnet/americanmasters/the-story-behind-nina-simones-protest-song-mississippi-goddam/16651/. Accessed 23 Feb. 2021.

Fleetwood, Nicole R. *On Racial Icons: Blackness and the Public Imagination*. Rutgers UP, 2015.
Franklin, Aretha. "Aretha Franklin—Respect [1967] (Aretha's Original Version)." *YouTube*, uploaded by Tatan Brown, 17 Oct. 2008, https://www.youtube.com/watch?v=6FOUqQt3Kg0. Accessed 21 Mar. 2021.
Foster, Eric K. "Research on Gossip: Taxonomy, Methods, and Future Discussions." *Review of General Psychology*, vol. 8, no. 2, 2004, pp. 78–99.
Fuss, Diana. *Essentially Speaking: Feminism, Nature and Difference*. Routledge, 1989.
Gavins, Raymond. "Sharecropping." *The Cambridge Guide to African American History*. Cambridge UP, 2015, p. 251.
Gilyard, Keith, and Adam Banks. *On African-American Rhetoric*. Routledge, 2018.
"Grammy Hall of Fame Award." *Recording Academy Grammy Award*, 2023, https://www.grammy.com/awards/hall-of-fame-award#s. Accessed 22 Mar. 2023.
Gramsci, Antonio. *Selections from the Prison Notebooks of Antonio Gramsci*. International Publishers, 1971.
Griffin, Farah Jasmine. *If You Can't Be Free, Be A Mystery: In Search of Billie Holiday*. Random House, 2002.
Greenfield, Robert. *The Last Sultan: The Life and Times of Ahmet Ertegun*. Apple Books, 2011.
Hallagan, William. "Self-Selection by Contractual Choice and the Theory of Sharecropping." *Bell Journal of Economics*, vol. 9, 1978, pp. 344–54.
Hannah-Jones, Nikole. *The 1619 Project: A New Origin Story*. The New York Times, 2019.
Harrington, Richard. "Nina Simone, A Voice to Be Reckoned With." *The Washington Post*, 22 Apr. 2003, https://www.washingtonpost.com/archive/lifestyle/2003/04/22/nina-simone-a-voice-to-be-reckoned-with/e5663b51-d1af-4b8f-959f-295314c2519f/. Accessed 4 Mar. 2021.
Harris-Perry, Melissa V. *Sister Citizen: Shame, Stereotypes, and Black Women in America*. Yale UP, 2011.
Hartman, Saidiya. *Scenes of Subjugation: Terror, Slavery, and Self-Making in Nineteenth-Century America*. Oxford UP, 1997.
Hawk, Byron. *Resounding the Rhetorical: Composition as a Quasi-Object*. U of Pittsburgh P, 2018.
Hill, Lauryn. "Lauryn Hill—Doo-Wop (That Thing) (Official Video)." *YouTube*, uploaded by Ms. Lauryn Hill, 23 June 2010, https://www.youtube.com/watch?v=T6QKqFPRZSA. Accessed 4 Mar. 2021.
Hill, Marc Lamont, and Emery Pretchaur, editors. *Schooling Hip Hop: Expanding Hip-Hop Based Education across the Curriculum*. Teachers College P, 2013.
"History." *American Federation of Musicians*, https://www.afm.org/about/history/
Hoare, Quintin, and Geoffrey Nowell Smith, editors and translators. "The Intellectuals." *Selections From the Prison Notebooks of Antonio Gramsci*. 12th ed., International Publishers, 1995, pp. 1–5.
Holiday, Billie. "Strange Fruit," Commodore, 1939.

Holiday, Billie, and William Duffy. *Lady Sings the Blues*. 50th anniversary ed., Harlem Moon, 2006.

hooks, bell. *Ain't I A Woman: Black Women and Feminism*. South End Press, 1981.

Jackson, Janet. *Rhythm Nation 1814*, A&M Records, 1989.

Jackson, Michael. *Thriller*, Epic Records, 1984.

"Janelle Monáe—Who Is Cindi Mayweather?" Recording Academy, 2 Dec. 2014, https://www.grammy.com/grammys/videos/janelle-monae-who-cindi-mayweather. Accessed 18 Feb. 2021.

Jones, Charisse, and Kumea Shorter-Gooden. *Shifting: The Double Lives of Black Women in America*. Perennial, 2003.

Journet, Debra, et al. *Narrative Acts: Rhetoric, Race and Identity, Knowledge*. Hampton P, 2011.

Kaufman, Gil. "Cardi B's Attempt to Trademark 'Okurrr' Turned Down by U.S. Patent Office." *Billboard*, 2 July 2019, https://www.billboard.com/articles/columns/hip-hop/8518263/cardi-b-trademark-okurrr-turned-down-us-patent-office. Accessed 4 Mar. 2021.

Knowles-Carter, Beyoncé. *Lemonade*, Parkwood. 2016.

Knowles, Solange. *A Seat at the Table*, Columbia, 2016.

Knowles, Tina. "Tina Taught Me." *A Seat at the Table*, produced by Solange Knowles, Columbia, 2016.

Lathan, Rhea Estelle. *Freedom Writing: African American Civil Rights Literacy Activism, 1955–1967*. Conference on College Composition and Communication and National Council of Teachers of English, 2016.

Lamarre, Carl. "Every Song Ranked on Megan Thee Stallion's 'Good News': Critic's Picks." *Billboard*, 20 Nov. 2020, https://www.billboard.com/articles/columns/hip-hop/9487557/megan-thee-stallion-good-news-song-rankings/. Accessed 4 Mar. 2021.

Lanehart, Sonja. *Sista Speak!: Black Women Kinfolk Talk About Language and Literacy*. U of Texas P, 2002.

Liu, Ying, et al. "Effects of Musical Tempo on Musicians' and Non-Musicians' Emotional Experience When Listening to Music." *Frontiers in Psychology*, vol. 9, Nov. 2018, https://www.ncbi.nlm.nih.gov/pmc/articles/PMC6243583/pdf/fpsyg-09-02118.pdf. Accessed 4 Mar. 2021.

Lizzo. "Lizzo—Tempo (feat. Missy Elliott) [Official Video]." *YouTube,* uploaded by Lizzo Music, 26 July 2019, https://www.youtube.com/watch?v=Srq1FqFPwj0. Accessed 4 Mar. 2021.

Lordi, Emily J. *Black Resonance: Iconic Women Singers and African American Literature*. Rutgers UP, 2013.

———. *The Meaning of Soul: Black Music and Resilience Since the 1960s*. Duke UP, 2020.

Love, Bettina L. *Hip Hop's Li'l Sistas Speak: Negotiating Hip Hop Identities and Politics in the New South*. Peter Lang Publishing, 2012.

———. *We Want to Do More Than Survive: Abolitionist Teaching and the Pursuit of Educational Freedom*. Beacon P, 2019.

Mackey, Nathaniel. "The Changing Same: Black Music in the Poetry of Amiri Baraka." *boundary 2*, vol. 6, no. 2, 1978, pp. 355–86.

Mankarious, Sarah-Grace, and AJ Willingham. "How American Police Gear Up to Respond to Protests." *CNN*, https://edition.cnn.com/interactive/2020/07/us/police-gear-trnd/, 3 Aug. 2020. Accessed 11 Feb. 2021.

Maraj, Louis M. *Black or Right: Anti/Racist Campus Rhetorics*. Utah State UP, 2019.

McGee, Alexis. *Legacies of Black Womenhood in Blues, and Hip Hop: A Critique of Feminism, Sonic Rhetoric, and Language*. Aug. 2018. U of Texas at San Antonio, PhD dissertation.

———. "The Language of Lemonade: The Sociolinguistic and Rhetorical Strategies of Beyoncé's *Lemonade*." *The Lemonade Reader*, edited by Kinitra D. Brooks and Kameelah L. Martin, Routledge, 2019, pp. 55–68.

———. "Horatio Alger, Jr." *Critical Survey of American Literature*. 3rd ed., edited by Steven Kellman, vol. 1, Salem P, 2016, pp. 53–58.

McKittrick, Katherine. *Demonic Grounds: Black Women and the Cartographies of Struggle*. U of Minnesota P, 2006.

McWhorter, John. *All About the Beat: Why Hip Hop Can't Save Black America*. Gotham Books, 2008.

Meeropol, Abel. "Bitter Fruit." *The New York Teacher*. US Library of Congress. Jan. 1937, https://perspectives.ushmm.org/item/abel-meeropol-bitter-fruit. Retrieved 20 Mar. 2020.

Miller, Elizabeth Ellis. "Remembering Freedom Songs: Repurposing an Activists Genre." *College English*, vol. 81, no. 1, 2018, pp. 50–72.

Mills, Charles. *The Racial Contract*. Cornell UP, 1997.

Minaj, Nicki. "Nicki Minaj—Beez in the Trap ft. 2 Chainz." *YouTube*, uploaded by Nicki Minaj, 12 Dec. 2012, https://www.youtube.com/watch?v=yDwMsx6LSos. Accessed 8 Feb. 2021.

"Missy Elliott Is Just Better When It Comes to Making Music Videos," https://ambrosiaforheads.com/2017/01/missy-Elliottt-dancing-music-video/

"Missy Elliott Discusses Her Album 'Iconology' | Rap Rotation | Amazon Music." *YouTube*, uploaded by Amazon Music, 21 Oct. 2019, https://www.youtube.com/watch?v=R8W3l-dUp80. Accessed 21 Feb. 2020.

Moody, Joycelyn. Personal Communication. Black Feminist Theory [class introduction]. 2016, U of Texas at San Antonio.

Moraga, Cherríe, and Gloria Anzaldúa, editors. "Entering the Lives of Others." *This Bridge Called My Back: Writings by Radical Women of Color*. 4th ed., State U of New York P, 2015, pp. 19–65.

Morgan, Marcyleina. *The Real Hiphop: Battling for Knowledge, Power, and Respect in the LA Underground*. Duke UP, 2009.

Moten, Fred. *In the Break: The Aesthetics of the Black Radical Tradition*. U of Minnesota P, 2003.

Moynihan, Daniel Patrick. "*The Negro Family: A Case for National Action.*" 1965, https://web.stanford.edu/~mrosenfe/Moynihan%27s%20The%20Negro%20Family.pdf. Accessed 4 Mar. 2021.

Newby, Blake. "Twitter Gave Megan Thee Stallion Her Own Emoji, and It's About Time:

"It's a Hot Girl Summer, so you know she got it lit." *Revelist*, 30 Aug. 2019, https://www.revelist.com/celebrity/megan-thee-stallion-emoji/16297/the-emoji-design-is-a-megan-signature/3. Accessed 4 Mar. 2021.

"Nicki Minaj Hilariously Explains 'Beez in the Tap' | The Graham Norton Show." *YouTube*, uploaded by The Graham Norton Show, 22 June 2020, https://www.youtube.com/watch?v=2C-BVg5tBA8. Accessed 4 Mar. 2021.

Nunnley, Vorris. *Keepin' It Hushed: The Barbershop and African American Hush Harbor Rhetoric*. Wayne State UP, 2011.

"Okurrr | Pepsi 30." *YouTube*, 7 Feb. 2019, https://www.youtube.com/watch?v=NXO1PK9LO2E. Accessed 4 Mar. 2021.

Ore, Ersula. *Lynching, Violence, Rhetoric and American Identity*. U of Mississippi P, 2019.

Owens, Dana [Queen Latifah], with Karen Hunter. *Ladies First: Revelations of a Strong Woman*. William Morrow and Co., 1999.

Pagden, Anthony. *Lords of All the World: Ideologies of Empire in Spain, Britain and France c.1500-c.1800*. Yale UP, 1995.

Perry, Samuel. " 'Strange Fruit,' Ekphrasis, and the Lynching Scene." *Rhetoric Society Quarterly*, vol. 43, no. 5, pp. 224–74.

Petchauer, Emery. *Hip-Hop Culture in College Student's Lives: Elements, Embodiment, and Higher Edutainment*. Routledge, 2012.

Pi, Jiancai. "Altruism, Moral Hazard, and Sharecropping." *Agricultural Economics*, vol. 62, no. 12, 2016, pp. 575-84, doi:10.17221/219/2015-. Accessed 7 Feb. 2022.

Pierpont, Claudia Roth. "A Raised Voice: How Nina Simone Turned the Movement into Music." *The New Yorker*, 3 Aug. 2014, https://www.newyorker.com/magazine/2014/08/11/raised-voice. Accessed 4 Mar. 2021.

Pough, Gwendolyn D. *Check It While I Wreck It: Black Womanhood, Hip-Hop Culture, and the Public Sphere*. Northeastern, 2004.

Pritchard, Eric Darnell. " 'Because of Their Fearlessness, I Felt Empowered': Ancestors, Fictive Kin, and Elders." *Fashioning Lives: Black Queers and the Politics of Literacy*. Southern Illinois UP, 2016.

Prasad, Pirtha. " 'Coalition Is Not Done in Your Home': From Idealized Coalitions to Livable Lives." *Spark: A 4C4Equality Journal*, vol. 3, 2021, https://sparkactivism.com/volume-3-call/from-idealized-coalitions-to-livable-lives/. Accessed 7 Feb. 2022.

———. "Backchannel Pedagogies: Unsettling Racial Teaching Moments and White Futurity." *Present Tense*, vol. 9, no. 2, 1 Mar. 2022, http://www.presenttensejournal.org/volume-9/backchannel-pedagogies-unsettling-racial-teaching-moments-and-white-futurity/. Accessed 4 Mar. 2022.

Queen. *Queen's Greatest Hit, Vol. 1*. Elektra, 1981.

"Ranking Member Waters Q&A with Secretary Mnuchin—07/27/2017." Uploaded by U.S. House Committee on Financial Services." *YouTube*, 27 July 2017, https://www.youtube.com/watch?v=yEYkxHXsdGI. Accessed 22 Apr. 2021.

Ratcliffe, Krista. *Rhetorical Listening: Identification, Gender, Whiteness*. Southern Illinois UP, 2005.

Redding, Otis. "OTIS REDDING-respect." *YouTube*, uploaded by pieroangelo2, 5 Mar. 2015, https://www.youtube.com/watch?v=KvC9V_lBnDQ

"Respect." https://songbpm.com/@aretha-franklin/respect-393ee2c9-501b-4e42-beb1-859658c9a1c1. Accessed 27 July 2023.

"Respect. Aretha Franklin." *Key & BPM/Tempo of Respect by Aretha Franklin | Note Discover*, https://www.notediscover.com/song/aretha-franklin-respect. Accessed 4 Mar. 2021.

"Reverb." *Merriam-Webster.com Dictionary*, Merriam-Webster, https://www.merriam-webster.com/dictionary/reverb. Accessed 22 Mar. 2023.

Richardson, Elaine. *African American Literacies*. Routledge, 2003.

———. *Hiphop Literacies*. Routledge, 2006.

Rickert, Thomas J. *Ambient Rhetoric: The Attunements of Rhetorical Being*. U of Pittsburgh P, 2013.

Robinson, Dylan. "Hungry Listening." *Hungry Listening: Resonant Theory for Indigenous Sound Studies*. U of Minnesota P, 2020, pp. 37–76.

Robinson, Janelle Monáe. *Dirty Computer* [Emotion Picture]. *YouTube*, uploaded by Janelle Monáe. 27 Apr. 2019, https://www.youtube.com/watch?v=jdH2Sy-BlNE. Accessed 21 Feb. 2021.

Rose, Tricia. *Black Noise: Rap Music and Black Culture in Contemporary America*. Wesleyan UP, 1994.

Rowe, Solána Imani [SZA]. *Ctrl*, Top Dawg Entertainment. 2017.

Rowe, Bruce M., and Diane P. Levine. "Introduction: The Nature of Communication." *A Concise Introduction to Linguistics*. 4th ed., Routledge, 2015, pp. 1–28.

Royster, Jacqueline Jones. *Southern Horrors and Other Writings: The Anti-Lynching Campaign of Ida B. Wells, 1892–1900*. Bedford/St. Martins, 1996.

———. "When the First Voice You Hear Is Not Your Own." *College Composition and Communication*, vol. 47, no. 1, Feb. 1996, pp. 29–40.

———. *Traces of a Stream: Literacy and Social Change Among African American Women*. U of Pittsburgh P, 2000.

Sandeen, Cathy. "Boomers, Xers, and Millennials: Who Are They and What Do They Really Want from Continuing Higher Education?" *Continuing Higher Education Review*, vol. 72, 2008, pp. 11–31.

Schafer, R. Murray. *The Soundscape: Our Sonic Environment and the Tuning of the World*. Destiny Books, 1994.

Schultz, David. "RICO Laws." *First Amendment Encyclopedia*. Middle Tennessee State U, 2009, https://www.mtsu.edu/first-amendment/article/1237/rico-laws

Selena. "Dreaming of You." *Dreaming of You*, EMI Latin, 1995.

Sen, Debapriya. "A Theory of Sharecropping: The Role of Price Behavior and Imperfect Competition." *The Journal of Economic Behavior & Organization*, vol. 80, 2001, pp. 181–99, https://doi.org/10.1016/j.jebo.2011.03.006. Accessed 7 Feb. 2022.

Sharpe, Christina. *In the Wake: On Blackness and Being*. Duke UP, 2016.

Simone, Nina. "Nina Simone—Mississippi Goddam (Official Audio—Live)." *YouTube*, uploaded by Nina Simone, 26 June 2015, https://www.youtube.com/watch?v=-HM2S6TVYII. Accessed 4 Mar. 2021.

Smith, Frankie. "Double Dutch Bus." *Double Dutch Bus*, Metronome, 1981.

Smith, Lillian. *Strange Fruit, A Novel*. Reynal and Hitchcock, 1944.

Smitherman, Geneva. "Soul 'n Style." *The English Journal*, vol. 65, no. 2, 1975, pp. 14–16.

———. *Talkin and Testifyin: The Language of Black America*. Wayne State UP, 1977.

———. "Black Language and the Education of Black Children: One Mo Once." *The Black Scholar*, vol. 27, no. 1, 1997, pp. 28–35.

———. *Word from the Mother: Language and African Americans*. Routledge, 2006.

Snead, James A. "On Repetition in Black Culture." *Black American Literature Forum*, vol. 15, no. 4, 1981, https://www.jstor.org/stable/2904326. Accessed 4 Mar. 2021.

Spillers, Hortense. "Mama's Baby, Papa's Maybe: An American Grammar Book." *Black, White, and in Color: Essays on American Literature and Culture*, by Hortense Spillers, U of Chicago P, 2003, pp. 203–29.

Stallion, Megan Thee. "Megan Thee Stallion—Body [Official Video]." *YouTube*, uploaded by Megan Thee Stallion, 19 Nov. 2020, https://www.youtube.com/watch?v=7PBYGu4Az8s. Accessed 4 Mar. 2022.

———. "Megan Thee Stallion—Big Ole Freak [Official Video]." *YouTube*, uploaded by Megan Thee Stallion, 28 Feb. 2019, https://www.youtube.com/watch?v=oBYf6gpVvRA&t=133s. Accessed 4 Mar. 2022.

"Strange Fruit—The Story Behind the 'Song of the Century.'" *YouTube*, uploaded by WYFIOnline, 7 Feb. 2017, https://www.youtube.com/watch?v=EZUoYg-PelY4. Accessed 7 Feb. 2021.

Stoever, Jennifer Lynn. *The Sonic Color Line: Race & The Cultural Politics of Listening*. New York UP, 2016.

"The Best of the Century." *Time Magazine*, vol. 154, no. 27, 31 Dec. 1999, p. 79, https://time.com/vault/issue/1999-12-31/page/79/. Accessed 7 Feb. 2021.

"The Combahee River Collection." *Words of Fire: Anthology of African-American Feminist Thought*, edited by Beverly Guy-Sheftall, The New Press, 1995, pp. 231–40.

"The Recording Ban of 1942." *Modern Songs of War And Conflict*, edited by Ben Jackson, Maryland: U of Maryland, Exhibition catalogue, https://exhibitions.lib.umd.edu/songsofwar/wwii/currents/recording-ban. Accessed 9 Dec. 2021.

"What Is a Trademark?" *United States Patent and Trademark Office*. 17 Jan. 2021, https://www.uspto.gov/trademarks/basics/what-trademark. Accessed 4 Mar. 2023.

Turner, Tina. "Tina Turner—Proud Mary (Live)." *YouTube*, uploaded by Tina Turner Official, 22 Nov. 2019, https://www.youtube.com/watch?v=TTfYnRQgKgY. Accessed 4 Mar. 2022.

United States Congress. Public Law 60-349. *An Act to Amend and Consolidate the Acts Respecting Copyright* [Copyright Act of 1909]. *US Government Publishing Office*, https://www.copyright.gov/history/1909act.pdf. Accessed 7 Feb. 2022.

United States Department of Justice [Archives]. "109. RICO Charges." *Criminal Resource Manual*, 22 Jan. 2020, https://www.justice.gov/archives/jm/criminal-resource-manual-109-rico-charges. Accessed 7 Feb. 2022.

US House of Representatives Committee on Rules Majority Office. *Floor Procedure In The U.S. House Of Representatives*, US House of Representatives Committee on Rules Majority Office, Jan. 1999, rules.house.gov/sites/democrats.rules.house.gov/files/documents/Archives/floor_man.htm. Accessed 23 Mar. 2021.

VanHaistma, Pamela. "Gossip as Rhetorical Methodology for Queer and Feminist Historiography." *Rhetoric Review*, vol. 35, no. 2, 2016, pp. 135–47.

Wade, Dorothy, and Justine Picardie. *Music Man: Ahmet Ertegun, Atlantic Records, and the Triumph of Rock'N'Roll*. W. W. Norton, 1990.

Walker, Alice. *In Search of Our Mothers' Gardens*. Harcourt Brace Jovanovich, 1983.

Walker, James A. "On the Syntax-Prosody Interface in African American English." *The Oxford Handbook of African American Language*, edited by Sonja Lanehart, Oxford UP, 2016, pp. 387–402.

Ward, Jerry W., Jr. *The Richard Wright Encyclopedia*, edited by Robert J. Butler and Robert J. Butler, ABC-CLIO, LLC, 2008, ProQuest Ebook Central, Greenwood Press, 2008, 349–50, https://ebookcentral.proquest.com/lib/ubc/detail.action?docID=617341. Accessed 21 Mar. 2021.

Waters, M. Billye Sankofa, et al., editors. *Celebrating Twenty Years of Black Girlhood: The Lauryn Hill Reader*. Peter Lang Publishing, 2018.

Watts, Eric King. *Hearing the Hurt: Rhetoric, Aesthetics, and Politics of the New Negro Movement*. U of Alabama P, 2012.

Weheliye, Alexander G. *Habeas Viscus: Racializing Assemblages, Biopolitics, and Black Feminist Theories of the Human*. Duke UP, 2014.

Well, Miriam J. "The Resurgence of Sharecropping: Historical Anomaly or Political Strategy?" *American Journal of Sociology*, vol. 90, no. 1, July 1984, pp. 1–29, https://www.jstor.org/stable/2779325. Accessed 21 Mar. 2021.

———. "Sharecropping." *The Dictionary of Human Geography*, edited by Derek Gregory, et al., John Wiley & Sons, ProQuest Ebook Central, https://

ebookcentral.proquest.com/lib/ubc/detail.action?docID=437431. Accessed 21 Mar. 2021.

Whitmore, Jon. *Directing Postmodern Theater: Shaping Signification in Performance*. U of Michigan P, 1994.

Wilson, Carl. "How Aretha Franklin Created 'Respect': The Greatest Cover Song of All Time and the Quintessential Empowerment Anthem." *Slate*, 16 Aug. 2018, https://slate.com/culture/2018/08/aretha-franklin-dead-the-story-of-respect-the-greatest-cover-of-all-time.html. Accessed 4 Mar. 2022.

Winnubst, Shannon. "The Many Lives of Fungibility: Anti-Blackness in Neoliberal Times." *Journal of Gender Studies*, vol. 29, 2018, pp. 102–12.

Wozolek, Boni. "The Mothership Connection: Utopian Funk from Bethune and Beyond." *The Urban Review: Issues and Ideas in Public Education*, vol. 45, no. 3, 2018, pp. 836–56.

"YouTube Presents: Janelle Monáe's Dirty Computer Q&A w/ Ari Fitz." *YouTube*, 27 Apr. 2018, https://www.youtube.com/watch?v=4tFEugP864o. Accessed 18 Feb. 2021.

Zackodnik, Teresa C. *'We Must Be Up and Doing': A Reader in Early African American Feminisms*. Broadview Press, 2010.

Zapp. *Zapp*, Warner Bros., 1980.

Index

Abramson, Herb Charles, 29, 30, 33–34, 36–39, 40, 52
a capella, 122
acknowledging the burden, 143
  in Black feminism, 164
ad libs, 128, 131
Adams, Tony E., 9
AFM. *See* American Federation of Musicians
Afrafeminism, 146–147. *See also* Black feminism
Afrocentrism, 154, 177
Afrodiaspora, 142
Afrofuturism, 73, 81, 189n14
agency
  Black grammar and, 137
  of Black women, 51–52, 149
Ain't I A Woman (hooks), 149–150
Alexander, Michelle, 22
Alim, H. Samy, 53
Allen, Lewis. *See* Meeropol, Abel
Almánzar, Belcalis Marlenis. *See* Cardi B
"Altruism, Moral Hazard, and Sharecropping" (Pi), 18
American Federation of Musicians (AFM), 30–32
  Ertegun, A., on, 33
Anderson, Tim, 33
Angélique, Marie-Joseph, 150–151

Angelou, Maya, 140
antiBlackness, 3, 11, 41, 56–57, 109–110
  capitalism and, 182–183
  mythic stereotypes, 165
  sonic sharecropping as, 28, 51–52
  violence of, 66, 131–132
Anzaldúa, Gloria, xv
Apollo Theater, 37
Asante, 157
aspect, 110–111, 191n7
assemblages, of Blackness, 41, 60
Atlantic Records, 29, 33
  artist compensation at, 34–36
  artist roster, 34
  Brown, R., on, 34, 36–40, 50–52
  legal case against, 47–48
  record keeping at, 47–48
audibility, 144. *See also* sonic mentorship
  defining, 141
  of generational sonic rhetorics, 166–167
autobiography, 171
autoethnography, 9–10
auxiliary verbs, 108, 191n6

backchannel pedagogies, 196n17
Bailey, Moya, 186n4
Baker, Houston, xvii

Baker, Lavern, 42–43
Banfield, William C., 195n13
Banks, Adam, 144, 147, 194n8
Baraka, Amiri, 66
be (verb), 108, 191n6. *See also* subjectivity
Beagle, Howell, 51
  Brown, R., and, 46–49
"Beez in the Trap," 101, 107, 112
Beitler, Lawrence, 65–69, 78
Bentham, Jeremy, 19
Benton, Brook, 172
Beyoncé, 1, 10, 120, 128, 182–183
  Super Bowl halftime show of, 95
Beyond Respectability (Cooper, B.), 144, 188n15
Bhabha, Homi, 156–157, 158
"Big Ole Freak," 129
"Bitter Fruit" (Meeropol), 70
Black bodies
  in Black grammar, 125
  fungibility of, 166
  repetition and, 125–126
  sound and, 124–125, 180
  surveillance of, 166
  of women, 130, 166
Black communication, xvii
Black feminism, 105, 122–123, 181
  acknowledging the burden in, 164
  Collins on, 142, 151–152
  Davis, A. Y., on, 155
  defining, 151–152
  development of, 142
  Lathan on, 143
  public intellectuals, 144, 145–156
  sonic sharecropping resisted by, 36–40
Black Feminist Thought (Collins), 151–152
Black fungibility, 41, 180
  of bodies, 166

Black grammar, 99–100, 103–107
  agency and, 137
  Black body in, 125
  copula in, 108–109
  duration in, 132
  Nicki Minaj using, 111
  prosody of, 101, 118, 123
  queer Black time in, 107–111
  repetition in, 118–119, 124
  of Simone, 114
  Smitherman on, 160
  subjectivity and, 104–105
  temporality of, 138
Black LGBTQ history, 181–182
Black music
  identity and, xvii
  recording industry and, 53–54
Black Noise (Rose), 115
Black Panthers, 95
Black performance, xvii–xviii
Black women, 2
  agency of, 51–52, 149
  bodies of, 130, 166
  in Canada, 181
  cross-generational communication of, 4
  discriminatory practices against, 135
  double bind of, 149–150
  generational sonic rhetorics of, 4–8, 13–14, 121, 180
  labor of, 25
  lynching of, 60–62
  in oral traditions, 152
  as public intellectuals, 144–145, 177–178
  in recording industry, 53–54
  redefinition of common archetypes, 147–156
  sonic rhetoric of, 180
  sonic traditions of, 4–5, 102

strong Black woman myth, 164–165
voice of, 145–146, 176–177
white supremacy challenged by, 4–5
#BlackLifeMatters, 76
Blackness, xiii, 78
conceptualizing, 185n1
diversity of, 2
public gaze on, 162
racializing assemblages of, 41, 60
as social measurement, 56
stereotypes about, 88
subjectivity and, 97–99, 114–115, 117–118, 162
Blair, Elizabeth, 70
Blues Legacies (Davis), 8
bodies. *See* Black bodies
"Body," 125
Boomers, 53
bootstraps motif, 74, 189n11
Bradley, Regina, 5
branding, 40
Brandt, Deborah, 142, 193n3
Branstetter, Heather Lee, 168
Braun, Scooter, 12
Braverman, Avishay, 18
Brooks, Daphne A., 5, 35
Brooks, Gwendolyn, 154
Brown, Mary Ellen, 171
on gossip, 171, 172–173
Brown, Mildrey, 60
Brown, Ruth, 2, 15, 53, 71, 174
on Atlantic Records, 34, 36–40, 50–52
Beagle and, 46–49
Ertegun and, 41, 44–46
on sonic sharecropping, 16
Browne, Simone, 19, 40, 180
Bryant, Jacquline, 152
burden, acknowledging, 143, 164
Burke, Kenneth, 92–93
Bursey, Gerry, 49

Cabaret Tax, 32
call-and-response, 143
gossip in, 172–173
Lathan on, 148–149
voice in, 173
Calloway, Blanche, 36–37, 39
Cameron, James, 64–66, 84
Campt, Tina, 67
Canada, 181
capitalism, 182–183
Carby, Hazel, 131
Cardi B, 2, 52–53, 128
lexicon of, 24–26
in Pepsi commercial, 26–27
on trademarks, 24–25
Carey, Tamika, 98, 100, 135, 137, 165, 179, 190n1
on rhetorical healing, 175
on vernacular, 177
Carr, Jesse, 59
Carr, Valerie, 171
changing same, 55
Holiday and, 63–64
Ore on, 58–59
past and, 58–64
psychic solidification of, 56
Chávez, Karma, 10
Christian, Barbara, 142
Cindi Mayweather. *See* Monáe Robinson, Janelle
citizenship, 68–69
Civil War, 21
Cohen, Cathy, 102
Collins, Patricia Hill, 10
on Black feminism, 142, 151–152
on politics of containment, 162
colonialism, 23
Columbia Records, 35
Commodore Records, 71
containment, politics of, 162
convict leasing. *See* sharecropping

convict photos, 188n7
Cooper, Anna J., 180
Cooper, Britney, 8, 97, 102–103, 135, 144, 177, 180, 188n15, 193n6
   on public intellectualism, 153
Cooper, Ralph, 88
copula, in Black grammar, 108–109
Cotton Club, 87
Crystal Cavern, 36–37
Ctrl, 161, 163–164
cultural codes, 195n13

"Daddy Lessons," 127–128
Dance, Daryl Cumber, 170, 174
dancing, xvi
D'Angelo, Frank J., 91
Darin, Bobby, 45
Dark Matters (Browne), 19
dark sousveillance, 28–29
Davis, Angela Y., 8, 146
   on Black feminism, 155
   on rhetoric, 168
   on "Strange Fruit," 72–73
Davis, Miles, 5
death, social, 53, 99
DeBose, Charles E., 191n7
debtor's prison, 22
Decca Records, 34, 70–71
Deeter, Claude, 64
DeGruy, Joy, 21
The Dictionary of Human Geography (Gregory), 17
Dirty Computer, 73, 80–81, 91
   as metaphor, 83
   Monáe Robinson on, 82
"Django Jane," 95
"Doo Wop (That Thing)," 101
   repetition in, 121–122
doo-wop, 121–122
Dowd, Tommy, 42
dreams, Holiday on, 175–176

"Drink Wine, Spo-Dee-O-Dee," 34, 36
duration
   in Black grammar, 132
   defining, 131
   Simone exploring, 131–135
Dylan, Bob, 12

Edgar, Amanda Nell, 141
edutainment, 71, 189n9
ekphrasis, 90
Elliot, Missy, 12, 58, 76, 88
Ellis, Carolyn, 9
emancipation, ideology of, 176–177, 196n18
erasure, 8–9
Ericson, Richard, 45
Ertegun, Ahmet, 29–31, 35, 36–39, 52
   on AFM, 33
   background of, 186n9
   Brown, R., and, 41, 44–46
Ertegun, Munir, 186n9
ethnicity, 98–99
experiential discourse, 168

Fanon, Frantz, 180
Federal Narcotics Bureau, 63
Feldstein, Ruth, 112, 135
feminism, xvi. *See also* Black feminism
Fields, Liz, 112–113
Fikes, Betty Mae, 113
Fine and Mellow, 57
Fleetwood, Nicole, 77
"Formation," 95
Foster, Eric K., 169
"Four Master Tropes," 92–93
Franklin, Aretha, 101, 112–113, 115, 116
   Hill and, 120–123, 124–125
freedom, 1–2, 133
   Baraka on, 55

Freedom Writing (Lathan), 142
Fuss, Diana, 92–93

Gabler, Milt, 71
"Garden (Say It Like That)," 164
gatekeeping, 155
Gavins, Raymond, 20
gender non-conforming sonic rhetoric, 181
generational sonic rhetorics, 133
   audibility of, 166–167
   of Black women, 4–8, 13–14, 121, 180
   conceptualizing, 182
   gossip as, 173
   sonic mentorship and, 144–145
   transmission of, 6
generational struggles, 174–178
Gibbs, Georgia, 42, 53
Gilyard, Keith, 157
gospel literacy
   gossip as, 172
   Lathan on, 142–143
   sonic mentorship and, 143–144
gossip, 167–174
   Brown, M. E., on, 171, 172–173
   in call-and-response, 172–173
   defining, 171
   as gendered, 171
   as generational sonic rhetoric, 173
   as gospel literacy, 172
   as literacy, 170–171
   misrepresentations of, 169
   reactions to, 174
   Smitherman on, 170
   sonic rhetoric of, 168, 170–171
   stigma, 169
The Graham Norton Show, 107
Gramsci, Antonio, 147, 152, 153, 168–169, 194n9

grandmother, xii–xiv
Greenfield, Robert, 30, 35, 36
Gregory, Derek, 17
Griffin, Farah Jasmine, 89
griot, 147, 194n8
grit, 189n10

habeas viscus, 41
Habeus Viscus (Weheliye), 8
Haggerty, Kevin, 45
Hallagan, William, 18
Hamer, Fannie Lou, 113, 135
Hanifan, Pat, 62
Hannah-Jones, Nikole, 159
Hansberry, Lorraine, 132
Head tart, 44
Hegel, G. W. F., 97, 118
Hill, Lauryn, 101
   Franklin and, 120–123, 124–125
   repetition used by, 123–124
hip-hop pedagogy, 8
historical rootedness, 8
Hoare, Quintin, 194n9
Holiday, Billie, 12, 55, 56, 58, 90–91, 130, 193n7
   changing same and, 63–64
   death of father of, 63
   on dreams, 175–176
   on "Strange Fruit," 64, 71
   voice of, 87–89
Honey, Hush!, 170
hooks, bell, 149–150
hope, 1–2
Howard University, 30
hush harbors, 143–144, 145. *See also* gossip
   defining, 193n5
   discourses, 156–174
   Nunnley on, 158–159
   sonic rhetoric of, 167
   voice and, 160–161

"I Got So Much Magic You Can Have It," 161
"I Like It," 27
Iconology, 73
Ideology of Emancipation, 176–177, 196n18
"I'm Better," 91
　lyrics of, 75–76
　music video, 73–75, 76–78
imitation, 41
In the Break (Moten), xvii
individualism, 151
intellectual labor, 147
interdisciplinarity, 7, 190n3
interludes, 161–167
　literacy and, 163
　oral traditions and, 167
intersectionality, 7, 25
　Monáe on, 86
intimate partner violence, 125
"It Jus Be's That Way Sometimes" (Carby), 132

Jackson, Janet, xv
Jackson, Jesse, 50
Jackson, Mahalia, 120
Jane Crow, 188n15
jazz, xvi
Jennings, John, 192n16
Jim Crow, 11–12, 22, 80–86
Johnson, E. Patrick, 102
Jones, Charisse, 164–165
Jones, LeRoi. *See* Baraka, Amiri
Jones, Stacy Holman, 9
Just Vibrations (Cheng), 6–7

kairos, 160
Kairos, 117
King, Deborah, 180
Knowles, Solange, 161–162
Knowles, Tina, 165, 176
　on racism, 161–162

Ku Klux Klan, 131
Kurtis Blow, xv

labor
　of Black women, 25
　free, 24
　intellectual, 147
　ownership and, 28
　sonic, 27–36, 187n14
　sound as, 15–23
Ladies First (Queen Latifah), 141
Lamb, 73–76
land
　ownership, 23
　sound as, 15–23
Lanehart, Sonja, 176, 196n18
The Last Sultan (Greenfield), 30
Lathan, Rhea Estelle, 74, 142, 193n4
　on Black feminism, 143
　on call-and-response, 148–149
　on gospel literacy, 142–143
　on leadership, 148
　on *mate masie*, 163
leadership, Lathan on, 148
Lemonade, 1, 120, 182–183
lexicon, 126. *See also* Black grammar
　of Cardi B, 24–26
　defining, 186n3
liable, 169
life writing, 167, 175. *See also* sonic mentorship
　autobiography, 171
　autoethnography, 9–10
　interludes, 161–167
Listening to Images (Campt), 67
literacy, xvii
　activism, 193n3
　as activist methodology, 145–146
　gospel, 142–143, 144, 172
　gossip as, 170–171
　interludes and, 163
　Pritchard on, 181–182

Royster on, 142, 146
  vernacular, 155–156
Little Miss Cornshucks, 41–42
Liu, Ying, 113
Lordi, Emily, 5
Love, Bettina, 78–79, 189n10
  on queerness, 101–102
"Love Galore," 163–164
lynching, 56–57, 188n3
  of Black women, 60–62
  as discourse community, 60
  history of, 64–69
  Ore analyzing, 58
  photographs, 65–68, 77–78
  as social control, 59–60
  spectators of, 68–69, 78
  as symbolic act, 58
  Wells on, 60–63, 83–84
Lynching, Violence, Rhetoric and American Identity (Ore), 58

Mackey, Nathaniel, 56
Maraj, Louis M., 195n11
Maraj, Onika Tanya. *See* Nicki Minaj
Martin, Trayvon, 77
Master P, 163
mate masie, 163
materialized sound, 192n1
McGhee, Brownie, 35, 36
McGhee, Stick, 34–35
McKittrick, Katherine, 150, 166
Meeropol, Abel, 55, 70, 91, 188n8
Megan Thee Stallion, 101, *129*
  paralexical language of, 127–130
  repetition used by, 125–127
metonymy
  defining, 92–93
  reverse, 93
  in "Strange Fruit," 93–94
Meyers, Dave, 73–74
Meyers, Elliott, 73–74
Middle Passage, 122, 159

Miller, Elizabeth Ellis, 113
Mills, Charles, 104, 190n2
miscegenation, xiii, xv
misogynoir, 25, 52
  defining, 186n4
Miss Rhythm (Brown), 34, 40
"Mississippi Goddam," 101, 112, 114, 131, 133
mixed-race, xiii–xv
Mnuchin, Steve, 192n14
modality, 110–111, 191n7
Monáe Robinson, Janelle, 12, 58, 73, 80–86, 88
  on *Dirty Computer*, 82
  on intersectionality, 86
Moody, Jocelyn, 151–152
Morrison, Toni, 5
Moten, Fred, xvii–xviii
Moynihan, Daniel Patrick, 98–100
Moynihan Report, 99
MTV, xvi
Murry, Pauli, 188n15
music, xv
music industry, 31–34
Music Performance Trust, 32
music videos, 57

narrative, 168–169
New Orleans, xvi
Newby, Blake, 128
Nicki Minaj, 101, 107–108, 128, 134
  Black grammar used by, 111
  meaning-making, 110–111
  sonic rhetoric of, 111
Nommos, 165–166
  defining, 157
Nunnley, Vorris, 145
  on hush harbors, 158–159
  on third spaces, 158–159

"Oh, What a Dream," 43
On Racial Icons (Fleetwood), 77

oral traditions
  Black women in, 152
  interludes and, 167
Ore, Ersula
  on changing same, 58–59
  lynching analyzed by, 58
Owens, Dana. *See* Queen Latifah
ownership, labor and, 28

Pagden, Anthony, 23
Page, Patti, 42, 43, 53
Panopticon, 19
paralexical language, of Megan Thee Stallion, 127–130
pedagogy
  backchannel, 196n17
  hip-hop, 8
Pennsylvania, xiii
"Pep Rally," 73
Pepsi, 26–27
Perry, Samuel, 8–9, 90
personal, politicization of, 167
Petchauer, Emery, 189n9
Pete, Megan. *See* Megan Thee Stallion
Petrillo, James, 32
Petrillo Strikes, 16, 32
  Anderson on, 33
photographs
  convict, 188n7
  lynching, 65–68, 77–78
Pi, Jiancai, 18
Pierce, Ponchitta, 153
politicizing the personal, 167
politics of containment, 162
popular culture, repetition in, 119
Pos Traumatic Slave Syndrome (DeGruy), 21
postcolonialism, 158
Pough, Gwendolyne, 1, 2, 5, 8–9, 180
poverty penalties, 22
Prasad, Pritha, 191n12
Pretchauer, Emory, 71

Pritchard, Eric Darnell, 8, 9
  on literacy, 181–182
privilege, 29
prosody, 27, 124, 126, 137
  of Black grammar, 101, 118, 123
  defining, 106–107, 186n5, 191n5
  of Simone, 136
  voice, 130–131
  Walker, J. A., on, 106
public gaze, 162
public intellectuals, 161, 194n9
  Black feminist, 144, 145–156
  Black women as, 144–145, 177–178
  Cooper, B., on, 153
  defining, 147, 153
  redefinition of common archetypes, 147–156
public sphere, 166

quare studies, 102, 182
Queen, xv
Queen Latifah, 139–140, 145, 182
queer and queering
  defining, 101–102
  grammar, 100–101
  Love on, 101–102
  queer Black time in grammar, 107–111
  of temporality, 102–103, 136, 137–138

race music, 50
the Racial Contract, 104
racism, xv
  Knowles, T., on, 161–162
racketeering, 49
"The Radical Politics of Time," 97k
Ratcliffe, Krista, 92–93, 94
Reagon, Bernice Johnson, 113, 148
reciprocity, 173
record keeping, at Atlantic Records, 47–48

Index | 217

recording industry, Black women in, 53–54
A Red Record (Wells), 60–61, 188n5
Redding, Otis, 115, 117
Reese, Maggie, 62
repetition, 111–112
  Black body and, 125–126
  in Black grammar, 118–119, 124
  in "Doo Wop (That Thing)," 121–122
  Hill using, 123–124
  Megan Thee Stallion using, 125–127
  in popular culture, 119
  in "Respect," 116–117
  subjectivity and, 117–118
  temporality and, 119
repurposing sound, 119–120
res nullius, 23
"Respect," 112–113, 115
  influence of, 116
  repetition in, 116–17
Revelist, 128
reverb, 179
rhetoric, 11. *See also* sonic rhetoric
  Davis, A. Y., on, 168
  sound as, 90–95
rhetorical healing, 175
Rhetorical Healing (Carey), 179
rhetorical reclamation, 195n11
Richard, Cliff, 43
The Richard Wright Encyclopedia, 21
Richardson, Elaine, 139, 149, 171, 175
RICO Act, 16, 44–52
Ritz, David, 116
Robinson, Dylan, 123
ROC Nation, 54
Rose, Tricia, 115, 117–118, 119, 126
"A Rose Is Still A Rose," 120–121
Rowe, Solána Imani. *See* SZA
Royster, Jaqueline Jones, xvii, 59, 193n3
  on literacy, 142, 146

Sabit, Vahdi, 30–31
Sandeen, Cathy, 3–4
Sankofa, 138
sankofarration, 83, 95, 189n14, 192n16
Schafer, R. Murray, 188n6
Schiffman, Frank, 88
A Seat at the table, 161
Sekula, Allan, 67
Selena, xv
the self, sound and, 87
self-identification, 177–178
Sen, Debpriya, 17
Seven Arts, 51
sharecropping, 11–12, 27–28
  economic processes in, 17–18
  history of, 16–17, 20–21
  legacy of, 16
  mentality, 16–20
  normative applications of, 20–24
  praxis, 16–20
  from psychological standpoint, 18–19
  remnants of, 22
Sharpe, Christina, 195n11
Shifting (Jones and Shorter-Gooden), 164
Shipp, J. Thomas, 64–68
Shorter-Gooden, Kumea, 164–165
Simone, Nina, 98, 101
  Black grammar of, 114
  duration explored by, 131–135
  prosody of, 136
"The Singing Rage," 43
slander, 169
Slate, 116
Small, Christopher, 117
Smith, Abram S., 64–68, 106
Smith, Bessie, 193n7
Smith, Frankie, xv
Smith, Geoffrey Nowell, 194n9
Smith, Lillian, 91

218 | Index

Smitherman, Geneva, 103, 104, 109, 157
  on Black grammar, 160
  on gossip, 170
Snead, James A., 118–119
social death, 53, 99
social justice, 135–136
social life, 15, 99, 174
sonic color line, 94
The Sonic Color Line (Stoeve), 86–87
sonic labor, 27–36, 187n14
sonic mentorship, 12–13, 120, 142
  generational sonic rhetorics and, 144–145
  gospel literacy and, 143–144
  ontological development and, 149
  soothing by, 141
sonic rhetoric
  of Black women, 180
  gender non-conforming, 181
  generational, 4–8, 13–14, 121, 133
  of gossip, 168, 170–171
  of hush harbors, 167
  as methodology, 10
  of Nicki Minaj, 111
  sound as rhetoric, 90–95
  "Strange Fruit" as, 72–80, 86–95
sonic sharecropping
  as antiBlackness, 28, 51–52
  Black feminist resistance to, 36–40
  Brown, R., on, 16
  defining, 11, 28–29
  technology and, 29–31
  as vernacular, 28
sonority, 191n4
"Sorry," 10
Soul Train, xvi
sound
  Black body and, 124–125, 180
  Black communication and, xvii
  defining, 6–7
  as labor, 15–23
  as land, 15–23
  materialized, 192n1
  repurposing, 119–120
  as rhetoric, 90–95
  self and, 87
soundscape, 188n6
the South, xiii
Southern Horrors and Other Writings (Wells), 59–61
"Speaking Identities" (Edgar), 141–142
Spillers, Hortense, 41, 98, 105, 180
  on Black grammar, 99–100
spirit murder, 16
stereotypes, 5
  antiBlack mythic, 165
  about Blackness, 88
Stiglitz, Joseph E., 18
Stoever, Jennifer Lynn, 86–87, 94
strange fruit, 12
  defining, 93–94
"Strange Fruit," 8, 12, 56, 69, 77–78, 130
  Davis on, 72–73
  history, 64–69
  Holiday on, 64, 71
  metonymy in, 93–94
  as sonic rhetoric, 72–80, 86–95
  vernacular of, 92–93
  on YouTube, 57
Stroud, Andrew, 132
subjectivity
  Black grammar and, 104–105
  Blackness and, 97–99, 114–115, 117–118, 162
Sun Ra, 5
Super Bowl halftime show, of Beyoncé, 95
"Supermodel," 164
surveillance, 19
  of Black bodies, 166
  racializing, 45
Swift, Taylor, 12

syntactical morphemes, 192n15
SZA, 161, 165–166
  matriarchal figures for, 163–164

Taft Hartley Act, 49
Tagg, John, 67
"Take a Byte," 84, 85
Talkin and Testifyin (Smitherman), 157, 170
technology, sonic sharecropping and, 29–31
tempo, 113
temporal hegemony, 137
temporality, 112–113. *See also* duration
  of Black grammar, 138
  queering of, 102–103, 136, 137–138
  race and, 97–98
  repetition and, 119
tenant farming. *See* sharecropping
tense, modality, and aspect (TMA), 110–111, 191n7
Texas, xiv, xv
Tharpe, Rosetta, 182, 186n2
third spaces
  defining, 156–157, 158–159
  Nunnley on, 158–159
Time-Warner, 47, 50–51, 54
"Tina Taught Me," 161
TMA. *See* tense, modality, and aspect
Traces of a Stream (Royster), xvii, 146
trademarks, Cardi B on, 24–25
trauma, 56
"Trav'lin All Alone," 87–88
Trump, Donald, 192n14
Truth, Sojourner, 149–151
"Tweedle Dee," 42
"20 Something," 165

Ubuntu, 159
United States Patent and Trademark Office (USPTO), 24, 27

US Copyright Act of 1909, 187n13
USPTO. *See* United States Patent and Trademark Office

validation, 142
de Vattel, Emeric, 23, 42–43, 52
de Veaux, Alexis, 89
vernacular, 6
  Carey on, 177
  literacies, 155–156
  sonic sharecropping as, 28
  of "Strange Fruit," 92–93
violence
  of antiBlackness, 66, 131–132
  intimate partner, 125
vocality, 86–87
voice, 121–122
  of Black women, 145–146, 176–177
  in call-and-response, 173
  of Holiday, 87–89
  hush harbors and, 160–161

Walker, Alice, 145–146, 152
Walker, James A., 126–127
  on prosody, 106
Ward, Clara, 120
Ward, Jerry, 21
Ward Singers, 120
Waters, Maxine, 97, 98, 133, 192n14
Watts, Eric King, 80
Waymon, Eunice. *See* Simone, Nina
We Want to Do More Than Survive (Love), 189n10
Weheliye, Alexander, 8, 41
Well, Miriam, 17, 19
Wells, Ida B., 2, 59, 105, 188n5
  on lynching, 60–63, 83–84
Werner, Craig, 148
Weston, Ruth Alston, 6
Wexler, Jerry, 116
White, Deborah Gray, 146

white supremacy, 66
   Black women challenging, 4–5
   resistance to, 117–118
whiteness, 5, 59–60
Whitmore, Jon, 127
Williams, J. Mayo, 34
Williams, Marion, 120
Willis, Lucindy, 153
Wilson, Carl, 116–117, 120
Winnubst, Shannon, 41
Wondaland, 54, 81
Wozolek, Boni, 86
wrek, 8–9
writing studies, 103–104

YouTube, 57
Yule, Andrew, 34

Zackodnick, Teresa, 159
Zapp Band, xv
Zimmerman, George, 77